Does God Belong in Public Schools?

*

Does God Belong in Public Schools?

*

KENT GREENAWALT

PRINCETON UNIVERSITY PRESS

PRINCETON AND OXFORD

Library of Congress Cataloging-in-Publication Data

Greenawalt, Kent, 1936–
Does God belong in public schools? / Kent Greenawalt.
p.   cm.
Includes bibliographical references and index.
ISBN 0-691-12111-7 (alk. paper)
1. Religion in the public schools—United States.   2. Religion in the public schools—
Law and legislation—United States.   3. Education and state—United States.   I. Title.

LC111.G68   2004
379.28′0973—dc22   2004045779

British Library Cataloging-in-Publication Data is available

This book has been composed in Palatino

Printed on acid-free paper. ∞

pup.princeton.edu

Printed in the United States of America

1   3   5   7   9   10   8   6   4   2

TO MY SON DAVE,

WITH LOVE

*

Contents

Preface ix

Introduction 1

PART I
HISTORY AND PURPOSES 11

CHAPTER 1
A Brief History of American Public Schools and Religion 13

CHAPTER 2
Purposes of Public School Education 23

PART II
DEVOTIONS, CLUBS, AND TEACHING RELIGION AS TRUE 35

CHAPTER 3
Devotional Practices: Prayer and Bible Reading 37

CHAPTER 4
Moments of Silence 58

CHAPTER 5
Teaching Religious Propositions 64

CHAPTER 6
Equal Facilities 69

PART III
TEACHING ABOUT RELIGION 77

CHAPTER 7
Teaching and Religion in the Public School 79

CHAPTER 8
Teaching Natural Science I: Relation between Science
and Religion 88

CHAPTER 9
Teaching Natural Science II: Evolutionism, Creationism,
and Intelligent Design 101

CHAPTER 10
Teaching Natural Science III: What Amounts to
Teaching Religion?   116

CHAPTER 11
History, Economics, and Literature   126

CHAPTER 12
Morals, Civics, and Comparative Religion   138

CHAPTER 13
Constitutional Constraints and Other Legal Limits   152

PART IV
RIGHTS OF STUDENTS   161

CHAPTER 14
Student Rights to Religious Freedom and to Free
Speech on Religious Topics   163

CHAPTER 15
Excusing Students When They or Their Parents Object   174

Notes   189

Index   257

* *Preface* *

In the course of more extensive studies about religious liberty, both the free exercise of religion and the rule against establishing any religion, I became interested in the various ways in which issues about religion concern American public schools. After delving into topics such as school prayer, religious clubs, teaching about religion, and special treatment of students whose parents have religious objections to the curriculum, I concluded that most of the law about religion in schools could be explained by a principle that public schools should not sponsor religion; but that this principle, standing alone, fails to resolve many intricate issues of constitutional law and educational policy. This book explains and analyzes these problems.

My understanding of aspects of the subject increased greatly at presentations and conferences at the University of Virginia, the University of Colorado, the University of Notre Dame Law School, the University of Texas Law School, at Columbia University (at the "Fifteen Minute Paper Group" in the law school and at a meeting of the Center of Science and Religion). At the conference "Teaching about Religion in Public Schools," sponsored in May 2003 by the First Amendment Center and the Pew Forum on Religion and Public Life, organized by Charles C. Haynes and Melissa Rogers, I was able to talk to many of those who have been most active in trying to introduce more teaching about religion into public schools. Students participating in a seminar in the law of church and state that I have taught over the years have been a continuing source of insight.

I have benefited a great deal from the comments of many colleagues, including Barbara Armacost, Vincent Blasi, Michael Dorf, Melvin Eisenberg, David Mapel, Henry Monaghan, James Nickel, Lawrence Sager, Peter Strauss, Jeremy Waldron, and Jay Wexler. Philip Kitcher's help on the three chapters about science and religion was indispensable. He suggested research sources, and his critique of various drafts saved me from a good deal of imprecision and error. My brother Kim, a public high school teacher, provided an extremely valuable perspective. As readers of the manuscript for Princeton University Press, Christopher

Eisgruber and Stephen Macedo offered perceptive criticisms that allowed me to make the book clearer and more coherent. I also benefited from the comments of an anonymous reviewer of the chapters on science.

Darrell Cafasso, Michael Dowdle, Gregory Fayer, Mark Hulbert, Paul Horwitz, Kenneth Levy, Nancy Clare Morgan, Derrick Toddy, and Bethany Alsup contributed very useful and timely research assistance, and in the summer in which I was completing the manuscript, Rima Al-Mokarrab gave precise and very helpful assistance on virtually every chapter.

Before her death in the autumn of 2001, Sally Wrigley typed numerous drafts of chapters on free exercise and nonestablishment. Katherine Bobbitt and Jinah Paek carried the chapters of this book through to a conclusion; Ms. Bobbitt also did considerable research and made editorial improvements in every part of the book. She, Young Lee, and Sachin Pandya did a thoughtful and careful preparation of the index.

I have been fortunate indeed in having Ian Malcolm undertake substantive editing of the manuscript. He raised important questions I had not considered and identified many potential points of misunderstanding, as well as offering fruitful suggestions about how to deal with problems. Richard Isomaki copyedited the manuscript very carefully, eliminating numerous errors and obscurities in presentation. Ellen Foos graciously shepherded the book through production.

My wife Elaine has been a source of great support throughout the project. More directly, she significantly improved the writing in parts of the book and came up with the idea for its title.

Some of the material in the chapters on teaching about religion appeared in "Teaching about Religion in the Public Schools," 18 *Journal of Law and Politics* 329 (2002); "Establishing Religious Ideas: Evolution, Creationism, and Intelligent Design," 17 *Notre Dame Journal of Law, Ethics, and Public Policy* 321 (2003); and "Intelligent Design: Scientific Theory or Religious Conviction?" 45 *Journal of Church and State* 237 (2003).

CONTROVERSIAL CIRCUMSTANCES

1. On March 11, 2002, the Ohio school board heard conflicting testimony over what the state should teach about the history of life on earth. Parents had objected to their children being taught that Darwinian evolutionary theory is true. Believing that the theory is not only false but undermines sound religion and morality, the parents wanted teachers to present an account of life that recognizes God's creative hand. Two scientists testified that standard evolutionary theory cannot explain the complexity of organs like the eye and of many individual cells, which reveal an intelligent design. Unlike many so-called creationists, who claim that the earth is less than ten thousand years old and that all basic kinds of plants and animals were created at the same time, these scientists did not dispute that the earth is billions of years old, that single-cell life-forms were the ancestors of all life on earth, or that natural selection of organisms best suited for survival accounts for much of the development of life. Unlike Darwinians, however, they argued that natural selection cannot explain nearly as much as most modern biologists assume, and suggested instead that the history of life on earth demonstrates the activity of an intelligent designer. Opponents of teaching intelligent design claimed that teaching it, no less than teaching creationism according to the Genesis account, is teaching religion, not science. Should the board have directed its schools to teach intelligent design?

2. A junior high school course on sex education includes information about the use of condoms. Faced with extensive parental complaints that artificial contraception violates God's law and that schools should not teach it, should the school board direct that teaching about condoms stop?

3. The Edgemont public school long celebrated the Christmas season by having students gather in the central hall before classes and sing Christmas carols. All students attended a Christmas pageant put on by ninth and tenth graders, under the

music teacher's direction, involving Christmas music and dialogue about the birth of Jesus. Should the school have continued its caroling and pageant?

4. A ninth-grade English teacher assigned her students a research paper, for which they were to use at least four separate sources. Students picked their own topics. The teacher rejected as unsuitable one student's proposal to write on the life of Jesus. Was she mistaken?

5. Parents of fifth and sixth graders who have created a Christian club for their children apply to use an empty classroom during the lunch hour, when the students, with parents supervising, will engage in religious worship. Should the school provide the classroom?

6. An eleventh-grade civics teacher wishes to supplement the standard text with essays exploring religious perspectives on American society. She wants her students to consider claims that Americans are a "chosen people" and that the only firm basis for a belief in human equality rests on God's equal loving concern for all people. In her proposal to the principal, the teacher indicates that, beyond presenting these views, she will argue that both are valid, though leaving students free to believe otherwise. Should the principal approve her plan?

7. Educators in the New York City school system proposed a "Rainbow Curriculum" for elementary schools that emphasized broad tolerance for individuals and groups. Parents in some districts objected to teaching respect for gays and lesbians and appreciation for family structures involving homosexual parents. The basis for their objections was largely religious. Should the schools have refrained from teaching this aspect of the "Rainbow Curriculum"?

8. High school seniors choose a classmate to speak at their graduation. During a rehearsal two days before graduation, the principal learns that the speaker will urge her audience to turn their lives over to Jesus. Should the principal intervene?

9. Ten of the twenty-two books on the shelf of a fifth-grade classroom are religious, and the teacher keeps a Bible on his desk. During the daily period of "free reading," he always reads

silently from his Bible. After a few parents complain, should the principal tell the teacher to change the selections in his little "library" or his reading habits?

10. Having reviewed the district's literature texts for elementary school, fundamentalist Christian parents discover that both in specific aspects and overall impression, the readings deeply offend their religious convictions. When they ask to withdraw their children from class use of the texts, should the district accede?

Religion, Educational Purposes, and Constitutional Law

These ten problems all involve judgments about how public schools should respect religious freedom, and all of them reach beyond sound educational decisions to constitutional interpretation. Officials must determine the meaning and application of language forbidding the government from establishing religion and protecting the free exercise of religion and freedom of speech. Within our political system, constitutional questions involve judges: how often should they constrain the educational choices of legislators, school boards, administrators, and teachers?

Our ten problems implicate fundamental controversies over the purposes of public education. How should schools aim to educate our children? What should they take on; what should they leave to parents and private groups?

Most of the critical questions arise out of an assumption that the government, and its schools, should be neutral about religion. According to the Supreme Court, American states may not prefer one religion over others and may not prefer religion over nonreligion. Some Supreme Court justices and critics believe government should be able to prefer religion in general; a smaller number of people (not including any Supreme Court justices) think states should be able to prefer Christianity. Almost no one believes the Constitution allows officials to prefer one version of Christianity over all others. Thus, virtually everyone agrees that certain preferences or endorsements in respect to religion are forbidden. It follows that public schools may not teach that particu-

3

lar religious doctrines, such as the virgin birth and transubstantiation, are true; nor may they endorse particular religious practices, such as Communion with wine or infant baptism.

Aiming to inculcate various moral and political virtues, public
schools teach students that they should respect their fellows, tolerate diverse views, and deliberate about alternatives. This instruction may affect the attractiveness of various religions. Most
obviously, students may be discouraged from accepting religious views directly opposed to what they are taught in school.
For example, a white supremacist religion that advocates de-
priving minorities of all political rights will find few recruits
among students taught to believe in racial equality.

Although tracing the connections between the teaching of
civic virtues and the appeal of various religions may be haz-
ardous, we can imagine that the influences reach beyond instances of direct opposition. A teacher recommending tolerance
and reasoned consideration for political life may emphasize that
he is not addressing how people should develop religious beliefs
and practices; a church that demands strict adherence to higher
religious authority and takes a harsh view of other religious perspectives may say little about politics. Hierarchical, intolerant religion is not opposed in strict logic to participatory, deliberative,
tolerant politics. But there is a tension. Unable to compartmen-
talize, or to perceive why attitudes appropriate for religious understanding are inapt for politics, a student might be drawn to a
religion that fits her ideas of desirable political life, and vice
versa. Thus, what schools teach apart from religion can have
spillover effects for the ways students approach religion.

About these possible spillover effects, educators might adopt
a range of attitudes. They could regard the effects as beyond
their mandate; unintended influences on religious beliefs and
practices would not be their concern.

Alternatively, educators could welcome certain of these effects. Although schools cannot teach against hierarchical, intolerant religion, educators might recognize that the civil life of liberal democracies will fare better if fewer people adhere to such
religious faiths. So long as they assume that schools should not
aim, even indirectly, to promote or discourage religious views,
educators who welcome various spillover effects will *act* like
those who disregard them.

4

Finally, educators might regard spillover effects as a cause for regret, drawing schools away from a neutrality about religion they might otherwise achieve. On this view, perhaps schools should try to counter spillover effects in various ways—much as we might hope that officials planning a new highway would not stick with an otherwise appealing route that would require the destruction of six Roman Catholic churches and no other houses of worship. One way to minimize spillovers would be to show believers in a hierarchical, intolerant religion how they can harmonize their views with democratic politics.

A related concern about spillover involves religion more broadly. Education that disregards religion may implicitly communicate its unimportance. Do public schools need to try counter this possible effect by presenting religious perspectives as options for students to consider? This troubling question about public school curriculums easily outranks in practical significance more confrontational issues about practices such as prayer and Bible reading.

In the pages that follow, we will examine these ten problems and others like them, analyzing ways in which religion touches the public school system, and exploring what courts have said about constitutional limits. The book is not restricted to discerning what public schools *may* do, given prevailing constitutional law; it also considers the exercise of educational judgment and the range of choice that judges should allow. Judicial decisions and opinions serve as subjects for critical examination, as well as setting the parameters for what now counts as constitutionally permissible. Avoiding the oversimplifications and automatic dismissals of opposing arguments that one finds at all points along the religious and political spectrums, the book aims to provide readers with bases on which to make judgments of their own that go deeper than visceral like or dislike of competing positions or groups. These bases are not easy formulas but a range of normative principles and practical considerations that should inform educational and constitutional choices.

Public school systems surely rank among the most important of American social institutions. According to tradition, they are our primary vehicle for forging a unified civic identity and for creating opportunities for children to transcend their parents' economic and social status. Yet we all know that, nationwide, public schools suffer grave problems. Inner-city schools, beset by budgetary constraints and acute disciplinary difficulties, are failing miserably in the endeavor to afford fair opportunities for many of their students. Some critics level the further charge that even schools in favored geographical locations do not provide students a coherent moral structure, and they attribute this failure to the absence of religion.

One proposed "remedy" for religionless public schools is public financing of private education, dominantly education under religious auspices. Although arguments about such aid connect to debates about what public schools should undertake, we can quickly see that neither "vouchers," approved by the Supreme Court in the summer of 2002, nor other assistance to private education will "solve" issues about public school religion.

At present, few legislators are willing to vote in favor of vouchers for all students that approximate the costs of public education. Even if they did so, many parents would not find within easy reach private schools that offer a religious education they approve. For the foreseeable future, most American children will be educated in public schools. The proper place of religion and religious judgment in those schools will remain a central political and constitutional issue for a long, long time.

To explore these issues, we begin by sketching briefly the historical development of public schools as it relates to religion, and constitutional doctrines that apply to religion in the schools. Next we turn to modern controversies over the proper purposes of public schools that bear significantly on the place of religion.

These initial chapters set the stage for the more detailed treatments that follow. Each of the remaining chapters discusses a set of specific problems, such as school prayer or teaching science, providing an analysis that takes into account constitutional law and educational policy in our liberal democratic political order. All our subjects can be loosely categorized under four major questions: (1) Do devotional practices belong in public schools? (2) When should the religious convictions and interests of students be treated like their nonreligious interests and convictions? (3) What should schools teach about religion and about topics, such as evolution or use of condoms, whose content conflicts with widespread religious views? (4) When should students, and teachers, be exempted from ordinary educational requirements because of their religious convictions?

By way of brief summary, the United States Supreme Court, in its exercises of constitutional interpretation, has said that officially sponsored devotional practices do not belong in public schools; that, in general, voluntary student groups devoted to religion should be treated like other student groups; that schools should not teach particular religious propositions as true but may teach about religion; that government should not, in short, sponsor particular religious views or engage in religious practices. I shall suggest that these positions represent an approach to the place of religion in public schools that is coherent and reflective of the fundamental values of a diverse liberal democracy. These are values that I embrace. The positions also represent sound constitutional doctrine. But these positions alone, at this level of generality, leave many sensitive issues unresolved. Much of the book is taken up with addressing these issues from the standpoint of educational choice and constitutional doctrine.

In part II, we inquire mainly about religious practices, reviewing general devotional exercises such as prayer and Bible reading and use of school facilities by religious clubs. We also address the bar on teaching religious propositions as true.

We concentrate in part III primarily on the subtle problems of teaching *about* religion, something allowed, and even encouraged, by the language of Supreme Court opinions. Individual chapters address different branches of learning and forms of teacher expression that do not directly involve the curriculum.

In part IV, we consider students' expressions of religious perspectives within the context of public education and claims by parents to have their children opt out of education that offends their religious sensibilities.

Running through these chapters is a story of a changing relationship between religion and public education, in which the courts have played a role, but only a modest one.

The schooling of children became mainly public in the first half of the nineteenth century. Although church membership was then lower than it is now, writers widely supposed that religious conviction was the key to personal morality and good citizenship; a nondenominational Protestantism was taught and practiced within the schools. By the end of the nineteenth century, texts and educators were treating their subject matters as essentially secular; religion was no longer a significant aspect of what students were taught. But in a great many schools, morning prayers and brief devotional Bible reading continued, the husks of a once serious effort to instruct students in the Christian religion.

During the late nineteenth and early twentieth centuries, some state courts reviewed whether prayer and Bible reading in public schools violated clauses forbidding establishments of religion in their own state constitutions. Most, but not all, concluded that these devotions were all right. When the United States Supreme Court finally addressed the practices in 1962 and 1963, it decisively ruled that they violated the Establishment Clause in the First Amendment of the federal Constitution. The Court indicated that schools could teach *about* religion but not attempt to indoctrinate.

The legal history of the last four decades has involved a working out of many of the implications of this basic principle. The Supreme Court itself has considered moments of silence, prayer at graduations and football games, posting of the Ten Commandments, the status of student groups that engage in religious worship, and the teaching of evolution and creationism. Lower courts have inquired about rights of teachers to express religious views, and rights of students to fulfill assignments with religious topics and to withdraw from parts of courses that offend their religious convictions.

During the past two decades, the Supreme Court has revamped the law of free exercise and establishment to an extraordinary degree. One component of this restructuring has been a reliance on a concept of equality, drawn from the Free Speech Clause, to require that, among voluntary student groups, religious groups be treated no less favorably than other groups. But the main engines of reform have been a sharp cutting back of both free exercise and establishment restrictions. The consequence is that other branches of government now have much broader discretion to decide how to treat religious claims and religious groups than they once did. But in this era of striking change, most of the standards relating to public school education have proved remarkably stable.

They have done so despite the fact that public schools have been a major battleground in what some have described as the country's "culture wars." A large segment of the American populace persists in condemning the Supreme Court for taking religion out of schools and thus contributing to a secular, immoral, materialist cultural ethos. Others insist that religion has no place within public schools. Within recent years, a third approach has attracted the support of a surprisingly diverse range of groups: public schools should make a much more serious effort to teach about religion but without engaging in devotional practices or teaching the truth of particular religious views. Everything the courts have said so far leaves wide room for debate about the constitutional limits of teaching about religion and about how a program conceived in those terms can best be carried forward.

Although the chapters that follow provide an account of "where we are now" and "how we got there," their main focus is analytical and normative. They undertake to examine the decisions and doctrines of the courts from a critical perspective, explaining their bases and evaluating their strengths and weaknesses. They focus on the central principle that public schools should not teach religious views as true, exploring what that principle entails and whether it is a solid basis for the aspirations of public schools. Most of the chapters involve a mixture of constitutional law and educational judgment. What is the range of approaches that schools may undertake? Within that range, which approaches make the most sense in terms of educational objectives and the values of the religion clauses? In no small part, the normative analysis of the book can be seen as a reflection on the constitutional "specialness" of religion. A pervasive question in modern law about the religion clauses is how far religion should be treated differently from other subjects of human understanding. A foundational assumption about religion and public schools is that religion is not the same as other subjects; this study helps show why that assumption has arisen and why it should continue.

PART I

HISTORY AND PURPOSES

*

A Brief History of American Public Schools and Religion

As we have seen, although American public schools have continually aimed to educate children to be moral persons and good citizens, the place of religion has undergone a fundamental shift: from colonial times to the mid–twentieth century, primary and secondary education became increasingly public, universal, and secular.

Here we consider the growth of public education in the United States, looking at the complex motivations of the innovators of the public school movement, at the "nonsectarian" religious teaching and devotions in which those schools engaged, and at the schools' growing secularity in the late nineteenth century. History cannot solve our present problems, but it offers a context in which to understand them.

This chapter also traces major Supreme Court cases and doctrines, which later chapters analyze more closely. Since 1947, Supreme Court interpretations of the Constitution's religion clauses have set sharp limits on religious teaching and practice within public schools; but these decisions leave open crucial issues of educational policy and constitutional judgment.

THE DEVELOPMENT OF PUBLIC SCHOOLS

Education in the early American colonies was almost entirely private and substantially religious. In 1647 Massachusetts adopted an "Old Deluder Satan" act requiring tax-supported town schools, but throughout the other colonies "formal schooling was typically a mix of private academies and local denominational religious schools."[1] By the latter stage of the eighteenth century, Stephen Macedo writes, the "profound democratic currents that fed the American Revolution greatly increased the concern with popular enlightenment."[2] Noah Webster urged that all citizens should be fitted for "places of trust" and that education should be a legislature's "first care."[3] As legislatures abandoned property qualifications for voting, as immigrants poured into cities, as fathers increasingly toiled in industries rather than at home, reformers conceived general education as a means to prevent disorder and to promote progress and civic virtue.[4]

In the early nineteenth century, states and cities often subsidized charity schools and religious schools on a per pupil basis.[5] Most of these schools complemented the values of families in the community, although urban charity schools self-consciously intervened against what their organizers perceived as the alien cultures of parents.[6] Between 1830 and 1860, many cities instituted their own schools and terminated support of private schools.[7]

Free public schools, drawing students from all social classes and national and religious heritages, aimed to create a "common republican culture."[8] Although reformers believed that public schools would increase academic effectiveness, for Horace Mann, the leader of the common school movement, "schooling was necessary to preserve republican institutions and to create a political community."[9]

Anti-Catholic attitudes undoubtedly affected the growth of public schools, as the number of American Catholics increased from thirty-five thousand in 1790 to over three million in 1860.[10] Not only the importance but the quality of those attitudes varied; unthinking bias against the Roman Catholic religion and the peoples of Catholic lands[11] combined with apprehension about the church's teachings, which not only defended a powerful form of hierarchical religious authority, but also stridently opposed religious liberty as an ideal.[12]

Whatever the precise effect of anti-Catholicism on their development, the character of the original public schools was indisputably a broad nondenominational Protestantism.[13] Although schools were "nonsectarian," their teaching and practice were significantly religious. Americans then believed, as some still do, that moral education could not be sundered from belief in God and an afterlife. Horace Mann wrote that "religious instruction in our schools, to the extent which the constitution and the laws of the State allowed and prescribed, was indispensable to the students' highest welfare, and essential to the vitality of moral education."[14] Filled with biblical stories, the commonly used McGuffey readers conveyed the message, in the words of Henry Steele Commager, that "God was omnipresent. He had His eye on every child for every moment. . . . He was a just God, but a stern one, and would not hesitate to punish even the smallest children who broke his commandments."[15] Popular nineteenth-century texts for the first eight grades "accepted without question the biblical account of the world, Adam and Eve included."[16] Nature was ordered by God, and so was history, including instances of God's frequent interposition that showed "that Americans are the people chosen by God in the modern world for a special destiny."[17] Prior to 1870, many texts denounced the Catholic religion as false and dangerous.[18] Although emphasizing religion less, secondary-school texts also "were laced with Christian, Protestant beliefs."[19]

The primary devotional practice was reading the Bible without commentary.[20] Mann remarked, "Our system earnestly inculcates all Christian morals; . . . in receiving the Bible, it allows it to do what is allowed to do in no other system,—*to speak for itself*. But here it stops."[21] The Bible used was the King James Version, acceptable to Protestants but not Catholics; and the very practice of reading without commentary was antithetical to Catholic teaching that Scripture should be understood as interpreted by the church. When Philadelphia school officials, having declined to let Catholic children read their Douay Bible, released them from classrooms during Bible reading, riots between nativist and Catholic mobs cost twelve lives.[22] Although American Roman Catholic leaders complained that public schools should be fairer to their faith, they increasingly insisted that the only remedy for the nonsectarian Protestant character of the schools was Catholic children attending Catholic schools and being assisted by state funds.[23]

One lesson from the Bible-reading conflicts is that no form of devotional practice is universally acceptable. If devotions are watered down not to conflict with anyone's beliefs about straightforwardly religious topics, such as the nature of God, they will offend those who reject watered-down religion.[24]

As the nineteenth century progressed, the religious content of public school teaching decreased dramatically, to such an extent that Warren Nord can write, "[B]y the year 1900 . . . there was little religion left in schools or universities. True, some prayer and Bible reading took place in many schools. But [religion] was no longer to be found in the heart of education, in the curriculum or in textbooks. The governing purposes of education had changed."[25] This dramatic shift was not mainly in response to the relatively few state judicial decisions restricting religious exercises within public schools.[26] The fundamental underlying causes had to do with the disintegration of a unified religious culture in Western civilization,[27] a consequence of complex influences including the Renaissance revival of classical studies, with their focus on human perspectives, the Reformation's elevation of individual thought and conscience, the breakdown of traditional structures wrought by the market economy and Industrial Revolution, and the growth of empirical natural sciences freed from religious premises. Nord remarks, "The secularization of the modern world is not the work of secularists."[28]

Devotional practices continued in many schools; they came increasingly to be justified in civil rather than religious terms. One 1870 defender of Bible reading urged that religion is taught so "that pupils may become intelligent and virtuous citizens."[29]

Although the idea that public schools should educate children to become moral citizens never disappeared, an ideal of liberal education gave way to a view that instruction should be practically useful, helping students to make their way in the world.[30] Nord writes that this utilitarian approach to education was part of the general Progressive movement, which, in "contrast to traditional religions and classical education," "placed a powerful emphasis on personal experience, on openness, on nonauthoritarian teaching, and on the uniqueness of the individual child."[31]

John Dewey, the most influential educational theorist of the twentieth century, emphasized learning by doing; his notion of community recognized cultural difference to a far greater degree than had the early school reformers.[32] During the latter part of the twentieth century, progressive education competed with more traditional approaches for dominance.[33] According to one account, from 1900 to 1925, educators primarily emphasized assimilation of a large immigrant population; from 1925 to 1954, they aimed largely to help children "adjust to life" (the progressive education approach); from 1954 to 1983, they responded to public demands that minorities, the poor, and the handicapped acquire educational opportunities; from 1983, after publication of the report *A Nation at Risk*, which warned of a rising tide of educational mediocrity, they focused on academic skills that workers need in a modern economy.[34]

We shall leave our historical sketch of public school philosophies at this point, relying on the subsequent discussions of educational purposes and specific subjects of educational policy to highlight major perspectives of the recent past.

CENTRAL CONSTITUTIONAL DECISIONS

Not until the mid–twentieth century did the United States Supreme Court develop constitutional doctrines that constrained public schools, well after their essentially secular character was already entrenched. The Court's decisions, some highly controversial, set certain clear boundaries; they leave unresolved other troubling problems we shall explore.

The Court's late entry is largely explained by the Constitution's distribution of state and federal powers. The First Amendment, which provides that "Congress shall make no law respecting an establishment of religion or prohibiting the free exercise thereof," originally applied only against the national government. States remained free to establish their own religions and to inhibit religious exercise as they saw fit. After the Civil War, the Fourteenth Amendment significantly restricted state power: states cannot "abridge the privileges or immunities of citizens," nor deprive persons "of life, liberty, or property without due process of law," nor deny them "the equal protection of the laws." Over time, judicial doctrine has settled that the Fourteenth Amendment makes the fundamental protections of the Bill of Rights applicable against the states, but this occurred with respect to the religion clauses only in 1940, and not until 1947 did the Supreme Court render its first significant Establishment Clause decision.

In two 1920s decisions that preceded this development, the Court determined that a state may not prohibit the teaching of foreign languages prior to ninth grade,[35] and may not bar children from attending private schools, including parochial schools.[36] Neither case concerned religion in public schools, but each reflects a kind of constitutional protection of pluralism in education; and their reliance on the liberty of parents to determine children's education bears obliquely on how public schools should treat religious topics and respond to parental complaints that the curriculum offends their religious convictions.

The 1947 case of *Everson v. Board of Education*[37] adopted an expansive view of what the Establishment Clause forbids. By a bare five-to-four margin, the justices allowed localities to provide free bus transportation for children attending nonprofit schools, including parochial schools. Justice Black regarded this assistance as a peripheral service, like fire and police protection, not a subsidy to the schools themselves. He penned more general language about the Establishment Clause that many jurists have quoted subsequently:

> Neither a state nor the Federal Government . . . can pass laws which aid one religion, aid all religions, or prefer one religion over another. . . . No tax in any amount, large or small, can be levied to support any religious activities or institutions, whatever they may be called, or whatever form they may adopt to teach or practice religion. . . . [T]he clause . . . was intended to erect "a wall of separation" between church and state.[38]

More remarkable than the Court's division over bus transportation was its unanimous adoption of this highly separationist account of nonestablishment. All the justices relied heavily on the views of Jefferson and Madison and the movement toward nonestablishment in Virginia. This approach was dubious from a historical point of view, given that the amendment actually protected existing state establishments from federal interference. Those inclined to political interpretations of Supreme Court doctrine have noted that in the mid–twentieth century the overriding issue about establishment was public aid to Roman Catholic parochial schools and that the great majority of Protestants united with Jews and secularists in opposing it.[39]

One year after *Everson* construed the Establishment Clause to forbid government promotion of religion, the Court first considered a public school program. During each week schools in Champaign, Illinois, set aside a period for religious instruction, which was offered by teachers of various faiths who were subject to approval and supervision by the school superintendent. Noting that students released for religious instruction had to attend those classes, Justice Black wrote that the use of school property for teaching religion and the close cooperation of school authorities and the private Council for Religious Education constituted an impermissible support of religious groups in spreading their faiths.[40]

The Court followed this controversial ruling four years later by upholding a similar plan, under which the religious classes were taught off school property.[41] Justice Douglas wrote that New York had made a wholesome accommodation of the public service to the spiritual needs of its people. The opinion's broad language about accommodation gave hope to those who opposed strict separation that government might support religion to a degree that far exceeded what *Everson* foretold.

In 1962 and 1963 the Court declared that schools could not begin their days with a school-sponsored class prayer[42] or devotional Bible reading,[43] thus rejecting a characteristic feature of public education from its inception. These decisions were so unpopular that many school districts simply have disregarded them. Nonetheless, during a later period when the Court was retreating from its hostile attitude toward aid to private religious education, it extended its bar on prayers to graduation ceremonies and football games.[44]

The Bible-reading opinion, *Abington Township v. Schempp*, contains comment of much wider significance: the Court's most definitive statement on teaching *about* religion:

> [I]t might well be said that one's education is not complete without a study of comparative religion or the history of religion and its relationship to the advancement of civilization. It certainly may be said that the Bible is worthy of study for its literary and historic qualities. Nothing we have said here indicates that such study of the Bible or of religion, when presented objectively as part of a secular program of education, may not be effected consistently with the First Amendment.[45]

What exactly is an appropriate teaching about religion as part of secular education is the central question about religion and the public schools; our examination of how to implement the Court's proposal occupies much of this book.

Beyond its specific ruling, the *Schempp* case is also significant in the general doctrinal test the Court employed: to be acceptable, a law or practice must have a "secular legislative purpose and a primary effect that neither advances nor inhibits religion."[46] Courts applying general constitutional language usually develop intermediate "tests" through which they strain the facts. Here, the Court indicated that if Bible reading was instituted for the purpose of promoting religion or if it has that effect, it is a forbidden establishment.[47] This inquiry about purpose and effect became the core of the Court's standard test in reviewing all varieties of Establishment Clause challenges for four decades.

The full test, developed eight years later in *Lemon v. Kurtzman*,[48] a case striking down aid to parochial schools, joined the elements of purpose and effect to an examination of excessive entanglement. If the government and religious authority were unduly intertwined, that constituted an establishment.[49] A 1997 opinion characterized all entanglement as an aspect of effect rather than an analytically separate element.[50]

By now, most of the justices sitting on the Court have either rejected the *Lemon* test outright or have remarked that it should not be applied in its full form in every establishment case. But a majority opinion of the Court has yet to abandon that test. This posture leaves lower-court judges in a bind, having been instructed by the Supreme Court *not* to abandon a prevailing standard before the Supreme Court itself does.[51] These judges must apply the *Lemon* test *and* be sensitive to other approaches that might command a Supreme Court majority or persuade individual justices. The major alternatives at this stage are (1) endorsement: does a law (or practice) endorse a particular religion or religion in general? (2) coercion: is a law coercive? (3) history: would a law have been regarded as an establishment of religion when the First or Fourteenth Amendments were adopted? Subsequent chapters say more about these approaches.

For preferences or burdens that government directs toward one religion in comparison with others, the Court has employed the same test it uses for racial classifications. The preference or burden is acceptable only if it is a necessary means to accomplish a compelling government interest that cannot be achieved by less restrictive means. The government can rarely make this showing; patent discrimination among religions is doomed to failure.

One vital issue about religion and public schools is whether children whose parents object to what is going on—say, instruction in the use of contraceptives or the teaching of Darwinian evolutionary theory—may be excused from ordinary requirements.[52] Three Supreme Court cases stand out as critical. In *West Virginia Board of Education v. Barnette*,[53] the Court held that students who were Jehovah's Witnesses did not have to salute the flag. Although relying on the First Amendment as a whole, not just the Free Exercise Clause, *Barnette* definitively settled that persons who object out of religious conscience may not be compelled to comply with every standard practice of public schools.

Wisconsin v. Yoder[54] decided that the Amish had a free exercise right to withdraw their children from regular school at the end of the eighth grade. The Court said that, without a compelling interest, the state could not interfere with the Amish practice of community vocational education for teenagers.[55] The state failed to demonstrate that sending Amish children to school until they were sixteen, as the law required, served such an interest. *Yoder* is significant partly for its treatment of parental claims and the purposes of public education, a subject we take up in the next chapter.

In cases in which individuals sought exemptions from otherwise valid laws, states consistently had more success satisfying the compelling interest test than when they classified people by race or religion. Most claims by religious persons to be excused from standard legal requirements failed. Nonetheless, in *Employment Division v. Smith*,[56] in 1990, the Court abandoned that approach altogether for claims of special treatment. Native Americans who ingested peyote as the center of their worship services had no more basis than anyone else to violate antidrug laws. As far as federal constitutional law is concerned, *Smith* creates doubt whether parents possess *any* free exercise right to have children excused from school practices.[57] But Justice Scalia's opinion in *Smith* makes clear that legislatures and administrators may choose to provide exemptions much more broadly than the Constitution requires.[58]

Whether schools will respond favorably when parents voice religious objections to aspects of public education depends partly on how broadly *Barnette*'s right of conscience is construed, partly on how state courts interpret their own free exercise provisions and statutes (some of which explicitly grant greater protection than does *Smith*), and partly on their own educational judgments.

A person making a free exercise claim is usually asserting that a law or practice violates his exercise of religion; but free exercise can also function as a shield used by a state against an argument that it has violated the Establishment Clause. The state may argue that a challenged law relieves a burden on religious people and thus is justified as assisting free exercise. The Supreme Court has consistently refused to accept devotional exercises in schools or religious teaching on that basis. However, free exercise considerations *would* help sustain administrative choices to excuse religious objectors from practices in public schools.

An important free speech argument has proved effective in the last two decades in defeating various arguments that the Establishment Clause bars any assistance to religious associations. The basic theory is that the government cannot treat religious speech more restrictively than other speech. If a school allows use of its premises for all sorts of clubs but *not* religious clubs, it is engaging in "content regulation," and also, the Court has said, "viewpoint discrimination," a practice that is particularly hard to defend. The government cannot justify this discrimination as carrying forward a policy of nonestablishment. Thus, when school sponsorship of the ideas is absent, public schools may not (usually) differentiate between religious and nonreligious activities.[59]

Purposes of Public School Education

The constitutional principle that government should not establish religion sets limits on the place of religion in public schools, but the purposes of those schools provide powerful reasons not to disregard religion altogether. Reflection on this tension requires us to consider several issues. How does teaching about religion fit with the basic purposes of public education? Should schools aim to counter spillover effects on religious belief and affiliation caused by liberal education? How should the authority of parents, educators, school boards and legislators interact in determining what schools do?

What Is Public Education For?

Clearly, American education serves multiple, overlapping objectives. These include developing the vocational skills of students, their capacity for choice, their ability to participate in enriching activities, their civic virtue, and their moral character.

Vocational Training

Although liberal education is often contrasted with practical or vocational education, public education inevitably has a vital vocational component.[1] Much early learning—reading, writing, and counting—is required for ordinary work, as well as for larger educational purposes. Further, to perform work successfully, people need to be able to concentrate, to discipline themselves, and to work with associates—qualities schools aim to instill. And education that seems far from practical may help develop the kind of judgment that is crucial for making decisions about people and complex situations. Schools help students learn how to do the work required of them; the only serious question about this objective is how prominently it should figure in relation to other aims.

23

Enhancement of Capacity for Choice

Second, education helps students choose the lives they want to lead. Exposure to literature, history, and science gives young people a sense of possibilities and perspectives, a basis to decide for themselves how to live, rather than conform to someone's preordained program.

Knowledge and Enrichment

Apart from helping students make major life choices, study increases their knowledge of the world and helps them enrich their lives. As Amy Gutmann says, citizens value education prior to college "for helping children learn how to live a good life in the nonmoral sense by teaching them knowledge and appreciation of (among other things) literature, science, history, and sports."[2]

Education for Life as a Citizen

Training children to participate in the civic life of our republican government was, as we have seen, a primary motivation of early school reformers. Good citizens must be able to consider and discuss political possibilities; they must respect other citizens and tolerate their views. Many scholars believe that this civic education remains highly important for public schools. In her *Democratic Education*, Amy Gutmann, for example, writes that "a society that supports conscious social reproduction must educate all educable children to be capable of participating in collectively shaping their society."[3]

The objective of preparing students for democratic citizenship affects the material of courses, the way events and historical personalities are cast, and techniques of instruction. Courses cover the country's history and form of government. Patriots of the Revolution are depicted more favorably, for example, than the Ku Klux Klan. Teachers aiming to teach gender and racial equality treat students of all kinds with equal respect, and insist that their students do so. They encourage students to think for themselves, to express their views and respond thoughtfully to the opinions of others.[4]

24

Where the main responsibility lies to educate children for democratic citizenship is disputed. This issue bears on what public schools teach, but less than might appear at first glance. Michael McConnell contends that our country was committed from its origins to the idea that moral and civic education should rest in the hands of parents and private groups.[5] The government should "disestablish" education, as it has disestablished religion, and support parental choices to educate children in the way they think best.[6] Were such a view taken to mean that we should have no public schools, only a set of private options, it would suggest that any issues about religion in public schools are about what to do with an educational system that would die out in a just society. But McConnell himself believes that public schools will properly remain in place and continue to educate many students.[7] Like private schools, these public schools presumably will still need to do some educating for civic virtue,[8] although it remains a central question how much of the job they should leave to families and private groups, including religious organizations.

Moral Character and Ideals

Public schools have traditionally aimed to instill in students desirable moral characters and ideals, beyond those connected to liberal democracy. Of course, that was completely natural so long as education was conceived as substantially religious; instruction grounded in religious premises would include teaching about how to live. But some theorists now argue that liberal democracies should be neutral among competing versions of the good life, and this logic might extend to public schools.[9]

Understood in its widest form, the argument that schools should not teach morality is unappealing. *Most moral virtues* concern how people can live amicably together. Schools certainly should encourage students to be honest and respectful, even when these qualities do not relate to politics.[10] Further, any mandate of neutrality reaches nonmoral, as well as moral, aspects of the good life. If schools should not teach aspects of morality except those concerning civic virtue, they should not tell students that they should appreciate art and music or, for that matter, regard knowledge as intrinsically valuable as well as useful. Such

25

a restraint would be very broad; that alone should induce skepticism about proposals that schools should adopt a neutral stance toward morality. The most one can plausibly argue is that schools should avoid moral instruction about matters that are substantially controversial and do not concern responsibilities individuals have toward their fellows.

Overlapping Domains

One who relates educational purposes to what might be taught quickly realizes that many subject matters and forms of teaching accomplish multiple purposes. To take a single example, if students are taught to think carefully about actions that a protagonist of a novel, say David Copperfield, might have taken, this could enrich their appreciation of literature, help them develop their own capacity for choice, contribute to their moral character, and involve them in deliberation of a kind that could be productive in political life. Purposes do not match subjects and forms of teaching in any simple one-to-one relationship.[11] Nevertheless, disagreements about legitimate purposes and about priorities among these can affect what subjects are taught and exactly how they are presented.

How Does Religion Fit?

Given their educational purposes, what should schools do about religion? A person who believes that faithfulness to a true religion is the primary purpose of life may respond that the best education must include religion; a skeptic who regards religions as foolish delusions may think their only place is as objects of criticism for the miseries they have caused. Is it possible to reach any conclusions on which we could agree if we did not evaluate all the merits and flaws of religions? Can we say anything if we suspend judgment about the truth and value of various religions?

It helps first to ask ourselves these questions freed from worries about state involvement and classroom conflict, imagining that we are private tutors with individual students. We know that people ignorant about religion can manage quite well in most modern jobs, but we can see that religion is a relevant subject for each of the other major educational purposes. It has been a central aspect of human culture throughout history. Knowledge of civilization includes knowledge of religion. A high percentage of Americans profess belief in God;[12] most participate in worship services fairly regularly;[13] and many say that religion is important in their lives.[14] Judged by what members of our society believe, religion is a serious object of choice for people deciding how to live. Many people draw from religions as sources of insight about morality, social justice, and civic duty. No doubt, one *can* be a moral person and a good citizen without being religious and without well understanding why religion means as much as it does to many of our fellows, but whatever the sources of one's own public and private values, one will develop a better sense of how to treat others and make political choices if one grasps how people who do care about religion see themselves and the wider society. As private tutors suspending judgment about the merits of religion, we would engage our students in its study.[15]

Are matters different for public schools? Given religious liberty and nonestablishment, perhaps these schools simply have no business teaching religion. Up to a point, this reservation about the legitimate role of public schools is sound; they may not teach that particular religious ideas are true or that particular practices are required. But, in theory at least, schools can explore the place of religion in history and in people's lives without reaching judgments about religious truth.[16]

Another concern about public schools and religion is competence. Most history teachers know something about the Protestant Reformation and Puritan Massachusetts, but relatively few schoolteachers are now trained to teach about religion in any depth; and how many teachers would wish to explore the question of religion in ways appropriate for public schools is uncertain. But whether better-trained teachers, inclined to explore dimensions of religion without proselytizing, could function well in the public school setting is itself a serious issue.

The contention that religion is best left to parents and other private organizations weaves together threads of legitimacy and competence. But most parents and affiliated private organizations, presenting their own religion as the truth and developing its implications, are unlikely even to attempt to offer a detached,

27

nonjudgmental account of various religions in historical context. Thus, what public schools could aspire to do differs qualitatively from what private sources usually provide.

One conceivable basis for schools to omit much education about religion is that citizens of liberal democracies should discuss and determine major political issues in terms of shared political premises that do not rely on any religious view.[17] Students do need to understand that political issues often are debated without reference to religious premises, and that such constrained debates may be more constructive than ones in which competing religious views are thrust into mutual opposition. But religious perspectives commonly provide support for ideas, such as human equality, that may also be reached on other grounds; and an understanding of religious perspectives helps us to grasp the political currents of our society. Further, the question of whether political discourse *should* be free of religious premises is itself hotly contested.[18] The basic idea of deliberative consideration would be contradicted if mature students were merely presented with religion-free discussions of politics, and not given a chance to consider whether that is indeed an ideal for all liberal democracies.[19] Finally, most importantly, any purely political argument for disregarding religion does not touch the powerful claims that religion should be presented as an important subject for individuals deciding how to live.

A different reason why public schools might steer clear of religion is that what they say will inevitably have the effect of favoring some religious views over others. Even presenting the Puritans in a positive light without saying much about their actual religious beliefs may seem a kind of endorsement of their Protestant vision over the orthodoxy of the Church of England and Roman Catholicism. But similar effects occur if the schools remain silent. Whatever they mention or omit will have some effect on religious convictions and affiliations.

RESPONSES TO SPILLOVER EFFECTS ON RELIGION

These effects raise the secondary question about the purposes of public schools that were discussed in the introduction: how should educators regard the influence of liberal instruction on their students' religious perspectives? If the schools say very little about religion, this may incline students to believe that religion, contrary to the convictions of many religious people, is not of central importance for most domains of life.[20] And how schools teach various subjects can influence students' views about particular religions. Most straightforwardly, if a school teaches as true what a religion asserts is false—say, the Darwinian theory of evolution—that can undercut belief in the religion, for better or worse. More subtle interrelations are likely to be pervasive. Authoritarian, dogmatic school teaching about other subjects seems to go hand in glove with authoritarian, dogmatic religion. Teaching that emphasizes skepticism, critical judgment, and deliberation fits better with democratic, less dogmatic religion. Should educators concern themselves with the negative influence their teaching may have on various religions?

Some may say that once schools figure out what they should do in light of legitimate purposes and restraints on teaching religion, they should disregard unintended effects. This may be *one* defensible strategy for a government that is supposed to remain neutral about religious truth; but it is unduly harsh as a general approach. Suppose planners have proposed alternative routes A and B for a new road; members of the Highway Authority conclude that if they discounted all effects on religious groups, they would slightly prefer route A. But that route entails the destruction of the community's only six Roman Catholic churches. Constructing route B would destroy two Catholic churches, and one each of Episcopalian, Presbyterian, and Methodist churches, leaving at least one church of each of those denominations. Because route B will have a less disproportionate effect on the fate of various religious groups, its choice seems not only acceptable but preferable.[21] If so, a counsel that public educators should be indifferent to effects on religious convictions and affiliation can be defended only on the grounds that such effects are too difficult to assess and that responding to them becomes too complicated and dangerous in the school context.

Uncertainties about actual influences raise a very large caution about concentrating much on spillover effects. Undoubtedly, both our education and our society have become more secular over the last two hundred years; it is intuitively plausible that tolerant, critical teaching must incline students toward less dogmatic religions and that inattention to religion in school must make religion seem less important. But what are we to make of the fact that in Western European countries (including Great Britain) in which religion has been a part of general education over most of the last century,[22] involvement in religious groups is much lower than in the United States and skepticism about religion is much more widespread. Given the complex threads of historical influence, it would, of course, be silly to attribute these differences in attitudes about religion mainly to how religion has been treated in schools; but the European experience at least generates a serious doubt whether more or less objective teaching about religion, combined with well-worn rituals, is likely to help produce religious commitment. And during a modern era in the United States in which public school teaching became less directive and placed a greater emphasis on critical thinking, membership has shifted from traditional, now fairly liberal, churches to more evangelical, less liberal, churches. One wonders whether young people, wanting a solid authority for some aspects of their lives, will be more likely to turn to evangelical religion if schools (and family) fail to provide that authority.

Even if educators had greater confidence than now seems warranted about the exact influences of educational strategies on religious convictions, they might be worried that any self-conscious effort to respond would be inept and uneven, making disregard a preferable strategy.

Instead of disregarding influences on religious views, educators might welcome influences on religious understanding and affiliation that indirectly promote civic virtues. The idea here, developed forcefully by Stephen Macedo,[23] is that authoritarian, intolerant, dogmatic religions that discourage critical thinking are less desirable *from a civic point of view* than open, tolerant religions that encourage critical deliberation. If the effect of public education is indirectly to favor the second kind of religion, that is a cause for satisfaction, not regret.[24]

A sharply contrasting attitude is that such negative influences are at odds with an ideal of neutrality according to which government actions would not influence religious beliefs and practices. One such account is provided by John Tomasi,[25] who argues that the way "[l]iberal regimes shape the ethical outlooks of their citizens, deeply and relentlessly influenc[ing] even their most personal commitments over time,"[26] threatens the legitimacy of the political order.[27] No one can achieve complete neutrality of effect, but that does "not excuse liberals from seeking out ways to *minimize* the unintended effects of spillover so far as liberal justice allows."[28] Because educators should help them to fit the norms of public reason to the broader views they affirm,[29] civic education should invite students to consider the meaning of their rights as citizens within the context of their full perspectives.[30] Thus, Roman Catholic children "must be helped to understand what it means to be a Catholic within the liberal social world they are about to enter."[31]

Tomasi's suggestion has considerable intuitive appeal for possible spillover effects on religion.[32] If I were teaching a few like-minded students, I would relate education about civic virtue to their understanding of life's ultimate meaning. For example, if my students were evangelical Protestants convinced that only those who accept Jesus Christ as their personal savior are redeemed, I would suggest how religious liberty and disestablishment could make sense from their perspective. Public school teachers would have difficulty designing individual treatment for each religious group of diverse student bodies; but Tomasi seems to have in mind rather teachers exploring a range of religious understandings and how they relate to the civic life of liberal democracies.[33]

Even taken in this way, Tomasi's suggestion does not set an easy task for the public school teacher. We may initially rule out any conscious distortion, or silence about important subjects, that is designed to minimize spillover effects. (Tomasi does not propose this.) A teacher aiming to avoid having students think badly of Roman Catholicism should not fail to mention the Spanish Inquisition or soften its horror. A science teacher should not fail to teach that the earth is outside the physical center of the universe even if the doctrine of some religion puts the earth there.

A much thornier problem for a teacher aiming to counter spillover effects is drawing necessary distinctions. The teacher will have to figure out what are (1) irreconcilable conflicts of religious perspectives with civic ideals, (2) serious tensions between the two, and (3) potential spillovers that reflect no genuine incompatibilities or tensions. The opinion of some Muslims that blasphemy should be severely punished[34] directly conflicts with modern liberal democratic ideas of freedom of speech and religion. Perhaps we can take adherence to a Christian Church that is universal (in some sense) as fully compatible with appropriate national patriotism in the political realm (so long as we accept that someone's Christian commitment always stands in potential judgment on national politics). The right kind of teaching about patriotism might generate no real tension with acceptance of a universal Church. But how are we to understand the relation between civic equality for women and religious rules against ordaining females, as well as the traditional view of many religions that wives have special responsibilities within the family? And how should we perceive the relation of biblical literalism to a teacher's claim that our Constitution has been served well by not being interpreted literally? No doubt, devoted Roman Catholics or Orthodox Jews who accept every teaching of their religion can believe in civic equality; no doubt, biblical literalists can endorse nonliteralist constitutional interpretation. But is a teacher to deny any tensions among the paired positions? Many people believe that the justice of civic equality for women has implications for how churches should organize their internal affairs; many believe that the reasons why constitutional literalism is unwise also bear on biblical interpretation. Even attempting to discern whether significant tensions do exist drives the teacher deep into religious understandings and their relation to civic ideals, a topic that may not be appropriate for school classrooms.

Perhaps the teacher is better off stressing that he or she is only talking about political and secular moral ideals, that religion is a different subject, and that many excellent citizens adhere to religions whose structure and tenets differ significantly from the parallel norms of liberal democracies. The main work of countering spillover effects would be left to parents and other private individuals.

The insights of Macedo and Tomasi, apparently in direct opposition, might be joined in the following way.[35] Because potential spillover effects may often be desirable from a civic standpoint (and because teachers cannot confidently say when tensions between perspectives are serious), teachers should counter these effects only when doing so does not undercut the educational policy that may cause the spillover and when they need not decide whether an arguable tension is genuine. By way of illustration, students should be shown how a believer in authoritarian religion can accept liberal democracy;[36] they should not be told that ideas of secular tolerance and respect have no relevance for religion.

AUTHORITY TO DECIDE

Thus far we have considered desirable educational approaches, putting to one side the question of who should decide what policies any school system should adopt. As Amy Gutmann points out, liberal democrats cannot simply favor the best approach; they must ask who should be able to make that determination. After she contrasts approaches that emphasize the place of the state, of families, and of individual children,[37] she proposes a division of responsibility among politically representative bodies, individual parents, and professional educators.[38]

The main competitor to an account such as this, which places considerable educational authority in school boards and other elected bodies, is one that grants authority to individual parents. On this theory, a majority of parents should not impose on a minority who objects. Thus, even if a majority approves of sex education, such education would be out of bounds for public schools or should not be imposed on children of dissenting parents.[39] Given all the social regulations on behalf of children's welfare that may conflict with parental judgments,[40] any absolute priority for parental judgment is not a political tenet of modern liberal democracies.[41] The special authority of parents is now mainly conceived as conducing to the welfare of children, as the broader society assesses that welfare.

The main thrust of a parental rights approach is to support a pluralist approach to education, with the state providing financial support to private and parochial schools. It is of little help in deciding exactly what public schools should teach. When parents whose children are in the same public schools have sharply different educational opinions, obviously they cannot all be satisfied. Claims of parental rights, however, *can* underpin arguments to assign more authority to local communities rather than larger units of government[42] and to allow individual exemptions from standard requirements.

33

The broad political question of comparative authority links to constitutional law and the role of courts. Some questions of relative authority are (merely) ones of political and educational theory, not law. The best educational theory may assign professional educators primary responsibility to determine how math should be taught; but a school board may have legal power to usurp that responsibility. Other questions of authority raise constitutional issues. Most commonly, unhappy parents claim that no one within the educational system has the power to do what they challenge, such as engage students in classroom prayer; but sometimes people complain that a decision has been made by the wrong body or according to the wrong standard of judgment.

The religion clauses of the Constitution make educational decisions respecting religion peculiarly susceptible to legal challenge. School officials have the power to do many foolish things, but they must tread extremely carefully when the subject is religion.

Whenever judicial interference emerges as a serious possibility, courts must consider more than ideal standards of constitutional judgment. They have to worry about what facts they are able to determine[43] and what workable remedies they can grant. To take a simple example, a judge can much more easily determine the content of a textbook and specify what needs to be altered than she can determine that a teacher is favoring a particular religion in oral comments and tell him just what he needs to say instead, with what inflection and with what degree of enthusiasm. If what teachers say—and how they say it—matters more than the content of texts, judges have a decidedly limited capacity to control instruction.[44] Judges who recognize that questions are very hard to determine commonly defer to the authority of officials, here teachers, principals, and school boards, who make initial decisions.

CONCLUSION

In this chapter, we have reviewed a wide array of issues about educational purposes, negative spillover effects, and the distribution of educational authority. In subsequent chapters, we consider practical consequences of the various contending positions.

PART II

DEVOTIONS, CLUBS, AND
TEACHING RELIGION AS TRUE

*

CHAPTER 3

Devotional Practices: Prayer and Bible Reading

Almighty God, we acknowledge our dependence upon Thee, and we beg Thy blessing upon us, our parents, our teachers and our Country.

In 1951, New York's State Board of Regents, with broad supervisory powers over the public schools, composed this nondenominational prayer that it recommended classes recite each day.[1] After a group of parents in New Hyde Park objected to students' saying the prayer, New York courts sustained the prayer, assuming that participation in it was voluntary. In Pennsylvania and the city of Baltimore, laws required that the school day begin with a reading of the Bible, without comment.[2] A Unitarian father in Pennsylvania objected to the state's practice of Bible reading, and the famous atheist Madalyn Murray (O'Hair) complained about Baltimore's. The Supreme Court resolved these cases in 1963, a year after its ruling on the New York prayer.

In both instances, the Court held that the practices violated the Establishment Clause. Although the margins were a comfortable six to one[3] and eight to one, these rulings have proved enduringly controversial. Many school districts maintained class prayer and Bible reading well after the decisions, and it was said more than thirty years later that "flagrant disregard of the law banning school prayer [continues] in many parts of the country. In the deep south, daily prayer and Bible reading in schools are commonplace."[4] A number of constitutional amendments have been proposed in Congress to alter the outcomes.[5]

 We begin our discussion of particular legal and educational issues with prayer and Bible reading for a number of reasons. These were the key devotional practices in nineteenth-century schools. The Supreme Court's invalidation of them marks a significant shift in what is regarded as constitutionally acceptable involvement of public schools in religious activities. Further, these cases set the framework for much of what follows, both the rejection of sponsored devotions and the basic idea that public schools may not teach religious truth but may teach about religion. We can understand a good deal about religion in public schools if we grasp why these decisions make constitutional sense in a liberal democracy whose people accept diverse religious perspectives.

By any fair appraisal, the prayer and Bible-reading decisions—*Engel v. Vitale* and *Abington Township v. Schempp*—have not influenced people's lives as directly as the landmark rulings requiring school desegregation and creating a constitutional right to abortion (*Brown v. Board of Education* and *Roe v. Wade*). Routine prayers and Bible reading in public schools rarely transform children's lives. But for many religious conservatives, the decisions powerfully symbolize the secularization of American public life, a deplorable drift away from our society's recognition of its dependence on God. And these critics are right to understand the decisions as carrying negative implications for the place of religion in public schools, beyond the particular actions they condemn.

How is it that practices so common in the United States were outlawed by such substantial majorities of the Court? From the beginning of the Republic, prayers have been offered at official occasions to bless the endeavors of political authorities and citizens; and we have seen in chapter 1 that Bible reading without comment was widespread in public schools from their origin. If prayer and devotional Bible reading were constitutionally unacceptable, why did the Court did not say so before 1962 and 1963? To answer this question, we need to repair to some historical facts sketched in chapter 1.

The First Amendment to the U.S. Constitution contains two clauses relating to religion: it says, "Congress shall make no law respecting an establishment of religion or prohibiting the free exercise thereof." The original Bill of Rights applied only against the federal government. According to now settled judicial interpretation, the Fourteenth Amendment afforded citizens the protections of the Bill of Rights against the states and localities as well; but the first application of the Establishment Clause to the states occurred only in 1947, in the seminal case of *Everson v. Board of Education.*[6] This helps explain why the prayer and Bible-reading decisions came so late.

But we need briefly to explore another perplexity about the Establishment Clause's application to the states. People disagree about exactly what the Free Exercise Clause protects, but few dispute that coverage of the clause against states should be the same as coverage against the federal government. Analysis is more complex for the Establishment Clause, which initially protected state establishments from federal interference.[7] Some scholars have complained that a provision designed to safeguard state establishments should not be understood to forbid state establishments.[8] The answer is that the initial Establishment Clause not only protected state decisions about establishment, it also precluded any establishment within the domains of the federal government. No state establishments remained when Congress proposed the Fourteenth Amendment, so at that stage the practical significance of the clause was to restrict any federal establishment. Given the extension through the Fourteenth Amendment to the states of many other protections that originally concerned only the federal government, extending the prohibition against federal establishments to the states is not at all odd.

A separate question is whether the Fourteenth Amendment's guarantee of individual rights should be taken to forbid establishments of religion that do not violate any particular individual's personal liberty. The Supreme Court has rightly assumed that the guarantee of "no establishment" ties directly to the protection of individuals' free exercise of religion, although the justices may be faulted for failing to explain that connection more carefully.[9]

SCHOOL-SPONSORED PRAYER AND BIBLE READING

To understand why the decisions about prayer and Bible reading were so one-sided, we look to the *Everson* case. The majority upheld the state provision of bus transportation for parochial school children, but Justice Black's opinion emphasized the "'wall of separation' between church and state."[10] In language with which the dissenters agreed, he wrote that a state may not "pass laws which aid one religion, aid all religions, or prefer one religion over another."[11]

Although Justice Douglas's rhetoric of accommodation to religion in the decision upholding New York's "released time" system[12] gave temporary encouragement to those who favored a more permissive understanding of the Establishment Clause, *Engel v. Vitale* and *Abington Township v. Schempp* dashed these hopes for direct devotional practices sponsored by schools. In *Engel*, Justice Black, after reviewing colonial history, wrote that the government's placing its stamp of approval on a particular kind of prayer exercised "indirect coercive pressure on minorities to conform" and constituted "one of the greatest dangers" to individual religious liberty.[13] "[I]n this country it is no part of the business of government to compose official prayers for any group of the American people to recite as part of a religious program carried on by the government."[14]

Brushing aside arguments that Bible reading was designed for nonreligious moral inspiration, Justice Clark declared in *Schempp* that the state cannot prescribe religious exercises as "curricular activities of students who are required by law to attend school."[15] States must observe a wholesome neutrality, not place their official support "behind the tenets of one or of all orthodoxies."[16] The Establishment Clause "withdrew all legislative power respecting religious belief and the expression thereof."[17] To be acceptable, a practice must have "a secular legislative purpose and a primary effect that neither advances nor inhibits religion,"[18] a test of constitutionality that mandatory Bible reading fails. Responding to the worry that a "religion of secularism" will be established unless religious exercises are permitted, Clark wrote that schools may neither promote religion nor affirmatively oppose religion. The strict neutrality they must maintain allows studying the Bible "for its literary and historic qualities" and permits "a study of comparative religion or the history of religion and its relationship to the advancement of civilization."[19]

Earlier in his opinion, Justice Clark quoted approvingly from the language of two *Everson* dissents. In one of these, Justice Jackson had remarked that our public schools are organized "on the premise that secular education can be isolated from all reli-

gious teaching so that the school can inculcate all needed temporal knowledge and also maintain a strict and lofty neutrality as
to religion. The assumption is that after the individual has been
instructed in worldly wisdom he will be better fitted to choose
his religion."[20] The most difficult problems of religion and public
schools require us to recognize that Justice Jackson's premise is
wholly unrealistic.[21]

In a lengthy concurring opinion that broadly surveyed church-
state issues in constitutional law, Justice Brennan urged that "organs of government" cannot be used for "essentially religious
purposes."[22] The purpose of public schools was to serve a public
function, Brennan said, "the training of American citizens in an
atmosphere free of parochial, divisive or separatist influences of
any sort—an atmosphere in which children may assimilate a
heritage common to all American groups and religions."[23]

Justice Stewart dissented in both *Engel* and *Schempp*.[24] Objecting to the "wall of separation" metaphor, he argued in *Engel* that
letting students who wish say the Regents prayer would not establish an official religion.[25] In *Schempp*, he contended that a ban
on religious exercises in school would place religion "at an artificial and state-created disadvantage."[26] Parents who want the
school day to begin with Bible reading have "a substantial free
exercise claim."[27] It is not that the parents have, strictly speaking,
a constitutional right to have Bible reading, but the state may decide to afford that exercise of religion.[28]

Schempp sets the outlines of Establishment Clause doctrine for
public schools. They can neither sponsor devotional religious exercises nor instruct that religious propositions are true or false,
but they may teach about religious understandings, and they
may teach religious texts in the course of secular education. In
the next chapters, we take up the question of moments of silence
and the bar on teaching religious propositions, and in part III the
complex problems of teaching about religion.

But here, let us take stock and ask what may be said against
the decisions regarding prayer and Bible reading. Opponents of
both rulings make legalistic arguments and a commonsense appeal that the great majority of parents and students want devotional practices,[29] that since students who do not want to participate may be excused, allowing those who wish to join in would
be far better than satisfying the small minority who object.

Such advocates support their assertions that parents enjoy a free exercise claim to have their children involved in school devotions by referring to the Framers' acceptance of publicly sponsored prayers. With a rather narrow sense of what establishes religion, the Framers would not have objected to sponsored nonsectarian prayers and Bible reading in public schools (had they existed), any more than did the nineteenth-century creators of those schools.

Although the issue of nonpreferential aid to all religions has generated intense controversy, with extensive criticism of the Supreme Court's position that government cannot favor religion in general,[30] that issue, on examination, has little bearing on most public school problems. No devotional practices are wholly nonpreferential. Bible reading has a significance for Christians and Jews that it does not have for Buddhists and Hindus. The reference to "Almighty God" in the New York State prayer does not suit those who believe in many or no gods; and a watered-down prayer that does not refer to Jesus offends some Christians who believe that true religion centers on Christ. Although states could give tax benefits to all religions, schools are inherently incapable of discovering devotional practices that are equally acceptable to all religions.

If we cannot find completely nonpreferential devotional practices, should we accept devotional practices that are nondenominationally Christian, or satisfy the majority, or are left to individual students? Each of these approaches fails.

Some historians have asserted that the authors of the Bill of Rights assumed that government could favor Christianity over other religions.[31] No modern justice has advocated this approach for modern American society, and we can easily see why. Our country's religious diversity has continually increased. Most notably, a 1965 immigration law, which sharply reduced discrimination in favor of Europeans,[32] has brought an influx of Muslim, Hindu, and Buddhist immigrants. General preferences for Christianity would make many such families into second-class citizens.

Allowing the majority to dictate devotional practices in various school districts would, in effect, support their religion at the expense of those of minorities. Much of the point of nonestablishment is to protect religious minorities. And having individual students take turns selecting a prayer or reading for the group could work to similar effect, since a student in a small religious minority would only rarely be able to choose or experience a devotion she feels is suitable.

Proponents of prayer and Bible reading may urge that these activities are appropriate because education is compulsory and occupies much of the time of students and because the start of the school day is an important occasion that should be entered into with a devotional practice. An argument based on time and compulsion is powerful for combat troops and prisoners, but it has little force for students, who have plenty of time outside the formal classroom setting to undertake religious devotion.[33]

The more weighty argument, perhaps, is the one about important occasions. Parents and children may believe that major activities in life should begin with a group prayer, in which all who wish may share. If they honestly believe this about the start of the school day, they suffer a real deprivation if their wishes are frustrated. The availability of two alternatives partly meets this concern: those who wish to pray together may do so informally before the school day starts, or during lunch; and teachers may initiate the school day with a moment of silence.

What I have said so far does not directly meet the objection that however wise it may be to dispense with school-sponsored prayers, that course is not constitutionally required, because people at the time of the founding would have regarded such prayers as acceptable. The proponent of such a position takes as the proper test of constitutionality what those who enacted the First Amendment, or the citizenry at large, believed about its scope.[34]

The general question of how justices should interpret the Constitution is itself complex and controversial, and beyond the scope of this book; but a few comments may help to explain what I am assuming about sound constitutional doctrine.[35] First, whatever justices ideally should do and whatever individual justices sometimes say they do, the Court has developed constitutional doctrine in accordance with changing social conditions and values. In this respect, the religion clauses are by no means special; the Court uses general principles and values that it gleans from various constitutional texts to declare invalid practices that would undoubtedly have been accepted when those texts were adopted. To take just a few examples, the Court has declared that most classifications that disadvantage women are unconstitutional, it has prohibited racial segregation, it has created a right to have an abortion, it has ruled recently that states may not prohibit sexual relations between consenting adult homosexuals, it has curtailed the common law of libel and slander as that affects criticism of public officials, and it has forbidden the death penalty for rape. None of these rulings could be supported in terms of what specific practices those adopting the relevant provisions thought they were forbidding; but all of these decisions somehow implement fundamental principles that one can draw out of the provisions. The same may be said about the prayer and Bible-reading decisions, whether one focuses on the basic concept of "disestablishment" or "separation of church and state."[36] A school-sponsored prayer or devotional Bible reading tends to "establish" the favored religions *and* to merge the functions of government and religion.

Sketching how the Supreme Court has interpreted constitutional texts does not itself answer how the Court ideally should interpret. My own view is that, in general, interpretation of texts that tell us what to do should be flexible in light of changing conditions.[37] More specifically, when a Constitution is, like ours, very difficult to amend, rigid adherence to what a provision was narrowly intended to accomplish at the time of adoption would be a disaster. A more contextual development of principle over time is a requisite for a decently functioning constitutional order.

No reader will take the summary assertions of the last three sentences as constituting a persuasive defense of the Court's general approach. Those who disagree with that approach can understand many of the claims in the book as based on acceptance of a general strategy of constitutional interpretation that is now prevailing but which they themselves reject.

GRADUATIONS AND FOOTBALL GAMES

As controversial as its prayer and Bible-reading rulings have been, a majority of the Supreme Court has shown no inclination to back down.[38] Its next full decision on school prayer came only in 1992, when it declared in *Lee v. Weisman* that schools could not sponsor prayer at junior and senior high school graduation ceremonies.[39] Having chosen a rabbi to deliver an invocation and benediction at a middle school graduation, school officials had given him a pamphlet recommending that prayers for civic occasions be composed with "inclusiveness and sensitivity." The father of a student objected that any official prayers at public school graduations were impermissible.

Because graduation ceremonies are profound moments in the lives of many graduates and their families, the argument that students and parents who wish should be able to celebrate those occasions by invoking the blessings of God is much stronger than the analogous argument for ordinary classroom prayer. Four dissenting justices thought prayer in that context was acceptable, with Justice Scalia contending that public ceremonies had long involved prayers and that the meaning of the Establishment Clause should be marked by reference to historical practices and understandings.[40] Four of the justices applied standard Establishment Clause doctrines to hold the prayers invalid, as involving the states' promotion and endorsement of religion.[41]

Justice Kennedy wrote the majority opinion. A previous critic of the prevailing threefold test of purpose, effect, and entanglement,[42] Kennedy was evidently unwilling to join an opinion based on that approach. In order to attain a majority opinion, the other four justices voting against the prayers joined his two-step argument about coercion. Despite being formally voluntary, graduation ceremonies are among "life's most significant occasions" and attendance is effectively mandatory.[43] Standing or maintaining respectful silence during prayers might be viewed by students as signifying their adherence to the ideas expressed. Given the heightened concern with freedom of conscience in public schools, this "subtle and indirect" pressure, which "can be as real as any overt compulsion," is constitutionally unacceptable.[44]

At first glance, "coercion" seems an odd approach to Establishment Clause issues, since coercion about religion violates the Free Exercise Clause. Kennedy has claimed, apparently, that on occasion a subtle degree of coercion that is insufficient to violate free exercise does constitute a forbidden establishment of religion.

None of the opinions quite acknowledges the genuine dilemma about graduation prayers. In dissent, Justice Scalia ridiculed the idea that standing or sitting in silence would be thought by students to signify acceptance of a view.[45] The concern about students feeling that their silent participation would signify acceptance is not as ridiculous as Scalia claims. Anyone who knows teenagers recognizes just how sensitive they can be to the possibility that they will seem to endorse or accept behavior they do not like. But even if, as Scalia contends, dissenters may not feel they will be taken to signify adherence, they may well feel offended in conscience at having to sit through religious practices to which they object.

Justice Souter's concurring opinion, in which two other justices joined, responded directly to a free exercise argument offered on behalf of those who wished to pray. To be permissible under the Establishment Clause, an accommodation to religion "must lift a discernible burden on the free exercise of religion."[46] Omitting prayers at graduation ceremonies does not *burden* anyone's spiritual calling, because people can express their religious feelings before or after the ceremonies or organize privately sponsored baccalaureate services;[47] and no one is entitled to the government's symbolic affirmation of his religious view.[48] Yet, as I see it, Souter's argument does not recognize the special significance of expressing one's religious feelings as part of the main ceremony itself, which is not mainly a wish for the government's symbolic approval.

Faced with an irreconcilable conflict between the understandable wishes of the majority to solemnize graduation with religious content, and the affronts to conscience of a minority of parents and students if the majority has its way,[49] the Court rightly chose to protect the minority. In my view, however, the justices would have been more honest had they acknowledged that no alternative can satisfy the sense of many parents and students that having a religion-free graduation sacrifices more than the states' symbolic affirmation.

In 2000, the Court extended the ban on school prayer to invocations at football games.[50] Students at a high school had voted for them and had selected a particular student to deliver them. The school's removal from the decision whether to have prayers and from their composition did not insulate it from the implicit coercion of the final message, Justice Stevens wrote. Some students were required to attend games, and others should not have to choose between staying away and facing an offensive religious ritual.[51] Stevens also drew from the Establishment Clause theme that the state should not perform actions that have the purpose or effect of endorsing religion. An objective observer would perceive in those acts a state endorsement of prayer.[52]

When Sponsorship Is Absent

Because the justices have emphasized different elements in various opinions, one cannot be sure exactly what it takes to make a prayer in a school setting unconstitutional, but we can discern the general parameters clearly enough. Unless the majority of the Court shifts dramatically,[53] prayers that are sponsored by a school directly or indirectly will be held unconstitutional. We lack reliable guidelines when such sponsorship is missing or remote.[54]

If school officials allow students to plan aspects of their graduation ceremony and the students decide to have a prayer and they pick someone to deliver it, the prayer would still violate the Establishment Clause.[55] Affording students this choice does not eliminate the element of school sponsorship, and the implicit coercion on dissenters is no less because students, not officials, have decided to have the prayer. Indeed, this example resembles the football prayer, except that the school might withdraw further from the content of the ceremony than it did in that situation.

A case that is closer to the constitutional border is when students choose a speaker, student or adult, and the speaker as part of her talk invites everyone to join in a prayer. If the invitation to pray is genuinely independent on the speaker's part (and school officials have not reviewed what the speaker will do), the school is not an obvious sponsor;[56] nonetheless, the invitation places students under pressure to participate in an action they may find offensive.[57] In my view, speakers at school graduations exhibit bad judgment if they undertake a group prayer, and I would regard such prayer as unconstitutional.[58] Crucial to this judgment is my sense that prayers are different from ordinary religious expressions, to which we now turn.

If school administrators or students choose a speaker for reasons having nothing to do with religion, *and* administrators do not supervise the message, the speaker should be free to offer some religious comments.[59] Anyone attending a graduation ceremony is aware that a speaker may say things with which he strongly disagrees, though he may reasonably expect what is mainly a unifying message.[60] Sitting and listening does not require a person to accept the speaker's opinions. If commencement speakers were told they could say anything that was other than religious, that would constitute an unacceptable form of censorship over the content of their messages.[61]

On the other hand, if a speaker is chosen just because of his likely religious message, the constitutional border has been crossed. If a principal chooses a famous Christian evangelist, expecting and hoping that he will preach his usual message, the school is sponsoring the religious message. The government's involvement is more remote if students do the choosing, but everyone assumes that school officials have *some* review over student choices of graduation speakers, and, in any event, a school should not sponsor an event at which a major aspect is predictably what comes close to a sermon.

What I have said about choosing speakers is subject to objections based on complexities of choice and the capacities of courts. Who can say *why* a speaker is chosen? A single individual may have multiple grounds of choice, picking televangelist Pat Robertson, for example, because he is a famous television personality *and* because he is a religious leader. Members of the graduating class may vote for someone for widely different reasons. Judges can assess the actual or predictable degree of religious content of a speech much more easily than why a speaker was chosen. Thus, judges might best decide that constitutionality depends on whether a speech is (or is highly likely to be) substantially religious.

The problem of why a speaker is chosen is eliminated if the valedictorian automatically has that responsibility.[62] One might conclude that a speaker who qualifies by objective criteria should be able to say what she wants, but many schools exercise some review of what such a person will say. The more extensive the review, the greater the school's responsibility for religious content.

This modest detour on the subject of religious speech helps show how prayer is different. Saying, "We should all be grateful to God for our blessings" is not to engage in an act of devotion;

saying a prayer is to do so. Speakers before an audience rarely say, "I will now offer a prayer." Rather they begin, "Let us pray."[63] The invitation is a demand, or at least a request, to members of the audience who must choose whether to "join" the prayer by their silent assent. They must also choose whether to adopt a physical posture associated with prayer. If they refuse to bow their heads or close their eyes, they know they risk offending other members of the audience. The issue here is not merely one of active state sponsorship. On the platform the public school offers for someone to address a general audience, certain proposed acts of devotion are inappropriate. We can see this clearly if we imagine a graduation speaker, having explained that school officials have not been involved in his decision, suggesting that members of the audience join him in a ceremony of Communion, and passing around bread and wine (or grape juice) for that purpose. Being invited to join in prayer does not put one "on the spot" to the same degree as an encouragement to take Communion, but it nevertheless calls on one to join an act of devotion. In overturning an injunction that forbade "the school district from *permitting* any prayer in a *public* context at any school function," the Court of Appeals for the Eleventh Circuit wrote that this "equated all student religious speech in any public context with state speech."[64] The court was insensitive to the significant difference between invitations to pray and ordinary expressions of religious points of view.

In a Guidance on Constitutionally Protected Prayer in Public Elementary and Secondary Schools, issued in February 2003 to state and local educational authorities, the Department of Education adopts positions about what the Constitution requires that are somewhat more favorable to prayer and religious speech than my analysis.[65] The department purports to be merely explaining the implications of Supreme Court doctrines, but, in doing so, it treats as settled certain issues that the Court has not resolved. The Guidance explicitly, and correctly, indicates that schools cannot sponsor religious speech. It says that speakers selected by neutral criteria who "retain primary control over the content of their expression" may not "be restricted because of the religious content of their speech";[66] and similar language under the heading "Prayer at Graduation" implies that the speakers may also engage the audience in prayer.

Lee v. Weisman recognizes that prayers aim to engage the audience in a way that ordinary speech does not. Nothing the Court has said about equal treatment of religion in other settings, much of it discussed in chapter 6, covers explicit prayers at public school ceremonies; my view that prayer should not be treated like all other religious expressions by a neutrally chosen speaker is consistent with everything the Court has yet decided.

In regard to the department's Guidance over "ordinary" religious speech, I agree that *some* religious content is permissible, and constitutionally protected, *if* the speaker is chosen on the basis of neutral criteria and the content of the speech is the speaker's own. But even if the speech is overwhelmingly religious—for example, a fervent plea to members of the audience to be born again—the Guidance would permit it, and, indeed, suggests that schools may not prevent it, if a speaker retains "primary control" over what he says, rather than the school "determining or substantially controlling" the content. I believe schools should not have such speeches at graduations, and that the approach of the Guidance not only well exceeds what the Supreme Court has indicated, but has serious flaws.

If a commencement speaker is chosen by student vote or a joint effort of school officials and students, who is to say whether selection has been by neutral criteria? Putting forward neutrality as the formal selection standard does not guarantee that those doing the selecting will refrain from choosing someone because they expect and hope to hear a religious message. If a student is selected by objective criteria, such as class rank, school officials often will hear the talk at a rehearsal and exercise some supervision over content. If their supervision falls short of "substantially controlling" content, the Guidance tells the schools to permit an explicit religious message—however dominant, narrow, and divisive—leaving the schools to disclaim sponsorship. I think, on the contrary, the school should treat a pervasively religious message as inappropriate.[67]

What Is Genuinely Devotional, or When Is the School Endorsing Religious Content?

Certain activities schools may engage in have a mixed religious and secular content. Whether these activities are acceptable depends mainly on whether their aims or effects amount to school endorsement of the religious message.

Not all devotion is verbal. Schools may place devotional decorations in classrooms, hallways, or elsewhere. In 1980, the Supreme Court reviewed a Kentucky law that required the posting of the Ten Commandments in every public school classroom.[68] Rejecting the legislature's asserted secular purpose, which connected the Ten Commandments to the common law, the Court declared that the aim of the display was impermissibly religious, to induce children to reflect upon a sacred text.

Much more complicated than the Ten Commandments law are presentations of sacred music by school choruses and the celebration of religious holidays. These two problems are related, because one typical form of celebrating the Christmas season is for students to gather and sing Christmas carols and for school choruses to offer concerts in which most of the pieces celebrate the birth of Christ. At the school I attended up through tenth grade, students joined together in the central hall to sing carols each morning in the week before Christmas, and the tenth-grade music class put on a Christmas pageant for the rest of the school.[69] These Christmas festivities are among my fondest memories of my eleven years at the school, yet they were unconstitutional according to the Supreme Court's approach to devotional exercises, with which I agree. The state was sponsoring practices that have serious religious significance for Christians. The element of coercion was less than with class and graduation prayers,[70] but the activities involved endorsement of a particular religious perspective.[71]

How to assess the performance of sacred music and the celebration of religious holidays has proved a thorny problem for the courts that have faced these issues. Given the prayer and Bible-reading decisions, it is clear that if the school is trying to convey a religious message or if its efforts will be perceived in that way, it acts unconstitutionally. Thus, a ruling that a school could not sing the Lord's Prayer at graduation was a straightforward application of *Lee v. Weisman*.[72]

Many classics of the musical repertoire, as well as popular pieces, have religious themes. According to one choir director, 60 to 70 percent of serious choral works are religious.[73] Public schools do not have to bar all such music from music classes and performances, any more than they are barred from having students read literature that is religious. Religious church music, such as Handel's *Messiah*, has significant aesthetic value, and it represents an important aspect of the history of music in Western Europe. Students may not only be told about such music. They may perform and listen to it. When religious choral music is presented as part of a concert, neither the participants nor the audience are necessarily expected to subscribe to the words that are sung.

So far, so good. But there is a crucial question of emphasis and coverage. If a school chorus's only performance each year is the *Messiah*, presented just before Christmas, the unavoidable inference is that religious significance is largely determining the choice. Similarly, if a concert involves *only* popular Christmas carols, the vast majority telling of the birth of Christ,[74] a suitable secular justification will be hard to find. On the other hand, including a few carols in a December concert is acceptable. According to one summary of factors, courts considering the teaching and performing of sacred choral music will consider the director's teaching style, including what he says during rehearsals, the site of a concert and its time of year, how selections are placed in a program, whether notes explain the musical significance of works, and the extent to which performance underscores aesthetic elements.[75] It may also matter just *how* religious the choral work is. Some of the greatest music of Bach, Haydn, Mozart, and Schubert was composed for masses, the central event in the worship of many Christian denominations.[76] Written precisely to be performed as part of a religious ceremony, such music is more indelibly religious than the song from Rodgers and Hammerstein's *Carousel*, "You'll Never Walk Alone." Whether courts should try to measure the religious strength of various works is doubtful, but music teachers and directors of choruses should pay attention to that; and it is hardly a surprise that we do not often come across public school performances of music written for masses.

The National Association of Music Educators, Music Educators National Conference, has adopted the following standards for the use of religious music in schools:

> 1. Is the music selected on the basis of its musical and educational value rather than its religious context?

2. Does the teaching of music with sacred texts focus on musical and artistic considerations?

3. Are the traditions of different people shared and respected?

4. Is the role of sacred music one of neutrality, neither promoting nor inhibiting religious views?

5. Are all local and school policies regarding school holidays and the use of sacred music observed?

6. Is the use of sacred music and religious symbols or scenery avoided?

7. Is performance in devotional settings avoided?

8. Is there sensitivity to the various religious beliefs represented by the students and parents?[77]

General as they are, these guidelines alert music educators to factors they should take into account. I think there is an air of unrealism or formalism about neutrality, the fourth factor. The great majority of serious sacred music in the Western musical tradition is Christian;[78] most Americans are Christian; many will be moved by the Christian message if they perform or hear Christian sacred music. Music educators can include pieces of sacred music from other traditions, and they can emphasize the musical and cultural elements of the Christian sacred music they perform; that is, they can aspire to neutrality. But if the great bulk of sacred music students sing is Christian, that is bound to have some effect of reinforcing Christian conviction.

In three cases, federal courts have taken a view about the performance of sacred music that is highly permissive—in my judgment, too permissive. In *Doe v. Duncanville Independent School Dist.,*[79] the Fifth Circuit Court of Appeals found no problem with a high school choir using as its theme song "The Lord Bless You and Keep You." Members of the choir sang this song at the end of class, at the end of some performances, and on the way home from performances. The words of the song are

> The Lord bless you and keep you, the Lord lift His countenance upon you; and give you peace, and give you peace, the Lord make His face to shine upon you, and be gracious unto you, be gracious, gracious unto you. Amen, Amen, Amen, Amen, Amen.[80]

The text is taken from Numbers 6:24–26, with some changes in the order of phrases and added "Amen's" and repetitions of phrases. This language is not specifically Christian, but the words happen to be those with which some Protestant churches close their worship services. In all probability, a significant number of students in the district attended such services. One could not expect them to do anything other than associate the sentiment of the song with which they close class and which they sing on bus rides home with the ending of their worship services. Despite what the court says about secular benefits, it is doubtful if a public school choir should identify as its theme any song that is seriously religious; certainly it should not be able to adopt a song with lyrics that resonate so closely with a standard part of Christian worship services.

In *Bauchman v. West High School*, the Tenth Circuit upheld a school choir's singing substantial amounts of Christian music, often at churches.[81] Performing a concert in a church is one thing; performing during devotional services is another. Absent some special connection between the school and the devotional service, such as exists in a baccalaureate service prior to graduation, public school choruses should not participate in worship services.

Florey v. Sioux Falls School Dist.[82] involved the singing of Christmas carols; the circuit court accepted as legitimate secular reasons for the caroling the district's policy to educate students on the historical and cultural significance of religion in the United States. This is a closer case than the other two. The court correctly points out that the music of carols is now associated with Christmas in many nonreligious settings, such as commercial television station programs and retail stores.[83] No doubt, explicitly Christian carols have transcended religious expression to become parts of the general culture during the Christmas season. But they have acquired this status because most people in the country are Christian. Perhaps carols are sung less than when I was a boy, but I doubt that most children in Sioux Falls, South Dakota, the school district involved, need much education about our heritage of Christmas carols. Singing carols at school is more a question of participating than learning;[84] as a mode of participating, singing carols is significantly religious for most people who sing them. For me, the secular reasons to sing carols in most American schools are far outweighed by their religious significance for the majority of students who will sing them.

As I have noted, the singing of sacred music relates closely to the more general topic of the celebration of religious holidays, which in turn might be seen as one small part of teaching about religion, a topic we shall examine in part III.

In regard to celebrations of religious holidays, schools should concern themselves with secular versus religious elements, with practicing devotions that are not in context really devotional, and with comparative emphasis.

The first point is simplest. Schools may freely engage students in various aspects of religious holidays that have become secular. The religious significance of Halloween and Valentine's Day is largely forgotten; schools can have students dress in scary costumes on Halloween and exchange cards of affection on Valentine's Day.[85] Christmas trees, Santa Claus, and an exchange of gifts are similar; they are no longer thought of as specifically Christian.[86]

One way to educate students, especially elementary students, about various religions is to have them participate in practices of those religions. The students may simulate what practitioners of the religion would do. One obvious danger here is endorsement; the school may seem to be recommending a particular practice as desirable. This will be a particular risk if the religion is that of the teacher and the majority of the school.

But there is also a danger in the opposite direction—a danger of disrespect. Since I do not have a very good sense of what rituals would be regarded as disrespectful by members of non-Christian religions, I will use an illustration that turns on how Communion is regarded by various Christians. Imagine the school is in a predominantly Baptist section of the country. Except for a few Catholics, all the students believe Communion is "merely" symbolic.[87] The teacher says, "Children, let's try to feel what it is like to be Roman Catholic and believe that this bread and 'wine' miraculously actually become the body and blood of Christ, what they call by the big name of 'transubstantiation.' I'll pass out some bread and grape juice, reciting the words that a Roman Catholic priest would say during the Mass, and you try to imagine what it would be for the bread and wine to be transformed, as Catholics believe." Then the teacher simulates the Mass as best she can. I have little doubt that Roman Catholics, parents and children, would be deeply offended by such a playing at this deeply mysterious rite that only Roman Catholic priests are authorized to perform. More generally, teachers must be careful not to engage students in practices that would offend members of the faith that is being presented to students. Judges may find it difficult to say when the line has been crossed, but they should treat clear instances of disrespect as unconstitutional, as doing avoidable harm to the religions involved.[88]

Comparative emphasis is crucial.[89] It is all very well for the school to celebrate or accommodate (in acceptable ways) the holidays of a number of faiths. But if a policy of cultural enrichment in regard to religious holidays turns out to be relied upon only to support carol singing and other religion-centered celebratory aspects of Christmas, it is hard to take the "secular" justification seriously.[90] Students are being invited to celebrate the one holiday with which most of them are deeply familiar; this is not serious education about the country's religious diversity. And the religious elements of Christmas are too strong to treat its celebration as an innocuous way to build community.

The aim of diverse education is not much enhanced if the school decides to throw in other December celebrations. A common complaint among Jews is that a December linking of Christmas and Hanukkah promotes a minor Jewish holiday that happens to be near Christmas in the calendar to the disregard of occasions in the year that are much more important to the Jewish faith. If the aim is really to educate students about the country's diverse religions, a school must make a serious effort to identify the most important occasions of major non-Christian religions and to present those to students in some form.

The Supreme Court addressed a different problem about the edges of sponsorship and devotion when, in the spring of 2004, it reviewed a challenge to the phrase "under God" in the Pledge of Allegiance.[91] A father of a daughter in public school who did not have custody over her and had never been married to her mother complained that the school district's policy of requiring teachers to lead willing students in the full pledge was unconstitutional, even though no students who objected were compelled to participate.[92] The Ninth Circuit of Appeals upheld his argument that the words "under God," inserted in the pledge in 1954 to distinguish this country from the godless U.S.S.R., endorsed a religious view, had a coercive effect of the kind condemned in *Lee v. Weisman*, and furthered a religious purpose in violation of the *Lemon* test.[93] Although the court's decision represented a fairly straightforward application of prevailing Establishment Clause tests, it triggered broad expressions of outrage; and many observers expected the Supreme Court to find some way to avoid the same ruling.[94] In the event, five justices decided that the father lacked standing to complain about the practice. Three justices wrote opinions sustaining "under God" in the pledge, and Justice Scalia, who recused himself, has expressed a similar opinion off the bench. The view that seems likely to attract at least one other justice is that expressed by Justice O'Connor.[95] The pledge is a patriotic exercise, not a religious devotion; "under God" now lacks real religious significance; the phrase is a kind of "ceremonial deism" that recognizes the country's religious traditions but does not endorse any particular religion or religion in general.[96]

What Neutrality?

One issue that lies behind all these cases about devotional practices is that of neutrality. Despite the disclaimers of the Supreme Court, many critics do not believe that the Court's approach is really neutral. In one sense, the critics are undoubtedly right. Most parents and children in a school district may strongly want prayer or Bible reading; a minority do not. If the minority is given what it wants, the majority, whose wishes about religion are frustrated, will not feel it is being treated equally. Further, the neglect of devotional practice can implicitly downplay the significance of religion, a message that can be conveyed by silent disregard as well as by explicit statement. Someone might defend minimal devotional practice as offsetting the negative effect on religion of secular education and helping religious students to integrate their nonpublic beliefs with the civic virtues of liberal democracy.[97] We will take up this issue about neutrality in chapter 5, which addresses the teaching of religious propositions.

Moments of Silence

MANY STATES and school districts have instituted moments of silence to replace oral prayer to begin the school day.[1] Students are free to use their moment of silence to pray, meditate, reflect on the day ahead, or remember last night's party. As we shall see, the Supreme Court has indicated by a kind of indirection that standard moment-of-silence laws are constitutional, but that does not settle whether observing a moment of silence is really consistent with the Supreme Court's approach to oral classroom prayer. Of course, many officials may not care about consistency—they may regard *Engel* and *Schempp* as misguided, or be responding to the outrage of religious parents; and they may be willing to do whatever they can to ameliorate the ban on oral prayer. But other officials who accept the underlying rationales behind that ban may wish to act in accord with it.

A moment of silence impinges less on dissenters than does oral prayer. In this case, no students need participate in an offensive practice, or listen to words that offend their conscience, or risk peer disapproval by asking to be excused. Virtually all religious traditions accept silent prayer and meditation.[2] Insofar as a moment of silence encourages prayer, it achieves nonpreference among religions more fully than can any oral prayer. Were silence freely chosen over oral prayer, that might give slight support to religious groups that accord silence great significance, such as the Society of Friends;[3] but for anyone who realizes that oral prayer is "out," silence appears not to involve such a preference.

As to whether a moment of silence encourages or favors prayer at all, the answer is more subtle. Certainly one can pray more easily during a moment of silence than during math instruction; in this minimal sense, silence encourages prayer. Further, everyone understands that when people are asked to pause for a moment of silence, prayer is *an* appropriate activity.[4] Whether a moment of silence somehow intrinsically encourages or favors prayer depends on the circumstances. If a host says before dinner starts, "Let us bow our heads for a moment of silence," the combination of "bow our heads" and a tradition of saying grace suggests that prayer in some form is expected, though of course not compelled. But at Memorial Day events, when people are asked to take a moment of silence for fallen heroes, concentrated remembrance is as appropriate as self-conscious prayer.

In the classroom setting, much will depend on just what the teacher says and on previous practice. If the teacher begins, "Let us bow our heads for a moment of silent prayer or reflection," she seems to encourage prayer; but if she says, "As always, we will begin our day with a moment of silence," that implication is largely removed. If mature students have actually participated in oral classroom prayer or are aware that students of a previous generation did so, and they are also aware that the Supreme Court has declared such prayer unconstitutional and that state legislators responded by instituting a moment of silence, they will probably assume that the main legislative object of a moment of silence is to allow silent prayer. Even as this sense of events weakens over time, students may retain a vague notion that moments of silence are provided largely so they can pray.

In what sense might we say that a moment of silence "favors" prayer or those who pray? Assuming that students are not asked what they do with their moments of silence, prayer could be "favored" only in a diluted sense. Students who do not pray could realize that they are not engaging in the most preferred activity, but they would face no consequence except, perhaps, a feeling of (slight) guilt; neither their teachers nor their fellow students would know how they had used their moment of silence. I once attended the Swarthmore Quaker meeting; during a part of the period of silence, I reflected on the previous night's basketball game, but with the somewhat uneasy feeling that I wasn't quite spending my time properly.[5] Only in such a sense could prayer and those who prayed be favored over those who recollect last night's party.

If we strip the issue down to its core, the question is whether public schools properly set aside a brief period of time during which silent prayer is obviously one appropriate activity, given the reality that many students will realize that the main reason parents and educators typically want the practice is to allow prayer. I think the answer is yes.[6] So long as legislators and teachers do not encourage prayer beyond these two minimal senses, this concession to those who would like to start the school day with prayer, a concession that does not impose on others, seems acceptable. But we should not fool ourselves into believing that the moment of silence is to be explained entirely apart from prayer. Someone might conceivably defend silence as an otherwise desirable practice, allowing students to collect their thoughts, and instituted for reasons having nothing to do with prayer; but the overarching reason why people in the United States are interested in classroom moments of silence is that they allow for prayer.[7]

Given Supreme Court doctrine about not promoting religion, moments of silence become unconstitutional if the push toward prayer is more substantial. As we have seen, a teacher may easily impart such a nudge, although courts are not likely to review the exact phraseology of instructors who tell their charges to take a moment of silence. The Supreme Court might have said that all moments of silence are unconstitutional because the risk of positive encouragement of prayer is so great, but it chose a different approach.

In the one moment-of-silence case the Court fully considered, *Wallace v. Jaffree*,[8] a majority of justices held that an Alabama law was invalid because it provided that a teacher may announce a period of silence "for meditation or voluntary prayer." The prior law had already provided silence for "meditation." The Court decided that the specific textual addition of "prayer" showed a forbidden purpose to encourage prayer, as borne out by the words of the act's sponsor and by a state acknowledgment during litigation.[9] The state "intended to characterize prayer as a favored practice"[10] and to convey a message of endorsement of religion.[11]

Three justices dissented, and Justices Powell and O'Connor, who concurred in the majority opinion, indicated that they would accept many moment-of-silence statutes, which typically say that students may meditate, pray, or reflect on the day's activities.[12] O'Connor suggested specifically that such statutes could mention prayer as one activity in which students might engage.[13] When we add the two concurring justices to the dissenters, we tally five votes in favor of most moment-of-silence statutes, and the majority as well hints that it may find many such statutes acceptable.[14] Changes in the Court since 1985 do not diminish the likelihood that it would approve most statutes authorizing moments of silence.[15]

O'Connor urged that moments of silence are distinguishable from oral prayer because they are not inherently religious and students who participate "need not compromise [their] beliefs."[16] A statute could be implemented to "effectively favor the child who prays" over the child who does not, if a teacher exhorts her pupils to pray.[17] "The crucial question is whether the State has conveyed or attempted to convey the message that children should use the moment of silence for prayer."[18]

Justice O'Connor's formulations obscure the critical issues in two respects. The simpler involves the idea of *favoring* the child who prays. As we have seen, even if the teacher exhorts students to pray, the only favoring *of children* is that those who do not pray may feel bad about not following the teacher's recommendation. No student is given an advantage or disadvantage because he does or does not pray. Thus, prayer can be favored as an activity without any tangible advantage for children who pray.

O'Connor's second obscurity is more subtle. The justice asks whether the message is that children *should* use the time for prayer. If I don't do something I should do, I have failed to perform a duty. Suppose the teacher says or implies that her students may pray, meditate, or reflect on the day's activities, but that the reason the school gives them this opportunity is that most parents and legislators believe prayer is important and hope many students will pray. One could then say the teacher "encourages" prayer over meditation and reflection, but no student is given the message that she *should* pray. O'Connor's opinion does not quite face up to how a court should assess an encouragement that is milder than telling students they should pray.[19] I have indicated that if such a weak encouragement is implicit rather than explicit, a moment of silence is acceptable, but we should acknowledge that many students will realize that those who institute moments of silence are not completely neutral between prayer and other possible uses of the moments.[20]

In the course of her opinion, O'Connor develops her "endorsement" approach to Establishment Clause issues.[21] She there presents "endorsement" as a kind of refinement of the purpose-and-effect elements of the Court's standard threefold establishment test.[22] The central question is whether a law has the purpose or effect of endorsing a particular religion or religion in general. The problem with government endorsement is that it makes religion relevant to a person's standing in the political community. According to O'Connor, endorsement is to be judged by an "objective observer," one who is familiar with the actual history of a statute and its implementation and who is acquainted with the values underlying the Free Exercise Clause.[23] This "objective observer" sounds suspiciously like a Supreme Court justice reviewing the record of a case; and indeed part of the strategy of the objective observer is that it does not assign to local juries and judges the final responsibility for determining whether a perceived endorsement is present.[24]

Unfortunately, the objectivity of O'Connor's approach detaches it to some degree from the concern that generates it; namely, that dissenters may feel themselves to be outsiders, not full members of the political community. It is perfectly possible that in some situation, most reasonable people in a community, both those whose religious values may be endorsed and nonadherents, would perceive an endorsement while an "objective observer" would not. Conversely, fully informed objective observers might see an endorsement, although most people would not.

We need not pursue all the complexities of endorsement approaches to see that "endorsement" is a possible alternative to inquiry about secular purpose and an effect of promoting religion. Usually the outcome will be the same whether or not a court asks specifically about endorsement or employs the standard *Lemon* test. In most establishment cases, prudent lower courts now inquire about endorsement, as well as applying the standard test.[25]

Given her version of the endorsement test, it is easy to see why Justice O'Connor agreed with four other justices that the Alabama law in *Wallace v. Jaffree* was invalid. Her approval of most other moment-of-silence laws is more difficult to explain. As I have indicated, a realistic appraisal would show that legislators do wish to encourage silent prayer even if they do not aim to have teachers tell students they *should* pray or to favor *the children* who pray. By obscuring degrees of encouragement, O'Con-

nor did not face the question of how the Court should treat a relatively mild encouragement with no practical implications for
individuals who resist the encouragement.[26] I have argued that,
at least as to silent prayer, such an encouragement is acceptable.
That conclusion is premised on the assumption that most of
those who pray do not kneel or engage in other physical movements that clearly signal prayer. Were those who prayed to identify themselves to their teachers and fellow students in such a
way, the pressure on others to pray (or to appear to pray) would
become constitutionally unacceptable.

Teaching Religious Propositions

In the cases we have examined so far, public schools did not actually teach that particular religious ideas are true, but the Supreme Court's decisions and opinions indicate clearly that such teaching is unconstitutional. The Court has consistently held that the government may not prefer one religion over another,[1] and in *Abington Township v. Schempp*, Justice Clark quoted approvingly Justice Jackson's conception of public schools as providing a "secular education," inculcating "needed temporal knowledge" and maintaining a "strict and lofty neutrality as to religion."[2] Writing for the Court in holding an antievolution law invalid, Justice Fortas was still more explicit: "Government . . . must be neutral in matters of religious theory, doctrine, and practice. . . . [I]t may not aid, foster, or promote one religion or religious theory against another or even against the militant opposite."[3]

The original common schools did not teach sectarian doctrines, religious ideas that would distinguish Episcopalians from Presbyterians, Congregationalists from Unitarians; but they did teach the existence of a beneficent God who rewards and punishes in this life and the next, and who has shown favor on the American people. Many texts and schools taught the superiority of Protestant understandings to Roman Catholicism. The modern idea that schools should not teach the truth of religious ideas is considerably more encompassing than this older vision. Schools should not teach propositions that are embraced by Christians but not Hindus, by theists but not atheists.[4]

One might well understand the idea that public schools should not teach religious truths as at the heart of the Supreme Court's approach to religion in the public schools. And, as we have seen, courts that struggle with whether and when school choirs can perform sacred music are asking in a sense whether the schools are endorsing the religious text or not. We live in a liberal democratic society in which people embrace highly diverse views about religion, including atheism and agnosticism, and in which people understand that religious groups can thrive and make a substantial contribution to the social order without the government adopting one religious position as true. In this setting, political philosophy suggests that public schools should refrain from teaching religious truth. I believe this principle is also a sound doctrine of constitutional law. It implements in a modern setting the fundamental idea that public authorities should not place their weight behind one religious view or another. Although many members of the founding generation may not have minded state support of Protestant Christianity, the modern principle traces a sensible evolutionary development from the earlier notion that no particular version of Protestant Christianity should be favored.

In previous chapters, we have come across various tests for what constitutes an establishment of religion. According to the so-called *Lemon* test, a law is invalid if it lacks a secular purpose or has a primary effect of advancing or inhibiting religion. The endorsement test, first proposed by Justice O'Connor, treats a law as invalid if it endorses (or disapproves) a religion.[5] If the core principle about religion in the public schools is that schools cannot teach religious truth, we can see that it makes little difference which of these two approaches a court adopts. To teach religious perspectives as true is to endorse the religions that embrace those propositions, and it is also to advance those religions in relation to others.

Although schools that refrain from teaching the truth or falsity of religious propositions achieve a kind of neutrality, we need to recognize three respects in which they fall short of complete impartiality about religious ideas. First, they are not neutral between people who want religious teaching and those who do not want religious teaching.[6] Second, as I shall explain, schools implicitly reject some religious ideas. And, third, their teaching of other aspects of human understanding without reference to religious ideas as true or false tends to detach those areas from religious understanding and to diminish its significance.[7] Nonetheless, if the government is not to promote Christianity or another particular religious perspective, steering clear of teaching the truth of religious propositions is the best that schools can do. Teaching that religion per se is true is logically impossible; although some commonalities exist, different religions assert different truths, and they do not all agree even about the existence of God.[8] The Supreme Court's instincts about teaching religion have been sound, and as our country's religious diversity increases, the greater becomes the importance of public schools staying away from pronouncements about the truth of religious propositions.

This straightforward conclusion raises three less than straightforward inquiries: (1) What are religious propositions? (2) May schools teach anything that accepts or rejects religious propositions? (3) What is it for schools to teach religious propositions as true?

The complex question of what counts as a religious proposition relates closely to the inquiry about what exactly constitutes a religion. Here we may settle for some brief generalizations. Claims about the existence, nature, and actions of God or gods are religious. Claims about life after death are religious.[9] Claims about the ultimate significance of physical reality and of human life are religious. Persons who deny the existence of any god, of life after death, and of ultimate significance provide negative answers to these fundamental religious questions. Whether or not one considers agnostic or atheist views to be themselves religious, they undoubtedly answer religious questions; schools may no more teach them than positive answers to the same questions.

Religions typically involve practices, such as prayer, baptism, and singing or chanting, that are held up as desirable or mandatory. Schools cannot teach that people should engage in these forms of worship and associated practices.

What we identify as religions typically also include ideas about how human beings should lead their lives—for example, they should be honest and generous toward others. For convenience, we may call these secondary religious propositions. Saying that schools cannot teach that particular views about gods, immortality, and worship are true or false is much simpler than deciding just what schools should teach about how to live. If schools are to teach any ethical standards at all, what they recommend will overlap with various religious perspectives that have a great deal to say about a moral life.

One tempting approach is to consider anything that people care about deeply enough as *religious for them*. We can see quickly why this approach does not work for what schools may teach. (In fact, it does not work for most other legal purposes.) If schools cannot teach as true or false answers to any questions about which some people care very deeply, they are barred from teaching respect for the environment, gender and racial equality, and a child's need for parental love. An excessively broad account of what count as religious propositions cannot be allowed to cripple the schools' efforts to provide ordinary moral and political education.

If we assume that (1) schools *may* teach some political and ethical ideas as sound, and (2) schools may not teach religious ideas as true, we need a basis to distinguish what count as religious ideas *that does not depend only* on how much people care about them. The best approach is to revert to the primary religious questions—about God, immortality, and worship—and to treat as religious whatever teaching about how to live connects closely to these primary religious questions. Thus, teaching that children need parental love does not answer a religious question, but teaching that parents should love their children *because the Bible tells them to* does answer a religious question.

The problem of discerning what are religious propositions flows naturally into our second inquiry: May schools say anything that accepts or rejects religious propositions? The answer is that some of what schools teach does implicitly reject certain religious ideas; it supports other religious ideas *only* in the sense of teaching ideas that fit comfortably with the religious ones.

Schools teach as true a range of physical facts, including the sun's place at the center of the planetary system. Schools also teach that members of different races, and women and men, are fundamentally equal. They teach that the American Revolution and American participation in World War II were morally justified. These teachings implicitly reject the following religious propositions: God created the sun to circle the earth; God instituted a strict racial and gender hierarchy and calls on us to perpetuate it; the saying of Jesus that we should "turn the other cheek" shows that God wants us to be pacifists. When school teachings contradict such religious propositions, teachers should not challenge the competing religious views head-on, but many students will grasp the negative implications for those views.

One might initially think that if the schools are rejecting some religious propositions, they *must* be accepting others, but this would be a mistake. Schools can offer *non*religious reasons for a position: they advance scientific bases for the earth's position vis-à-vis the sun; for nonpacifism and principles of equality, they offer moral and political arguments that do not rest on positive or negative answers to fundamental religious questions. If a school teaches that premises of liberal democracy commit us to racial equality, it does take a position that fits comfortably with a religious belief that God created human beings as fundamentally equal. But it does not directly support a religious understanding of human equality—an atheist or agnostic, as well as a theist, could accept the argument that democracy implies human equality.

To sum up, schools inevitably, unavoidably teach ideas that imply that particular religious doctrines about the natural world and social justice are incorrect. They need not, and should not, teach that *particular religious bases* for scientific, ethical, and political views are correct.

The inquiry that remains—what it is for schools to teach religious ideas as true—raises a double question. How far may individual texts and teachers say for themselves what a school may not say officially? Do teachers typically represent the schools, or may they offer individual opinions that they tell students are not official? And whether one focuses on schools, or teachers, or textbooks, how far should they delve into arguments for and against religious propositions, so long as they refrain from presenting any as officially correct? Later chapters examine these complicated questions in some depth.

CHAPTER 6

Equal Facilities

A CONCLUSION that public schools cannot teach religious propositions as true or sponsor religious devotions does not settle how they should treat student groups organized as independent clubs. A restrictive approach would be to bar religious groups from meeting on school facilities, on the theory that for schools to assist religion in this way is intrinsically inappropriate or will create the impression that the state is sponsoring religion. A diametrically opposed approach would be to confer special rights on students who organize in religious groups, because of the general value of free exercise and the school's inability to teach religious truths. A third approach is to treat religious groups like nonreligious ones.

The Supreme Court and Congress have adopted the third approach. Eschewing free exercise analysis, the Court has relied on the Free Speech Clause to forbid the exclusion of religious groups, and has declared that states cannot rely on the Establishment Clause as a basis to afford *less than equal* treatment.

Over the years, the Supreme Court's free speech cases have developed doctrines about various kinds of forums. In traditional public forums, such as parks and other open public spaces, states may restrict only the time, place, and manner of speech. Here, apart from speech that is independently illegal, such as incitement to criminal acts, states cannot forbid speech because of its content. Similar principles apply if a state chooses to make a forum widely available, as when a state university decides to allow student clubs of all types to use its classrooms for meetings. In more restricted forums, where the state reserves greater discretion about what speech to allow, it still may not discriminate against any particular viewpoints—for example, forbidding messages that oppose official policies and allowing messages that support them. This free speech law has dominated constitutional treatment of religious clubs.

In 1981, in *Widmar v. Vincent*,[1] the Court considered a state's explicit denial of equal facilities to religious groups. A branch of the University of Missouri made facilities available to registered student groups, but prohibited their use "for purposes of religious worship or religious teaching."[2] Members of Cornerstone, an evangelical Christian organization whose typical meetings included prayer, hymns, Bible commentary, and discussion of religious views and experiences, challenged the prohibition. The Supreme Court, by an eight to one margin, held that the prohibition was invalid. Once having created a forum that was generally open, the university could not discriminate against religious worship without a compelling interest in doing so.[3]

One compelling interest a state could have is avoiding Establishment Clause violations, and the Court turned to examine how an equal access policy would fare under the threefold test of purpose, effect, and entanglement that it developed in Lemon to determine if state regulation violates the Establishment Clause. The policy would have a secular purpose and would entangle the state less with religion than a regulation that requires a decision about what is "religious worship or teaching."[4] Although access could benefit Cornerstone, that would not be a "primary effect" of advancing religion, because the state would confer no approval of the group, which was only one of more than one hundred groups using university facilities.[5] Since equal access would not violate the Establishment Clause, the state had no compelling interest in excluding religious groups.[6]

In 1989 Congress enacted an Equal Access Act that extended the principle of Widmar to public secondary schools receiving federal financial assistance.[7] After school officials had denied students permission to form a Christian club that would use classrooms after school, the Supreme Court decided that the act had been violated and that the act was constitutional.[8] The statutory issue concerned the circumstances in which a school maintains a "limited open forum," requiring equal access to groups without discrimination based on "religious, political, philosophical, or other content" of speech.[9] The Westside High School had created a limited open forum when it made facilities available to groups such as a chess club and a community service club.[10] Upholding the statute's constitutionality, Justice O'Connor wrote that "the logic of Widmar applies with equal force to the Equal Access Act." Secondary students would understand that the school was not endorsing the religious message of the private student groups.[11]

Three justices were seriously concerned about the appearance of school sponsorship.[12] Justice Marshall claimed that the school actually endorsed the existing clubs as contributing to a well-rounded education, and that none of those clubs advocated controversial viewpoints; he believed that the school would have to take special steps to disassociate itself from the religious activity in order to avoid endorsement.[13]

Despite their basic right to equal treatment, religious clubs at public schools are not quite like other clubs. Reviewing the criteria for officers of a Christian club, the Second Circuit Court of Appeals reasonably concluded that the club could set religious standards for its key officers, but not for other positions.[14] This decision shows that even when religious clubs are student-initiated, they face some constitutional limits on how they order their affairs.[15]

The Supreme Court's most recent equal facilities decision extended the rule for high schools to elementary schools and held that equal treatment was constitutionally required.[16] School officials in a small town in central New York had refused to allow the Good News Club, for first to sixth graders, to use school facilities after school, under a community policy that did not allow use by "any . . . organization for religious purposes."[17] The club's meetings involved recitation and learning of Bible verses, singing, the telling of a Bible story and how it applies to the members' lives, and a closing prayer.[18] According to Justice Thomas, denying the Good News Club the use of facilities made available to other groups that promote moral and character development amounted to viewpoint discrimination.[19] There was neither a danger that children or parents would be under coercive pressure to participate nor a danger that people would perceive that the school was endorsing the Good News Club.[20] Unwilling to indulge some special assumption about what young children would perceive about endorsement, Justice Thomas pointed out that the risk that they would misperceive an endorsement was probably no greater than the risk "that they would perceive a hostility toward the religious viewpoint if the Club were excluded from the public forum."[21]

In suggesting that, because children could participate only if their parents gave permission, the pressure that counted was on parents, and adults would not be confused about endorsement,[22] Justice Thomas omitted a crucial aspect of pressure on parents. Given the insistence of many children between six and twelve years old who want something, Thomas's point cannot be that the parents would be entirely free from pressure; rather they would recognize that any pressure does not come from a state endorsement. But if children put pressure on their parents partly because they mistakenly believe their school sponsors the activity, children's misconceptions about endorsement could influence the parents indirectly.

The most interesting feature of *Good News Club* is its conception of religious meetings. Three dissenters contended that religious meetings were not analogous to other speech, and therefore could be treated differently. Justice Stevens undertook a threefold classification of (1) speech about topics from a religious point of view, (2) worship or its equivalent, and (3) speech aimed at proselytizing or inculcating belief in a faith.[23] Justice Souter considered the meetings of the Good News Club to be evangelical services of worship.[24] Both justices thought that a school's treating such meetings differently from meetings on other subjects did not amount to viewpoint discrimination. The majority of the Court disagreed.[25]

To understand this disagreement about viewpoint discrimination, we need to consider two other cases, including the Court's most difficult decision about equal facilities. Modern free speech jurisprudence clearly distinguishes between viewpoint discrimination and discrimination that is also according to content but not viewpoint. If a state allows speech praising officials and forbids speech criticizing them, it engages in straightforward viewpoint discrimination. A rule that prohibits any advertisements on public buses that endorse political candidates classifies according to the content of a message but not by viewpoint. Because the government should not permit or forbid speech depending on whether it likes the opinions expressed, viewpoint discrimination is particularly "suspect" and hard to justify.[26]

We can best understand the Court's subsequent difficulty over what counts as viewpoint discrimination in relation to a case where such discrimination was straightforward. In *Lamb's Chapel*

v. Center Moriches Union Free School District,[27] the district had refused to permit use of school facilities for a religiously oriented
film on family values and child rearing. Since the district would
have permitted films about family values and child rearing from
nonreligious perspectives, its refusal constituted impermissible
viewpoint discrimination.[28] *Lamb's Chapel* not only set the stage
for the next, more difficult case, it was relied upon by the Court
in a way that was obtuse to important differences between the
two situations.

In *Rosenberger v. Rector and Visitors of the University of Virginia*,[29]
the Court decided by one vote that a state university that funded
the printing of a broad range of independent student publications had also to fund a Christian evangelical journal urging
commitment to a Christian life. Under university guidelines,
funds were unavailable for a religious activity, one that "primarily promotes or manifests a particular belief in or about a deity or
an ultimate reality." The organizers of the magazine *Wide Awake*
complained that the university's refusal to support its publication financially violated the principle that the state should not
discriminate among speech on the basis of content. The university interposed the Establishment Clause as a justification for its
content-based guidelines.

The justices had an initial disagreement over the classification
created by the university guidelines. Justice Kennedy, citing
Lamb's Chapel, said that the guidelines involved viewpoint discrimination, favoring nonreligious messages over religious ones.[30]
Justice Souter, in dissent, responded that the guidelines afforded
equal treatment to religious,[31] atheist, and agnostic writings, all
writings that manifested a belief "in or about a deity or ultimate
reality." Competing viewpoints on that subject were treated
equally.

Each of the opinions is partly right.[32] Insofar as the guidelines
covered materials that mainly addressed the possible existence
and nature of God or ultimate reality, the classification did *not*
involve viewpoint discrimination, because all opinions on those
subjects were treated identically. Insofar as the guidelines covered comment on social problems, such as war or abortion, they
did discriminate against religious perspectives and in favor of
nonreligious ones. In that respect, the case did resemble *Lamb's
Chapel*.

Rosenberger shows, among other things, just how elusive the distinction can be between viewpoint discrimination and other content discrimination; but the adoption by five justices of a broad notion of viewpoint discrimination has come to be taken for granted by courts in subsequent cases. As in *Good News Club*, courts have assumed that viewpoint discrimination covers any differentiation of religious from nonreligious expression; and *Good News Club* blocks possible claims that worship and proselytizing within voluntary student groups are somehow special forms of speech warranting other than equal treatment.

Because student clubs involve voluntary participants, what the Court says in *Good News Club* about forms of speech does not address the problem I considered in chapter 3: whether a graduation speaker's invitation to prayer is indistinguishable from his expression of religious views. I have suggested that prayer *is* different in seeking to engage the audience in a way that ordinary speech does not. We should not suppose that the Court has resolved that the kinds of distinctions proposed by Justices Stevens and Souter are never relevant for constitutional purposes.

Rosenberger was difficult partly because the "equal facility" sought by *Wide Awake* was the actual expenditure of public money for an undeniably religious, evangelical message. Although the university's program of paying for student publications had an undoubted secular purpose, the particular disbursements for *Wide Awake* would support religious advocacy, something that had never been allowed in cases involving aid to parochial schools.

The implications of *Rosenberger* for the actual financing of student clubs are murky, thanks to qualifications in Justice Kennedy's majority opinion and Justice O'Connor's concurrence. Without doubt, a school may fund a chess club and a community service club, to take examples from the *Mergens* case. If a school does so, must it, may it, also provide similar financial support to a religious club?

The four dissenting justices in *Rosenberger* claimed that the financing that would be involved at the University of Virginia would itself be unconstitutional, a violation of the principle that public funds should never go for religious purposes.[33]

Both the Court's opinion and Justice O'Connor's concurrence walked a kind of tightrope. The opinions mentioned various factors that differentiated funding of a student religious publication from tax support of the religious activities of churches.[34] Wide Awake Productions, which published the journal at issue, was not itself a religious organization; the government program would be neutral toward religion if publications of all kinds were funded; no endorsement would be implied; funding money was derived from a student fee, not general taxes; students with a conscientious objection to use of their fees for political or religious messages (unlike ordinary taxpayers) might have a constitutional right not to pay;[35] and direct payments went to the printer, not to the organization sponsoring the religious publication.

Justice Kennedy reasoned that physical facilities require payment for upkeep, that computer facilities are not different in principle from meeting rooms, that paying printers is not different in principle from allowing use of computer facilities.[36] According to Justice O'Connor, the "case lies at the intersection of the principle of government neutrality and the prohibition on state funding of religious activity."[37] "When two bedrock principles so conflict," the Court, instead of relying on "categorical platitudes," must undertake "the hard task of judging—sifting through the details and determining whether the challenged program offends the Establishment Clause."[38] Although Kennedy's argument about use of computer facilities being closely analogous to paying for printing could be employed to defend payments for publications of a high school religious club, Kennedy and O'Connor both refrained from any broad endorsement of equal treatment for religious clubs that would include financial subsidy; and some material in the two opinions serves to differentiate *Rosenberger* from use of school taxes to aid religious clubs. When the Ninth Circuit considered funding from student payments, it concluded fairly easily that religious groups had to be treated equally with all others,[39] but it differentiated this support from direct use of tax money.

Few, if any, religious clubs will treat religious subjects in a detached or neutral way. They typically involve the practice of, and instruction about, the particular religion that their student members (and their parents) accept. Thus, the clubs do what the public schools, as such, cannot do. Although the difficulty young children will have in distinguishing what is merely *at* school from what is sponsored by the school makes the Supreme Court's extension of the equal treatment approach to elementary schools highly arguable, the basic doctrine that religious clubs should not be treated less favorably than other voluntary clubs is sound. So long as school officials have no significant role in the religious clubs, opening school facilities to them does not involve the state in promoting any particular religious view.

Parents who want devotional Bible reading or prayer as part of the school day are unlikely to be satisfied by having a voluntary club that meets once a week after school. But if those parents think of the school day as including such after-school programs, they can at least conceive their children as having some religious practice in connection with school.

To a limited degree, allowing religious clubs can also moderate objections to the failure of schools to teach about religion. Religious clubs can offer religious activities and teaching, although they will not alter the secularity of the basic courses. More to the point in terms of broad educational policy, clubs are most likely to present particular religions as true, not explore a range of religions or attempt to understand them in historical context. The manner in which voluntary religious clubs engage members is unlikely to mimic the way public schools would (or could) teach about religion. Although in some localities children (and their parents) are under some pressure to join Christian clubs, for the most part the clubs will not be joined by children with little interest in religion. Equal treatment for religious clubs may slightly relieve the pressure on schools to do something about religion, but the clubs have virtually no bearing on what the schools *should* do about religion in their curricula. It is to that important subject that we now turn.

PART III

TEACHING ABOUT RELIGION

*

CHAPTER 7

Teaching and Religion in the Public School

THE SUPREME COURT's decisions forbidding prayers and devotional Bible reading have proved among the most controversial the Court has ever rendered, yet whether to begin the school day with a few minutes of devotion matters far less than what schools teach about religion. Constitutional lawyers have given little attention to this nettlesome issue because the Court, having determined that teaching *about* religion is all right, has not reviewed programs that educators have labeled in this way.

Many citizens continue to resent the Court's assumption that schools cannot present Christianity, or theocratic religion, as true; but even people who agree that schools should not teach the truth of religious ideas diverge in their opinions about what precisely schools should do. At one end of the spectrum are those who want public schools virtually to ignore religion—leaving the subject to the home and private institutions. At the other end of the spectrum, people urge that schools, though refraining from any official doctrine, should present religious worldviews in a full way. In most schools, practice now lies closer to the former end of the spectrum—little is *said* about religion. Thoughtful critics have argued that this approach is unfair and even unconstitutional.

Part of the disagreement turns on how we should characterize present practice: is it neutral toward religion or does it teach a set of beliefs—secular humanism—that is opposed to traditional religious views? If public schools *are* inculcating one religion, albeit a nontheistic one, *or* ideas that are directly opposed to religious conceptions, fairness may require righting the balance. Of course, as the introduction suggests, we have no guarantee that teaching about religion will lead students to be more religious; learning a spectrum of religious views and learning more about what they take as negative aspects of religion could draw them away from faith they have accepted up to that point. But whatever the exact effects, schools should aim for fair treatment of major subjects of human concerns.

In approaching this subject, we need to ask both about desirable programs and the range within which educational authorities may choose. The best program at any place and time depends on the character of the local community and the competence of its teachers. Schools could entrust teachers who are well trained in the subject with instruction about religion that they should not assign to teachers who understand little about religion from an academic perspective or lack an ability to convey their understanding to public school students.

The range of choice to which I refer is one within which educational authorities can conform with the religion clauses.[1] Because individual boards of education and teachers should have considerable discretion,[2] less than ideal choices are nonetheless constitutionally acceptable.

We have seen in chapter 1 what the Supreme Court said about teaching religion four decades ago in the Bible reading case. The crucial sentence is this: "Nothing we have said here indicates that . . . study of the Bible or of religion, when presented objectively as part of a secular program of education, may not be effected consistently with the First Amendment."[3]

This language is carefully formulated to permit teaching about religion; it *does not* explicitly mandate such teaching.[4] It thus leaves open whether a school's failure to teach about religion violates the letter or the spirit of the religion clauses.

My central theses in this part of the book are straightforward. As chapter 5 indicates, public schools should not teach that particular religious propositions are true or false, sound or unsound.[5] The complaint that public schools teach secular humanism, taken at face value, is misinformed or misleading, but an actual devaluing of religious understandings may take place in public schools. Schools should pay considerably more attention to religious understandings than most of them now do. Exactly *what* should be taught about religious perspectives depends a great deal on the particular subject matter. For virtually all subjects, a serious question arises as to just how deeply teachers should probe religious perspectives. Although from the standpoint of a fully liberal education, much may be said in favor of a searching examination of religious perspectives, that ambition presents serious risks that educators may reasonably decide not to undertake. Educational authorities and individual teachers have a substantial range of choice about how much to cover religion and how deeply to examine what they cover. Schools may teach less religion less deeply than would be ideal, were all the teachers of that subject to be well trained and appropriately sensitive, and were parents to be fully accepting of diverse religions being taught from an academic perspective. Thus, although schools should say more about religion than they now do, their doing so is not constitutionally required.[6]

"Neutrality" and Secularization

Most public schools now largely ignore religion.[7] The benign appraisal of that stance is that secular education leaves religious claims for outside school—that it is neutral among religions and between religion and nonreligion. Justice Jackson, dissenting in *Everson v. Board of Education*, wrote of "the premise that secular education can be isolated from all religious teaching so that the school can inculcate all needed temporal knowledge and also maintain a strict and lofty neutrality as to religion. The assumption is that after the individual has been instructed in worldly wisdom he will be better fitted to choose his religion."[8] According to Warren Nord, the continually repeated assumption that schools sticking to secular education maintain neutrality "has become an article of the conventional wisdom."[9]

A strongly contrasting perspective, one many conservative Christians propound, is that the schools self-consciously teach the doctrines of "secular humanism," an atheist religion that opposes traditional religious beliefs and practices. Just what are "the doctrines" of secular humanism is not very precise,[10] but the central ideas include the absence of any deity, the capabilities of human reason (including science), individualism, and human autonomy. These ideas, critics contend, underlie self-centered behavior, materialism, moral weakness, and social decline; teaching them can have dire effects on the lives of students and on society.

The truth, as usual, lies between the rhetorical excesses involved in the benign appraisal of disregard of religion and claims about the inculcation of secular humanism. Although most academic disciplines no longer rely on religious premises, and American public school education was essentially secular by the beginning of the twentieth century,[11] a majority of Americans continue to say that religion is important to them. Religious worldviews compete with secular ones in our culture. Few text writers and school authorities aim to take sides on religiously contested matters; they do not set out to promote secular worldviews that oppose religious approaches.[12] Nonetheless, as Nord claims, "[T]he underlying worldview of modern education divorces humankind from its dependence on God."[13]

The conceptualization of what occurs that is most attractive for legal challenges is that secular humanism is a religion, and public schools are teaching it, in violation of the Establishment Clause. This argument has been markedly, and deservedly, unsuccessful. In *Smith v. Board of School Commissioners*, for example, the Eleventh Circuit Court of Appeals reviewed the use of forty-four texts in the Alabama schools, which were claimed to advance the religion of secular humanism.[14] The court said that "even assuming that secular humanism is a religion for purposes of the establishment clause," none of the challenged texts "convey[s] a message of governmental approval of secular humanism or government disapproval of theism."[15]

We need not pause long over the question of whether secular humanism is a religion. My own view is that the constitutional standard for determining if something whose status is in doubt is a religion is whether it exhibits enough features of standard religions.[16] According to this approach, an organized group subscribing to the tenets of secular humanism, and thus not subscribing to beliefs about human life and the world common for religions, can nevertheless be a religion if it engages in many of the practices of typical religions.[17] Whether or not, standing alone, people's adopting a set of religious propositions constitutes "a religion,"[18] public schools are not allowed to teach such propositions, positive ones—"God exists"—or negative ones—"There is no God."[19] Whatever the exact constitutional formulation, no justice has suggested that government has more latitude to inhibit or condemn religion than to promote or endorse it. Thus, if schools were teaching propositions about religion directly opposed to traditional views, they would be violating the Constitution, whether or not adherents of the negative views could be said to practice a religion.[20] Public school textbooks rarely set out to teach negative religious propositions; what they say is generally compatible with many religious perspectives. The crucial educational and constitutional question is not whether schools teach secular humanism, but whether they convey messages that reject or disfavor traditional religious worldviews.[21]

Some courses do teach as true propositions that many believers reject; instruction about evolution in biology classes is a notable example. Chapter 5 has explained why public schools inevitably teach as true or sound ideas that particular religious groups reject, but perhaps such teaching becomes much more troublesome when the ideas are antithetical to *many* religious believers and go to the core of their religious faith.

In some courses, texts and teachers pursue an exclusively secular analysis of issues that many citizens approach from religious premises. Various texts, for example, explicate the once popular "values clarification" approach to moral issues, suggesting that students need to clarify and choose their values. "Values clarification" in its usual form is diametrically opposed to the belief that moral standards derived from religion are binding and not a matter of choice.[22]

The most telling aspect of the complaint about secular education is not about individual courses or subjects, but overall effect: by treating all subjects from a secular point of view and by presenting secular modes of knowledge as sufficient for life, instruction within schools implies that religious understanding is not at the center of human understanding, but rather at its periphery. This message implicitly rejects traditional religious views, and thus fails to treat those religious views fairly and neutrally. The gist of this complaint falls close to what Sir Walter Hamilton Moberly once wrote about the modern university, which does not openly reject, but ignores, God.

> It is a fallacy to suppose that by omitting a subject you teach nothing about it. On the contrary, you teach that it is to be omitted, and that it is therefore a matter of secondary importance. And you teach this not openly and explicitly, which would invite criticism, you simply take it for granted and therefore insinuate it silently, insidiously, and all but irresistibly.[23]

Someone might respond to this challenge by claiming that so long as people understand that schools slight religion because of constitutional concerns, the schools convey no message denigrating traditional religious understandings.[24] The difficulty with this proposal is that whatever most adult citizens conceive as the reasons for the content of school curricula, the pervasive effect on their children who are being educated will not be *greatly* altered. Children may be influenced by the disregard of religion, even if their parents perceive a constitutional basis for it and explain that to their children.[25]

This assessment of religion-free public education is strongly critical, and we need to pause for a moment over its force. We can divide the straightforward implications of a certain kind of education from its causal effects in society.

If we disregard the actual effects of secular education on children, the critique directed at it is substantially accurate. When various subjects of human concern—history, morality, literature, and science—are presented without reference to religion, the irresistible implication is that these subjects can be well understood on their own without being placed in a religious perspective. This approach does not correspond with the view of many religious people that religious insight is crucial for true understanding of most other aspects of life. The approach also suggests (less strongly) that a relatively full life can be lived without involvement in religious practice.[26] Of course, public schools should not teach that an overarching religious perspective *is* necessary to comprehend other subjects or that religion *is* necessary for a full life, but they should not implicitly dismiss these possibilities.

If we turn to causal effects, the challenge to secular education is harder to evaluate. We may put the causal claim thus: students whose education refers very little to religion are less likely to take religion seriously in their own lives than students whose education includes appropriate references to religion. We can quickly see the intuitive plausibility of the causal claim—if, on its face, a religion-free education implies a diminished place for religion, it will probably have just that effect in the lives of its students. But here is where, short of being presented with convincing empirical data, we must be careful. We need to take into account what it is about religion that public schools may teach; what is happening outside school; and what social and psychological factors lead students (and adults) to embrace religious faith.

Drawing on our conclusion about teaching religious propositions in chapter 5 and oversimplifying the conclusions of the next five chapters, we may say that public schools must teach about religion in a relatively balanced and objective way, if they are to teach about it at all. Such teaching, when moderately competent, *is* likely to persuade students that religious convictions and practices have been an important force throughout human history and that many people in the United States and elsewhere continue to regard religion as very important. But is such teaching likely to lead students to accept religion in their own lives? Reading of New England's Great Awakening in the eighteenth century, one cannot help being struck by how strongly preachers who led listeners to religious conversions emphasized the horrible damnation awaiting those who remained mired in their own sins.[27] Such an appeal is vastly different from "detached" education about a variety of religious faiths. One can certainly imagine the latter indirectly leading students to the opinion that no particular religion has a monopoly on truth or lies at the center of human understanding, that all religions make some extravagant claims that reasonable, enlightened minds will reject.

What happens within school must be correlated to what happens outside school. The religious upbringings of public school students vary radically. For those whose parents are nonreligious and who are exposed to the heavily secular culture of our mass media, education about religion might spark an interest in whether religious involvement could enrich their lives. For children of deeply religious parents who are raised with unquestioning devotion to a single faith, public education about many religions might be more likely to dislodge them from a religious life than would a school's disregard of religion.

Finally, how can we estimate complex reactions? Regrettably, students may find they are "turned off" by some teaching. If religion is not mentioned (much), it might have a freshness of appeal, an excitement, that sets it off from the boring grind of ordinary study. (And, as I suggested in chapter 2, students whose education is nonhierarchical and nondogmatic might seek the more solid foundation of hierarchical, dogmatic religion, rather than an approach to religion that fits more coherently with their education.)

In sum, despite the intuitive plausibility of the thesis that disregard of religion in standard education will tend to downgrade its importance in students' lives, we cannot easily generalize about the comparative effects of schools disregarding religion and schools teaching "objectively" about religion.

I do not think any of the doubts I have sketched totally eliminate the intuitive force of the critique of religion-free education, taken causally, but they should encourage social scientists to gather empirical evidence about causes and effects. More to the point for my effort here, they support a focus on what is intrinsically sound education, a focus that does not rely heavily on how that education actually influences religious convictions and practices. Although educators should not mainly concern themselves with causal relations between sound teaching and religious involvement, they should be somewhat sensitive to parental concerns that schools are undermining their efforts to transmit religion to their children. (How much educators should be responsive to these concerns is a delicate question later chapters take up.)

The constitutional sensitivity of teaching about religion does not answer the concern that religion is now being unfairly treated (in a sense), but it does alert us to the relation between possible correctives and an evaluation of present practice. *Perhaps* a proposed remedy would be even worse in respect to the states' treatment of religion. If the prevailing approach is the best of admittedly imperfect alternatives, we must accept it. If that approach is arguably preferable to any remedies, it may remain a permissible alternative. What might *otherwise* be a violation of the Constitution could be acceptable because proposed remedies are not clearly better.

The obvious remedy for religion's present neglect is for schools to say more about it, while withholding judgments about religious truth. In certain limited respects, schools should undoubtedly adopt this remedy, which is consonant with the values of the religion clauses themselves. But a large measure of caution is needed. The wisdom of a proposed change can depend on how religion is now being neglected for particular subject matters, on the depth of treatment for religion that is proposed, on community acceptance of the schools' paying more attention to religion, and on teacher competence.

These issues are best addressed in the contexts of particular subject matters. In the following chapters, I begin with natural science, examining the issue of evolution and creationism in considerable detail. I then turn to history and economics; to civic and moral education; to literature; and to comparative religion. This survey does not cover the entire curriculum, but it is raises the major issues.[28]

Some of the key questions that the next five chapters address are these: (1) How far should texts and teachers talk about religious perspectives when these are not aspects of the subject matter as it has come to be defined? (2) Should texts and teachers cover religious perspectives when they do fall reasonably within a subject matter? (3) Should texts and teachers cover religious perspectives that provide answers that are implausible from the standpoint of the secular discipline? (4) Should courses in religion itself be offered to combat the implicit secular message of public school education? (5) How should one select material that relates to religion? (6) How much of an effort should be made to get students to see things *from* a religious perspective? (7) How far should teachers undertake close critical analysis of religious perspectives? (8) How far should teachers feel free to introduce their own convictions and practices?

Teaching Natural Science I: Relation between Science and Religion

THE FIERCEST CONTROVERSY over how religious perspectives might figure in public schools has centered on the teaching of evolution, a subject within natural science. In this and the next two chapters, I focus on that controversy, and on general issues about natural science and religion that it illustrates. These three chapters set a model for comparison of teaching other disciplines, which lack criteria of truth and methods as well settled as those of modern science.

Because the debate about evolution has endured so long, because the Supreme Court has twice dealt with laws that restricted the teaching of evolution, and because so much has been written about the persuasiveness of neo-Darwinian theory as compared with creationism and intelligent design, we shall engage this topic in greater detail than the ones that follow.

It may help at the outset to clarify the status of the claims I make in these chapters. I am neither a scientist nor a philosopher of science. As far as constitutional law is concerned, the crucial issue about what is or is not presented in science courses is what amounts to the teaching of religion. As these chapters show, that issue cannot be detached entirely from questions in the realm of science and its philosophy. This means that educators, judges, and scholars addressing the constitutional topic must do their best to appraise the literature that bears on the strength of scientific assertions. Somewhat more precisely, educators and others making curricular decisions will usually make these judgments directly; courts will determine whether the judgments others make about curriculum fall within a permissible constitutional range.

In the course of these chapters, I offer various suggestions concerning the state of scientific knowledge about the history of life on earth. At an initial glance, it may seem that I give more credence to critics of dominant evolutionary theory than would the overwhelming majority of practicing scientists, but it is not my intention to render a decisive judgment on that critique. The main aim, rather, is to assess whether the many people who would like to alter the teaching of evolution are making proposals that lie within constitutional boundaries. This requires that I spend at least some time explaining the substance of what they argue, and tentatively explore its plausibility. I believe that what I say is consistent with what modern scientists can reasonably assert about this domain. In any event, readers should keep in mind that my nonexpert assessments about the facts of biology and conceptualizations about what is science and what are theories about the limits of science are steps in an analysis of when the constitutional line that prohibits teaching religion has been crossed.

Natural Science and Religion

Although natural science is now taught without reference to religion, conflicts between scientific conclusions and religious understandings render that approach a source of continuing tension. In this respect, natural science differs from mathematics. Mathematical approaches have become increasingly central in the natural sciences, especially physics,[1] but almost everyone seems to agree that mathematics as a subject really is neutral among possible views about religion.[2] Its presuppositions do not reflect or reject religious faith; its content is rightly free of religion. One way to look at the natural sciences and other subject matters is to ask how they differ from math in this respect.

Texts and teachers in natural science courses typically do not refer to religion. This may seem less than neutral toward religion, because certain scientific claims conflict directly with widespread religious beliefs. Further, scientific perspectives may seem implicitly to exclude a religious reverence for the natural world as part of God's provenance,[3] and scientific solutions may implicitly displace religious approaches to practical problems such as human disease.

Some prominent scientists talk as if science yields conclusions— mostly negative ones—about the most fundamental religious questions. But science, as such, cannot tell us whether God exists, whether the universe has a purpose, or whether we can gain insights into reality through religious understanding.

The Controversy over Life's History

The long-standing conflict between evolutionary theorists and creationists has focused on America's public schools. If these schools had no need to teach about the origins of life, each side might content itself with promoting its favored worldview and proclaiming its opponents to be narrow-minded and dogmatic. But educators have to decide what to teach, and because public schools may not teach religious propositions as true, the First Amendment is crucially implicated.

On close examination, many of the contested constitutional issues turn out to be relatively simple, but others are not. After reviewing the basic controversy between evolutionary theorists and creationists, and the educational and constitutional questions that controversy raises, we shall explore five fundamental premises that, together, generate the most troubling questions about science, religion, and the public schools.

With this background set, we will inquire in the next chapter whether evolution, Genesis creationism, and intelligent design qualify as appropriate subjects for science courses in public schools. We will find that evolution definitely belongs in science courses, and that any account approximating the literal reading of Genesis does not. Students should be informed of uncertainties and possible gaps in dominant evolutionary theory and they may be told that, if any supplements are needed (a matter definitely in doubt), intelligent design is one, *but only one*, conceivable alternative.

The discussion in the following chapter shifts from what belongs in a science course to what counts as teaching religion. Teaching Genesis creationism is teaching religion, because the only substantial basis for believing in that account is religious. Teaching intelligent design is religious if that theory is presented as true or as *the* alternative to dominant evolutionary theory. A decision not to teach evolution is also religious, because religious views are the only likely basis for exclusion. Harder questions are raised by how a school treats perspectives that compete with scientific ones. Serious development of competing perspectives should be reserved for courses in history, culture, or comparative religion, or courses self-consciously adopting an interdisciplinary approach, such as "Perspectives on the Environment."

The Basic Conflict

Although not the first scientist to suggest the idea of evolution, Charles Darwin, in *On the Origin of Species* (1859), "was the first thinker to amass together, in one systematic volume . . . all the evidences from various scientific fields of study relevant to this topic."[4] The central thesis of evolution, Philip Kitcher has written, "is that species are not fixed and immutable. . . . From one original species, a number of different kinds may be generated."[5] Darwin's main explanation for this evolution with modification was a process of natural selection; whether individual animals would pass on to their offspring a characteristic they possessed from birth depended largely on whether the characteristic contributed to the animals' survival and reproduction.[6]

In the *Origin of Species* and in later works, Darwin drew from various sources to support his theory. Selective breeding by human beings provided an analogy to how natural selection could work. The remarkable similarity of embryos and of anatomical structures among widely variant species, such as lizards and human beings, suggested derivation from common ancestors. Fossils revealed that complex species developed from simple ones. Finally, variations in species in isolated locales, such as the Galápagos Islands, indicated an evolution from ancestors common to them and to related species found elsewhere. Darwin's own approach has been filled out and modified, but prevailing ideas are referred to as a neo-Darwinian synthesis.

Modern scientists, relying in part on astronomical physics and the use of radioactive isotopes to date rock fragments, place the age of the earth at somewhere between 4.2 and 4.8 billion years. Life appeared after several hundred million years or later, and for the next two billion years and more, all life-forms were single-celled organisms, such as bacteria and algae.[7] Not until the last billion years did these single-cell life-forms develop into all the complex plants and animals that have populated Earth.

Genetic theory helps confirm Darwin's idea of natural selection.[8] Changes in organisms over generations occur both because of recombinations of genetic characteristics[9] and mutations, alterations in the molecular structure and arrangement of genes.[10] Diversity among similar species is largely explained by reproductive isolation; thus animals in Australia differ from those in other places in the world. Modern evolutionists disagree about exactly how much natural selection explains. "Neutralists" contend against "selectionists" that chance—what is termed "genetic drift"—accounts for more change than has commonly been recognized.[11] Scientists also disagree to some extent over how steady or jerky evolution has been and over the size of particular changes.[12]

The neo-Darwinian synthesis is supported by the discovery that DNA molecules of closely related species are nearly identical in chemical composition and sequence,[13] and by studies of existing species that prove that over time the traits of organisms adjust to yield a better fit between organism and environment.[14]

Darwin's theory understandably disturbed many traditional Christians. If the history of human life can be explained without reference to God's creative hand, and if human beings are one link in a long continuous chain, no vast gulf may separate their rational and moral qualities from those of similar animals. Species far superior to our own may be in the offing if we do not manage to destroy life on Earth. The deterministic quality of Darwinian evolution and its dependence on random mutations also troubled those who believed that life is part of God's plan and that human beings can achieve their own true good by responding to that plan. Ever since Darwin wrote, many religious people have regarded his theory as threatening the grounds of religious belief and of morality.[15] Those who search for an alternative scientific theory have been largely motivated by this distress.

Evolutionary theory conflicts with a literal reading of Genesis, according to which God created other animals and human beings within a span of days.[16] And if one uses the Bible to mark the earth's age, taking the days of creation as days of ordinary length, one would arrive at roughly six thousand to ten thousand years. Creationists believe that God created all the basic "kinds" of animals at the same time. Any evolution that has occurred is within kinds, not from one kind to another. Although the notion of "kinds" is imprecise, cats are not of the same kind as dogs, and human beings are not of the same kind as apes. The fossils of simpler organisms tend to appear in lower strata of rocks because these creatures were less able to escape from waters of Noah's flood that engulfed the earth. At the time of the great flood, the nature of physical processes changed to such an extent that modern techniques of dating rocks, etc., are wholly unreliable.[17]

What scientific evidence supports the creationist story? For the most part, the argument is that the theory of evolution is unconvincing, and creationism thus wins by default. But positive evidence has also been claimed. Notably, some creationists have asserted that the bedrock along the Paluxy River in Texas contains fossils of human beings alongside those of dinosaurs, who became extinct long before human beings appeared on the scene, according to evolutionary theory. (The particular claim about Paluxy River fossils has been substantially discredited.)[18]

What proponents have called "intelligent design" is another theory that finds Darwinian evolutionary theory unconvincing as a complete explanation of life's development. That theory, which has been said to involve two basic assumptions—intelligent causes exist, and they can be detected empirically (by discerning specified complexity)[19]—rejects much less of the dominant scientific understanding than does standard creationism and makes far fewer claims about the details of what happened. I concentrate on the theory in its most modest form, because that form rejects the least of what scientists now assert.

Public School Teaching about the History of Life

Many Christian fundamentalists, accepting the literal truth of the Bible,[20] have tried to purge evolution from the public school curriculum or to have it balanced by "creation science" or labeled as "only a theory."

During the past century, a few states adopted laws forbidding the teaching of evolution.[21] Of more practical importance, up through the 1950s, was the marginalization of evolution by placing it at the end of biology courses, and successful opposition to textbooks containing evolutionary theory.[22] After the Soviet Union's launch of Sputnik in 1957, the first rocket to circle the earth, government officials, concerned with the quality of science education, helped finance new series of science texts, including biology texts that treated evolution more fully.[23]

In 1968, in *Epperson v. Arkansas*,[24] the Supreme Court held invalid a law that forbade teaching that mankind descended from a lower order of animals. Justice Fortas wrote that a state cannot tailor teaching to the principles of any religious dogma; the Arkansas law was based solely on "a particular interpretation of the Book of Genesis."[25] Since *Epperson*, creationists have sought to have evolution downplayed, treated as only unconfirmed theory, not truth, and "balanced" by teaching of creationism, in the form of "creation science," so that students can "make up their own minds." Both Arkansas and Louisiana adopted a Balanced Treatment Act. After a district court rejected the Arkansas law, which required schools to present both evolution and creation science,[26] the Supreme Court, in *Edwards v. Aguillard*,[27] concluded that the Louisiana legislature, in requiring that schools teach both evolution and creation science or neither, had a forbidden aim to advance religion.

In 1999, the Kansas Board of Education took a different tack, one it rescinded less than two years later. It removed evolution (and the Big Bang theory) from its seventy-one-page science curriculum.[28]

Basic Questions

Between literal-Genesis creationism and dominant evolutionary theory, science provides a decisive verdict for evolution. Even were these the only two alternatives, we would face educational questions about whether perspectives that reject dominant scientific theories belong in science courses, should be covered elsewhere in the curriculum, or should be omitted altogether from public education. We would also face related constitutional questions whether reliance on religious reasons to teach, or to refrain from teaching, material makes educational decisions unconstitutional.

Although these questions hold substantial interest, the gulf between Genesis creationism and dominant evolutionary theory conceals yet more perplexing issues. Suppose that educators, accepting major aspects of dominant evolutionary theory, are attracted by the idea that a full explanation of the development of complex forms of life may include a modest input of "intelligent design." Does that idea belong in a science course, or is it disqualified because it contains (or loosely implies) a religious conclusion, or because it fails to meet the requisites of scientific theory, or because it is implausible? And, relatedly, does "intelligent design" rest on a religious proposition?

Our examination of these questions can help us think more generally about the uncertain boundaries of science and religion, and about how to address other potential conflicts involving those domains.

SCIENCE, RELIGION, AND TRUTH

Five fundamental premises, in combination, generate the most troubling questions about science, religion, and the public schools, including the most nettlesome issues about teaching the history of life. (1) Schools should not teach the truth of religious propositions. (2) For many people, the domains of science and religion overlap significantly. (3) Anyone's assessment of what is true, overall, will include an evaluation of all relevant sources of truth, including any religious sources he or she credits. (4) Modern science is committed to methodological naturalism. (5) Scientific conclusions can bear on the likely truth of religious propositions.

Public School Teaching and Religious Propositions

As we have seen, the Supreme Court has made evident that public schools may not teach particular religious doctrines as true or as false. If a teacher's only possible basis for a claim is religious belief, her making the claim amounts to a teaching of religion, even though the claim does not involve any explicit religious proposition. Thus, if a teacher says, "The earth is exactly six thousand years old" and bases this claim solely on the words of the Bible, her assertion counts as religious.[29] On the other hand, as chapter 5 explains, when public schools teach as accurate certain factual propositions (such as the sun's place at the center of our planetary system) that conflict with the doctrines of particular religions, the teaching is not religious if its basis lies outside religious premises.

Domains of Science and Religion

In respect to the relation between science and religion, some people believe that the two domains do not overlap.[30] The idea that *natural science* does not overlap the domain of religion appeals to many people;[31] for others, a persuasive religious account of ultimate reality bears on subjects to which natural science speaks.

Even if science and religion address overlapping subject matters, we might escape conflicts if science and religion are completely separate discourses, *or* if what a religion asserts is compatible with what science discovers. The "separate discourses" approach founders on the reality that scientists and religious believers both care about what is really true, overall. Many scientists, including evolutionists, make claims about aspects of reality—about a series of events in the history of the universe or the earth;[32] the assertion that the earth is over four billion years old is *like* the assertion that I am more than sixty-five years old. Some religious believers understand what authoritative religious sources say about physical reality as mythic and symbolic, but many take these accounts more literally. Someone who accepts the literal truth of Genesis has a view about how life *really* developed historically that conflicts with evolutionary theory.

Although scientific and religious perspectives can conflict, two understandings common among traditional religions are compatible with what scientific investigation can establish. The first is that a creator created original matter and set things in motion according to scientific laws that the creator established. The second is that the creator continues to sustain the universe and life within it, even when things run wholly in accord with scientific principles.[33] Each of these two possibilities could be realized despite the universal operation of scientific principles.[34]

All Sources of Truth

A person who believes that various sources of truth point in different directions must evaluate them all to decide where the truth probably lies. Almost no one denies that scientific investigation is *a* source of truth. Numbers of scientists, and others, do not believe in religious sources of truth;[35] *they* will not consult any religious sources to decide what is true. But people who believe that both kinds of sources provide insights into truth[36] must decide what to believe when science, taken alone, marks as most likely a reality different from what religious sources they credit, taken alone, suggest. Many people will not credit a religious conclusion that conflicts directly with a powerful scientific one, such as the roundness of the earth. But if the evidence for the scientific conclusion is weak or full of gaps, and if the religious reasons for the competing conclusion are very strong, a person may well adhere to the religious view, believing that science will eventually revise its position.[37] The way in which persuasiveness from a religious perspective can affect judgments about scientific conclusions, and vice versa, is played out in religious arguments that evolutionary theory is at odds with the Genesis account or is at odds with how a divine creator would act.[38] For some religious believers, this possible conflict is a reason to reject evolution. Various evolutionary theorists from Darwin forward have made an argument from imperfection that when we look at animals as they now are, we cannot imagine that this is how a divine creator, acting directly with each kind of animal, would have created them.[39] Thus, debate over the scientific theory of evolution can draw us into theological and philosophical arguments about what a divine creator would do in creating individual kinds of animals directly. These arguments, not subject to scientific confirmation, are unavoidable, so long as our interest is in what is true overall; but they raise perplexities when we get to the subject matter of science courses and the teaching of religion.

Methodological Naturalism

Thus far, I have implicitly assumed a central characteristic of modern science, that it is methodologically naturalist—approaching scientific problems on the assumption that physical events have natural causes and can be explained according to uniform laws that need not refer to anything supernatural.[40] Methodological naturalism has proven very productive; scientists have discovered natural explanations for countless phenomena not previously explicable according to scientific principles. A scientist committed to methodological naturalism need not deny that science *may* prove unable to explain some physical phenomena.[41]

Science has not always been committed to methodological naturalism, and in the future it conceivably could move away from that position, however unlikely that eventuality may be. Alvin Plantinga, among others, has argued that Christian scientists should abandon methodological naturalism in favor of "theistic science" or "Augustinian" science.[42] Were the proposal of "theistic science" to entail not only that religious scientists should evaluate conclusions reached by methodological naturalism against their religious understandings before they make claims about what is true overall, but also that they employ a different way of *doing* science, it would abandon a shared, universal methodology that has proven highly valuable.

Scientific Conclusions and the Truth of Religious Propositions

1. *Counting negatively against the truth of religious propositions.* Committed as it is methodological naturalism, science may yield particular conclusions, and even theories, that bear on the truth of religious propositions. Most obviously, science may establish facts that are directly contrary to religious propositions. Thus, anyone who accepts scientific proof that the sun lies at the center of our planetary system cannot also believe the religious claim that God made the sun to circle the earth.

Scientific conclusions can threaten more fundamental religious propositions less directly. A number of prominent evolutionists have thought that the truth of evolution counts strongly against the possibility of a benign, omnipotent creator,[43] since such a creator would not have brought forth natural laws that produce imperfect life through the painful and arbitrary process of natural selection.[44] Scientists who assert that evolutionary theory supports atheism or warrants strong skepticism about all traditional religious views stray beyond the strict bounds of methodological naturalism; *but* we must understand that whenever scientific conclusions have a strong probability of being true overall, this can affect not only the likely truth of narrow religious doctrines that are directly opposed to the scientific conclusions, but also the persuasiveness of other, more basic, religious conceptions.

2. *Positive support.* Science may also provide a kind of positive support for religious propositions. Although the "Big Bang" theory of the origin of the universe can hardly be called evidence for God, some theorists do think the theory fits more congenially than the once popular "steady state" theory with belief in a God who creates ex nihilo.

And scientific investigations can relate more sharply to religious beliefs. Part of science is establishing the existence of things that science cannot yet explain. These phenomena might possibly point toward some supernatural power.

In a recent study of intercessory prayer reported in the press, the subjects of the experiment were 199 women in Korea who sought assistance at a fertility clinic to become pregnant.[45] The researchers said they expected that prayers by strangers would be shown to be useless. To their surprise, the rate of pregnancy for women who were beneficiaries of prayers was 50 percent— "an amazingly high success rate for any fertility program"; the pregnancy rate for the control group was 25 percent. Of course, the experiment may have been ill-designed;[46] it may prove not replicable by other experiments; the results may have been an astonishing coincidence. *If* the results were further confirmed by similar experiments, scientists might one day discover a forceful mental communication that affects physical processes and is subject to a natural explanation. Nonetheless, the experiment (if accurately reported) would lead an uncommitted observer to believe it at least somewhat more likely than he did before the experiment that a supernatural being or force responds to prayer.

Scientific methods may also be used to test a tentative religious explanation for a singular event, such as a startling recovery from physical affliction. If doctors who investigate to find a possible natural explanation begin with doubt that any such explanation may suffice, their inquiry follows the strictures of methodological naturalism only in a sense. The investigators do try to determine if they can explain what has occurred naturally, but they do not *assume* that such an explanation will work. An example of such investigations are the inquiries carried out by distinguished doctors under the auspices of the Roman Catholic

Church to determine if medical recoveries claimed to be miraculous are susceptible of a natural explanation.[47]

Although science cannot prove that miracles never happen, advances in science can make miracles seem less likely. As science keeps explaining events that once seemed miraculous, a person might reasonably conclude that no events are really at odds with accurate scientific principles.[48] But science alone cannot yield a decisive answer about miracles; a full evaluation reaches beyond science into the realm of persuasiveness from a religious and philosophical point of view. From the religious perspective, the reasons for and against miraculous interventions in human history look different from the reasons for and against creative intervention in natural processes of developing forms of life many millions of years before the origins of human beings.[49] For our purposes, the possibility of individual miracles matters largely as it bears on the likelihood of divine interventions in the processes of developing life.

The following two chapters explore the implications of these generalizations about science and religion for evolutionary theory and alternatives public schools might teach.

CHAPTER 9

Teaching Natural Science II: Evolutionism, Creationism, and Intelligent Design

A CAREFUL ASSESSMENT OF the place of evolution, creationism, and intelligent design in public schools requires matching the specific claims and methodological foundations of each against an analysis of what belongs in a science course and what counts as teaching religion.

SCIENCE AND MATERIAL FOR SCIENCE COURSES

Educators need to evaluate whether any theory about the development of life is "scientific," or nevertheless closely enough related to science to belong in a science course, and whether, from a scientific standpoint, the theory is minimally plausible.

Minimum Plausibility

Although I have no expertness in evaluating the plausibility of scientific claims, my appraisals are nevertheless worth stating, both because almost anyone trying to figure out what is true overall must engage a field in which he is not expert[1] and because many educational officials and virtually all judges who must discern if educational decisions are constitutional will lack special scientific competence.

Jeffrie Murphy says that scientific creationists regard their account as "a highly confirmed scientific hypothesis," which can be established by empirical evidence.[2] If evolution and creationism were both scientific theories and were about equally plausible from a scientific point of view, teaching them both in biology courses as alternatives would make sense.

If a theory, while relying on scientific evidence, has almost no scientific plausibility, science teachers, and textbook authors, should not present it as having a substantial probability of being true.[3] To warrant its being presented as possibly accurate, a theory should pass a threshold of plausibility. Although all scientific theories are revisable, and the most universally held theories—Newton's theory is the leading example—may later be supplemented or abandoned, it does not follow that every conceivable alternative is plausible or deserves equal consideration. The likelihood that further scientific advances will show that the earth is flat or that blood does not circulate from the heart is negligible.

Research scientists within the fields that count overwhelmingly accept evolution as the most convincing scientific theory about the development of species. Although some elements of the theory appear less subject to possible revision in the future than others, scientific evidence from various branches of science helps to support all of the crucial aspects. If any theory of the development of life on earth qualifies as plausible, evolution does so.

Certain objections to evolutionary theory turn out to be misconceived or not to be very substantial. The theory does not assume "progress," but merely the continuing adjustment of organisms to changing environmental conditions, and it does not assume that mutations are generally beneficial or harmful.[4] The theory of natural selection, properly understood, is not unfalsifiable in the sense of "explaining" any conceivable evidence.[5] With examples like the peppered moth (noted in chapter 8, note 14), we can clearly see that organisms better suited to survive in the environment do survive and pass on their characteristics to descendants. And scientists can predict that over generations viruses will develop resistance to antibiotics, as a theory of natural selection would indicate.

Negative Arguments

Both Genesis creationists and proponents of intelligent design present various negative arguments against the plausibility of evolutionary theory. In addition to disagreement about the strength of particular arguments, controversy swirls over the status of such arguments in general. We need to ask what force negative arguments of various kinds have.

In science, no less than other disciplines, negative arguments about an opposing position clearly are *one* proper part of a defense of one's own position. Creationists have complained that evolutionists arbitrarily rule their negative arguments out of bounds.[6] And, indeed, various assertions that scientists do not, and should not, abandon a dominant theory until a more persuasive scientific theory is offered in its place do suggest that the role for negative arguments is limited.[7]

Suppose that a critic presented a powerful argument that random mutation and natural selection, and other explanatory devices of neo-Darwinian theory, could not persuasively account for certain developments toward complex life as we know it. Such an argument, though it would neither establish the eventual unpersuasiveness of a neo-Darwinian explanation nor show the likely truth of any single alternative, should make us believe it is *somewhat less likely* that present neo-Darwinian theory affords an accurate account. Historically, perhaps the most familiar challenge to natural selection has been that imperceptible, gradual changes cannot explain the origin of complicated organs such as the eye and the wing: The eye and wing require a great many parts to function in a particular and precise way. Yet a slight development toward any one of these parts would confer no competitive advantage; therefore, mutations of genes producing physical features in any of these directions would not survive; therefore, the critics argued, the eye and wing could not develop by slow changes in a great many parts if these changes were "undirected" and depended on natural selection for their survival.

A similar argument about complex parts has been advanced about the molecules that make up cells. According to Michael Behe, "[T]he elegance and complexity of biological systems at the molecular level have paralyzed science's attempt to explain their origins."[8] For such systems, he writes, a neo-Darwinian explanation is implausible because elements serving no function before full development of the entire system would not survive. At present, because biologists have a fuller sense of how organs like the wing and eye have evolved than of the stages of single cells, the challenge to natural selection based on complex cells may seem the stronger; but biologists respond that as their knowledge grows of how these cells function, so will their ability to explain how the cells have evolved.[9]

Most evolutionary biologists, of course, disagree with the

view that any organs or cells pose serious difficulties for theories that ascribe a dominant role in evolution to natural selection. They argue, for example, that a degree of sensitivity to light could be very helpful in comparison with blindness (and various parts may also have served other purposes or have been genetically related to other valuable features), so we can imagine a slow progression from blindness to the full eye. But let us now for the sake of argument suppose that, contrary to what evolutionary biologists claim,[10] organs like the eye or biochemical processes within cells are very difficult for neo-Darwinian theory to explain. It hardly follows that Genesis creationism or intelligent design is true. A neo-Darwinian explanation may eventually prove adequate or new elements may be added to scientific explanations of evolution. One such possibility is offered by Stuart Kauffman, who has developed a "complexity theory," according to which the "order of the biological world . . . is not merely tinkered, but arises naturally and spontaneously because of . . . principles of self-organization—laws of complexity that we are just beginning to uncover and understand."[11]

At first glance we might suppose that if order or design has had a role in the historical development of life, it must have been intelligent. But when we think about the development of a single-cell human embryo into a multicell baby with bones, nerves, muscles, blood, and complex organs—programmed according to the DNA in its genes—we realize that order can have a natural explanation that does not depend on any premise about an intelligent creator.

Much scientific evidence of order, if it exists, is bound to be indecisive between intelligent design and natural principles of order. Lacking any full understanding of life's history, we cannot know whether scientists will discover how development over time might proceed by a nonrandom process that bears a resemblance to the progress from embryo to baby. Negative arguments about the role of natural selection do not support a single alternative that involves an intelligent creator.[12] But that does not mean the negative arguments lack all force. Were scientists to understand that a dominant theory has been rendered unpersuasive or highly vulnerable,[13] some of them, at least, should search for a better theory, even if the critic himself cannot provide one.[14]

A second reason for not automatically rejecting negative challenges to evolutionary theory is that creationist and intelligent-design criticisms are offered mainly on the issue of what is really true about life's historical development overall, that is, taking all relevant sources of truth into account. If their *positive claim* is that God has created by means that transcend ordinary natural processes, the critics do not have an alternative theory cast in terms of a *natural explanation*; their whole point is that any explanation that relies exclusively on standard science is false. Scientists, as scientists, may reiterate their commitment to methodological naturalism, but so long as they understand that the critic offers negative arguments for the proposition that some nonscientific explanation is accurate, they cannot fairly dismiss negative arguments about the role of natural selection on the question of what is true, overall.

Challenges to evolution that rely on disagreements among evolutionary experts present a variation on the overall theme of negative arguments. If two experts are strongly committed to a general theory, their disagreement about how a process occurs might or might not influence one's confidence in their shared conclusion. Suppose two sports fans who viewed the finish agree that A beat B in a cross-country race. The first fan thinks that B was trying her hardest but that she ran out of steam near the end. The second fan, aware that B and A are close friends, thinks he saw B intentionally slow down so that A could win. Their disagreement about *why* B lost does not diminish in the slightest our confidence that the fans correctly perceived who won. But suppose both fans say they are almost certain that A won, although neither saw the actual finish. The first fan says that A was well ahead at the halfway mark and looked as strong as did B. The second fan says that B was ahead by one hundred yards at that point, but was much more winded than A, who was closing fast. Here the disagreement about the reasons why A probably won would decrease our confidence in their shared assumption that A did win.

Our confidence in an aspect of evolutionary theory might be similarly shaken if two experts present powerful reasons why the theory of the other is not convincing. Opponents of gradualism, that is, imperceptible changes that slowly produce new features like complex cells, say that the standard explanation cannot show how such changes took place. Proponents of gradualism claim that no plausible scientific explanation suggests how larger, faster changes could have occurred.[15] If we think each negative criticism is convincing, we are left with the possibility of large, fast changes not easily explicable by present science.[16]

Probability claims present another variation on the force of negative arguments about evolutionary theory.[17] Let us suppose that, given the physical conditions of the earth four billion years ago, a very intelligent and informed observer from another galaxy would have concluded that the development of life-forms as complex as the "higher mammals" was extremely unlikely.[18] Does this show that natural processes did not produce life as we know it? No, the scientist responds, highly improbable events do happen, and we have no doubt what life-forms have developed. Before-the-fact probabilities are irrelevant once we are aware what actually happened. Imagine that someone throws a die five times. The probability that the sequence will be exactly what it turns out to be was only one in 7,776 (6^5), but that would have been true about any exact sequence of five throws of a die.

However, if a gambler threw a die five times and each time the die turned up six, we would wonder if the outcome was random or the die was weighted to show six. In an actual legal case, a Democratic official had the job of determining by a random process whether Democrats or Republicans would have the advantageous top line of the ballot; on forty of forty-one occasions the Democrats ended on top.[19]

For many, the force of the improbability argument for the creation of complex life is to render more plausible the argument that design has been involved in the history of life.[20]

How Plausible Are the Contending Positions?

Creationists and design theorists argue that the scientific evidence does not support neo-Darwinian evolutionary theory as a complete account of life's historical development. As I have mentioned, they contend that the development of complex life was extremely unlikely absent purposeful direction, that many links between species supposed by evolutionary theory are not supported by the fossil record, and that disagreements about the methods and timing of change show that proponents have no convincing version of evolutionary theory.

Evolutionists respond that improbable things do happen and that the fossil record is incomplete because it takes special conditions for fossils to be made, and soft tissue like eyes does not produce fossils at all. We can understand why only a very small percentage of species that have ever existed are revealed by fossils and why the gaps are as they are.[21] Biologists who disagree to some extent about the pace of evolution agree that evolutionary theory is correct in its major premises,[22] most notably that the earth is very old, that life somehow developed naturally from nonlife,[23] that all life proceeds from a common ancestor (or very few ancestors), and that natural selection explains much of that development.

Few research biologists and paleontologists believe that the attack on evolutionary theory is anything close to compelling. Although these professional scientists may conceivably be biased or locked into approaches in which they were educated,[24] the weight of scientific opinion must give nonexperts substantial pause about accepting challenges to neo-Darwinism, especially since evolutionary theorists have reasonable-sounding answers.

Creation science in its full-blown, literal-Genesis form lacks scientific support. I have already mentioned the many scientific disciplines that suggest that the earth is far more than 10,000 years old, a conclusion geologists had reached long before Darwin came along.[25] Modern estimates of the age of the earth, based on various methods of dating, range between 4.2 and 4.8 billion years.[26] The ratio between 10,000 years and 4.5 billion years is approximately the same as that between one hour and 50 years. (We wouldn't have much of a problem figuring out whether a human being had been alive one hour or 50 years.) The creationist claim that the Flood somehow altered natural processes, in a manner that makes all modern methods of dating unreliable, is implausible, at best (at least if one takes the claim as one of science). The evidence that simple life-forms preceded complex ones and that simpler species developed into more complex ones is very powerful. All in all, the scientific case for creationism in its standard modern form is extremely weak.

The comparatively modest claims on behalf of intelligent design are more plausible, if they do no more than challenge the completeness of the dominant account of how complex life developed and propose that intelligent design best accounts for details the dominant theory fails to explain. If an intelligent-design theorist is careful not to deny that the dominant account with all its features explains a great deal about life's development, he can render his own approach consistent with the empirical evidence, which itself cannot rule out a possible role, however minor, for creative intelligence that transcends ordinary scientific principles at various stages of the process. But intelligent design is not established by existing scientific evidence; the development of life may be entirely explicable without reference to any general design or order, or with reference to an order that is not intelligently designed.

It may be relevant in this connection that in many domains of science the areas of uncertainty are at least as great as they are with respect to processes of evolution; and in some of these domains, scientists have much less sense of how to proceed toward resolution of the uncertainties than do evolutionary biologists.[27] Given the progress of science across a wide range, one would be hesitant to invoke intelligent design as a way to fill various lacunae that will be highly likely to yield to scientific discovery in the future. From the standpoint of most scientists, any hypothesis of intelligent design seems no more apt for the history of life than other areas of scientific uncertainty. And it seems improbable that anyone would so strongly press the case for intelligent design in this particular domain, were it not for religious objections to the neo-Darwinian account.

Domains of Science and Science Courses

Could "scientific" creationism and intelligent design qualify as science, or belong in a science course?

We can identify at least four conceivable grounds for disqualification. First, the concepts of divine creator and intelligent designer are not scientific. Second, the theories provide explanations that are not according to natural laws. Third, their proponents may not be open to contrary evidence. Fourth, little scientific evidence favors the theories; the arguments against most aspects of evolutionary theory are unconvincing

and, in any event, do not establish the competing explanations. We have already disposed of the fourth ground by concluding that creationism in the literal Genesis version has little
scientific plausibility; were no more involved than that, it
would be hard to say whether creation science is exceptionally
bad science or not science at all. It remains to discuss the other
three grounds.

1. *Reference to divine intelligence.* Insofar as the terms of creation
science refer to a nonscientific divine creator, we can substitute
"abrupt appearance of species in complex form" for "divine creation." Although the language of "abrupt appearance" avoids
making any explicit theological claim, and the cause of abrupt
appearance might be aliens from another solar system, still in
the absence of any scientific explanation for how it has occurred,
"abrupt appearance" may seem to suggest the probability of a
supernatural creative force. The idea of intelligent design, though
not specifying what form the intelligence beyond natural cause
might take, suffers a similar disability.

However, as we have seen, a theory is *not* necessarily unscientific because its truth bears on the likelihood of some religious
tenet. If scores of skeptical researchers replicated the experiment
involving prayer by strangers and obtained similar positive results, that would constitute some evidence favorable to the
proposition that a divinity (or devil) intervenes in human affairs.[28] That fact would not make the studies, or their conclusions
about prayer, unscientific and religious.[29] A theory about the history of species is not *necessarily* unscientific because it makes the
existence of a divine creator seem more likely.

2. *An explanation that is not fully natural.* That the explanations
of creationists and intelligent-design theorists seem to transcend
scientific theory is a more troubling problem. Indeed, I believe
this turns out to be *the central theoretical* question about the status
of intelligent-design theory. Insofar as creationism purports to
explain the historical development of life on the basis of religious authority rather than scientific evidence, it definitely moves
away from the realm of science; but a proponent of intelligent
design may claim only that species, individual organs, and cell
structures have appeared in a manner that now defies standard

scientific explanations *and* seems likely to defy any future explanations that omit the action of some creative intelligence.[30]

In criticizing the district court's picture of science in the case rejecting Arkansas's Balanced Treatment Act,[31] Larry Laudan, a philosopher of science, pointed out that scientists may establish that certain physical events happen (or have happened) although they do not yet possess any plausible lawlike explanation of *how* they occur.[32] Intelligent design is not disqualified from the status of science simply because it offers no present scientific explanation of how surprising changes may have occurred; but its proponents *also* claim, relying on scientific evidence and understanding, that natural explanations will never suffice to explain these changes.

Two points are crucially important here. The first is that we can never be sure that ordinary scientific explanations will remain unsatisfactory.[33] The second point is that it is not reasonably part of science to be *certain* that a *scientific* explanation is conceivable for every physical event that occurs in the universe. Scientific explanations have been forthcoming for innumerable events that human beings once ascribed to supernatural causes, but it is a stretch to *assume* that science can explain everything factual.

Advocates of "scientific" creationism and intelligent design claim that the available scientific evidence suggests that a purely scientific explanation of the origin of species is not only unavailable now, but is unlikely in the future. So understood, the theories, relying on scientific evidence, are partly about the limits of science.

This insight is very important for whether intelligent design could qualify as science or belong in a science course. A particular theory that science "runs out" in some respect in explaining events *can be* subject to observation and falsification. If scientists develop new evidence or increase their understanding of available evidence, they may explain what was heretofore inexplicable in scientific terms. We could not, of course, expect *an explanation of occurrences that is according to natural laws*, when the whole point of a theory is that natural laws cannot explain all the data.[34] An investigation of a claimed miracle does not become unscientific if it concludes that probably no natural explanation suffices.

The idea that creation science and intelligent-design theory are substantially about the limits of science is a central assumption in what follows, and it is worth pausing over it. I am *not* claiming that any sharp line exists between ordinary observation and science, between ordinary observation and religion, or between positive theses and theories of limits; nonetheless I believe we can best understand creationism and intelligent-design theories as being about the limits of science.

If a scientist ascertains the length of a day on a planet in another solar system, using the most advanced technology, we regard that as a scientific discovery. Yet the method of learning is not qualitatively different from our ordinary experience that the time between one sunrise and the next is approximately what we have arbitrarily labeled as twenty-four hours.[35] In a somewhat similar way, ordinary observation can shade into, or toward, religious conclusions. If I observed that prayers to God for rain consistently were followed by rain, I would have some evidence that responses of a supernatural power to prayer can affect natural physical processes, a religious conclusion. And, as we have seen, a "scientific" experiment might also provide evidence for the power of prayer.

Could a claim about supernatural causation of life's development be *part* of a scientific explanation?[36] We may begin with the possibility that a creator has acted purposefully but for reasons we do not understand. Whether such a claim involves an *explanation* at all depends on how much one demands of explanations.[37] The claim does explain in a sense—it attributes a physical event to a powerful intelligent actor rather than to ordinary natural forces. Imagine you are walking along the beach and see a construction of twigs and pebbles that funnels water into a small dish. Aware that no beavers are around, you are sure that only a human being would have produced this funnel, but you have no idea what this particular builder was like or why she would have wanted to build what she did. You have no idea when, if ever, she will build another similar funnel or what precise conditions would cause her to do so. Suppose your six-year-old child asks where the funnel came from. You say, "Water and wind would not make this, and I'm sure no animal around here could. A person definitely built it, but I don't know why she wanted to get water into a dish this way." Intelligent-design theory, standing alone and without any input from religious premises, purports to provide an explanation to something like this degree. It excludes natural selection and other ordinary natural causes as the complete explanation for the development of the eye, or wing, or complex cells; it informs us that a designer with some intelligence played a role. It cannot tell us much about the qualities of the designer, except that the designer is very powerful. (Here, intelligent-design theory is much less informative than the parent on the beach, who at least can tell the child that the funnel's builder was a human being.) It can tell us that the designer created eyes so that animals can see—it can yield this minimal functional information—but it cannot tell us why the designer wanted creatures to be able to see—so that they can flourish or so that the designer can enjoy seeing them destroy each other in fascinating ways. It "explains" in roughly the same sense as the following comment: "Why did A die? B shot him, but I haven't the foggiest notion why." One who lacks any idea *why* the creator acted certainly has no scientific explanation for what has occurred.

We can fantasize about having the kind of knowledge of supernatural motivation that we find in Greek myths and parts of the Bible—Zeus punished Prometheus because he was angered by his presumption. That knowledge could give us causal explanations including motivations, but not ones formulated in terms of general principles.[38] We might even imagine explanations formulable in terms of general principles, such as "God responds favorably to every sincere prayer," based on evidence of a scientific sort.

When I say that creation science and intelligent-design theory are about the limits of scientific explanation, I mean that they offer neither an explanation of why a Creative Spirit acts that depends on scientific or ordinary observational evidence nor an explanation of physical events that can be cast in terms of general principles, much less scientific principles.

Do theories about the limits of science belong in science courses? When one cuts through the rhetoric and variant estimates whether evolutionary theory, in roughly its present form, provides an adequate explanation for the history of life, this issue emerges as a central conflict between those who think intelligent design is a proper topic and those who think it is not. In a debate before the Ohio school board, one critic said that proponents of intelligent design "were trying to force 'unanswerable questions' about some theoretical instigation of life into a school curriculum properly limited to the rigorous proofs of science."[39] A proponent of intelligent design countered that "the methods of science are part of the debate that teachers should air."

In this debate, evolutionists are implicitly claiming that theories about where scientific explanations may fall short do not belong in science classes; proponents of intelligent design strongly disagree. The answer to this fundamental theoretical issue is that the limits of science *could* be an appropriate subject for science courses; but this answer needs explication, and it may have little practical bearing on whether schools should teach about intelligent design.

We need first to distinguish between two kinds of limits: limits of science's subject matter and possible limits within the range that scientific principles ordinarily cover. Science cannot explain why anything at all exists, why our lives have meaning, if they do, and why we should be ethical.[40] These intrinsic limits, set by the nature of the scientific enterprise, should definitely be mentioned in science courses, and it would be appropriate for texts and teachers to discuss controversies over the exact nature of these limits, including competing suppositions about the relations of science and religion. The full development of intrinsic limits belongs outside the domain of science. By contrast, suppose a subject matter falls broadly within the domain of science, and yet scientific evidence may suggest that no natural explanation suffices for physical events. So it is with claims about medical miracles and creative interventions in the historical development of life. If convincing evidence of such limits lay within science itself, their analysis would appropriately fall within the scope of science courses. To draw an analogy, a course in economics or political science would properly discuss the reasons why models fall short of predicting real-world consequences.[41]

Scientists might concede the logic of this suggestion and deny its practical relevance. According to the premise of methodological naturalism, scientists proceed on the assumption that natural explanations will be forthcoming for physical events that are now inexplicable. We lack convincing evidence that science will be unable to fully explain the development of life in the future.[42]

And, as I have said, in respect to the number of uncertainties, evolutionary theory does not differ from many domains of science. Instead of talking about limits, perhaps science teachers should follow scientists and tell students that science looks for natural explanations.

Although a strong connection exists between what practicing scientists do and the content of science courses, I believe the teacher should (or at least may) explore certain issues the scientist may put to one side. Ideally, a science teacher or text might say something like this:

> Modern science seeks to discover natural explanations for physical events. We cannot be certain that natural explanations will always suffice, but physics, chemistry, and biology have made amazing advances by assuming that they will. If we had powerful evidence that science could not conceivably explain some phenomena, this evidence of limits could be one small part of science courses; some people believe such evidence exists about evolutionary processes, but the uncertainties there are matched by those in other areas of science. In any event, it is too soon to conclude that any difficulties with evolutionary theory, even if they exist, cannot be rectified by scientific explanation.[43]

3. *Close-mindedness.* Our third possible difficulty with creation science is that its proponents are not open to evidence that counts against their theory. No doubt, receptivity varies to some degree, but members of important creation science organizations, the Creation Research Society and the Institute for Creation Science, must affirm—indeed, must *take an oath*—that they believe in the Genesis account of creation.[44] Those who are certain on religious grounds that Genesis is literally true are not the best people to consider the scientific evidence in a suitably detached way, especially if they are firmly convinced, on theological grounds, that scientific evidence *must* support the account religious authority reveals. Someone who believes only in an undefined degree of intelligent design has much less of a precommitment. He can be open to the possibility that science will establish other explanations for what he now thinks can best be explained by intelligent design. Although most proponents of intelligent design undoubtedly have religious reasons for resisting the persuasiveness of the neo-Darwinian synthesis,[45] that

alone is not an adequate reason to discount their arguments about its *scientific* inadequacy.

In its typical Genesis form, creation science does not belong in the science curriculum. Either it is nonscience or very bad science. It does not present a reasonable scientific explanation of the history of life on earth, and it lacks substantial argument and evidence that anything other than Darwinian evolution is the primary explanation for that development. Any appeal for "fair treatment" is misplaced. School students should not be expected to choose between a powerful scientific theory and one without merit that happens to coincide with many of their religious beliefs. As Kitcher writes, "It is educationally irresponsible to pretend that an idea that is scientifically worthless deserves scientific discussion."[46]

However, science teachers should cover the evidential gaps and controversies surrounding the neo-Darwinian synthesis. Any evidence for a kind of order of a sort not yet integrated into the dominant theory should be fairly presented. Teachers should indicate that present uncertainties by no means show that the dominant theory is incapable of explaining everything important. They should also explain that if the development of life has proceeded partly on the basis of an order that present neo-Darwinian theory neglects, that order may or may not reflect an intelligent designer; but that modern science has discovered naturally explicable principles of order for much that once seemed beyond explaining. Science teachers should *not* get far into the question of whether any as yet undiscovered principles of order in evolution, were they to exist, are likely to have proceeded from a creative intelligence.[47] One reason not to engage this possibility at any length is that students with religious objections to standard evolutionary theory may build much more than is warranted from any scientific perspective from conjectures about intelligent design.

Teaching Natural Science III: What Amounts to Teaching Religion?

TEACHING RELIGION

Thus far, we have concentrated on what counts as science or belongs in a science course. We now approach our topic from the perspective that matters for constitutional law: what counts as teaching religion? We shall focus first on the responsibilities of educators, saving judicial enforcement of the Establishment Clause for the last section.

Teaching Religion: Creationism and Intelligent Design

Teaching creationism in its full-blown, Genesis version is teaching religion, even if the material is taught as creation science, Scripture is not mentioned, and terms like *abrupt appearance* are substituted for divine creation. The difficulty is not that the theory has implications for some religious propositions, it is the absence of any real scientific basis for the theory. One could believe in the theory only for religious reasons. Creation science is not genuine science because neither its theses nor the techniques of its practitioners are genuinely scientific, and its conclusions conflict with the overwhelming weight of scientific evidence;[1] what makes the theory religious is that religious premises explain why the practitioners reach the conclusions they do.[2]

The status of intelligent design is less easily fixed. If the theory accepts most features of the neo-Darwinian synthesis, including natural selection as an explanation for many evolutionary changes, it does not conflict sharply with what scientists can comfortably assert. My present state of understanding is that a scientist looking at the scientific evidence could reasonably doubt the power of natural selection to explain *as much* as is often claimed for it, and might suppose that constraints of order, as yet unexplained, are a plausible basis for some changes that might be difficult to explain by natural selection. (This not to say that this view is more sound than any other, just that it is within the bounds of what one might find it reasonable to believe.) However, as we have seen, there could be principles of order in the evolutionary process that do not involve *intelligent* purpose, just as we can find order in the growth of embryo to baby without assuming intelligent design. To assert that problems with evolutionary theory must be resolved by intelligent design is to rely on a religious premise; all one could say based on present science (and likely future science) is that intelligent design is one conceivable component of a full theory of how complex life developed.[3]

Decisions Not to Teach Evolution

Can a decision not to teach a subject matter amount to a teaching of religion? If a subject matter, according to standards within the discipline, would undoubtedly be taught but for religious views, and it is not taught primarily because of religious views, it amounts to a kind of teaching of religion. Although the religious view is not itself directly taught, opposed ideas are suppressed for religious reasons.

As we have seen, scientists regard evolution as by far the most convincing scientific explanation for the development of species. Further, theories of natural selection and common descent are important not only in evolutionary biology, but in the wide range of biological sciences, including molecular and cell biology, ecology, physiology, classical genetics, and environmental biology. In any biology course developed without respect to religious opinions, evolution would figure prominently, with whatever reservations might be offered about gaps and uncertainties. Were evolution not taught only because it conflicts with religious views, religious premises would be dictating the content of the curriculum. Such a decision would be unfaithful to the idea that the state must remain neutral about religion; it would implicitly endorse and promote the religious view that is opposed to evolution. So also would be decisions at the state level to leave evolution off a state's required curriculum[4] or to teach evolution as only "a theory" (if that implies that it is less well confirmed than most scientific explanations).[5] If either of these downgradings of

117

evolution is done for religious reasons, the competing religious approach is being promoted, though to a lesser degree than if the teaching of evolution is forbidden outright.

An opponent of teaching evolution might respond that if a school teaches evolution as the leading explanation of species development, it takes a position *against* religion. This would be a mistake. Teaching evolutionary theory as accurate does imply that some religious accounts of the history of life are mistaken, but we have seen in chapter 5 that some school instruction inevitably offends particular religious views. If the criteria for what is taught as true do not rest on any religious judgment, a conflict with religious opinions does not establish that the state is taking an antireligious position.

Science and Other Ways of Understanding

This problem, however, raises more subtle and difficult questions about *how* evolution is taught as true: questions about the authority of scientific claims of truth, and the relation between science and other methods to reach judgments about reality. These questions are far deeper and more general than the particular issue about evolution, creationism, and intelligent design.[6]

Because many scientific theories are overthrown and revised as understanding increases, one would be foolish to think that just the presently dominant scientific accounts of evolution contain no errors or omissions. What is misleading about the statement that "evolution is *only* a theory" is that it obscures degrees of likelihood of revision, and the relation of evolution to other scientific theories. Before William Harvey's discoveries in the seventeenth century, scientists did not understand that blood circulates, from the heart back to the heart, in the bodies of mammals. Given overwhelming evidence of various sorts that blood does circulate, the chance that this scientific finding will be overthrown is extremely slight; one would not now speak of a mere "theory" that blood circulates. Much of evolutionary theory is no more insecure than many other prominent scientific views. It is extraordinarily unlikely that scientists will discover that the earth has existed only six thousand years, that unicellular organisms did not precede multicellular organisms, and that natural selection had *no* role in the development of life.

The relation of science to other means of discerning truth is more complicated. Some people have always resisted the view that science reliably indicates what is true. If the Bible is the authoritative word of God, perhaps it is a better source of what is really true overall than any purely human discipline. In an odd way, postmodernist approaches to knowledge give a degree of support to this kind of claim. If one believes that *all* human modes of thought are partial, ideological, and inevitably subjective, one might think that science has no favored status over competing avenues to truth (although most people do assume that a great many scientific conclusions provide accurate knowledge).

A crucial issue for public schools is just what teachers should say to students about these issues. Science teachers should explain something about scientific methodology, about how the claims of science are conceived, and about the possibility of competing perspectives, concluding that science itself cannot establish with certainty that its modes of inquiry about what is true in the external world are more reliable than alternatives, although in many respects scientific conclusions are confirmed by direct observations[7] and by real-world consequences, such as successful medical results based on the assumption that blood circulates. Science teachers cannot be expected to teach nonscientific alternatives to science in detail, but probably they should suggest how science fits among human ways of conceiving reality and why some members of the community believe there are more reliable ways of ascertaining truth than scientific inquiry. Ideally, these alternatives should appear elsewhere in the school curriculum, say in history or in courses on comparative religion, where they can be given fuller treatment.[8]

Special problems concerning science and other ways of understanding arise when arguments for a particular position are mixed and when religious conclusions are taken as the basis for beliefs about science or vice versa. Scriptural or theological arguments for and against the truth of evolutionary theory are straightforwardly religious. A science teacher may tell students about them, but should not discuss whether they are sound or unsound. The same conclusion holds for arguments that begin from the truth of evolution and proceed to atheist or theist conclusions.[9]

119

The most troubling category includes arguments over "imperfection" and evolutionary theory. The positive aspect of the argument from imperfection is that, given a process in which developments occur according to imperceptible changes that build on the qualities of existing organisms, we should not expect anything approximating perfection in design.[10] The claim that the life-forms we find correspond with what evolutionary theory says we should find falls within the domain of science, and outside the domain of religion.

The negative aspect of the argument differs. It asserts that a divine creator, acting directly, would not have made such a hash of things; God, or at least the God assumed by Western religions, would not have designed so badly. Therefore, evolution is much more plausible than divine creation. This argument is one of religion, or religious philosophy, drawing conclusions about what we should expect from a divine being with certain characteristics. Because this argument was made by Darwin and can be significant in a culture in which many people begin by assuming direct creation by God, a science teacher may raise the issue whether the record science reveals is what we should expect from a creator acting directly; but the teacher should not attempt to resolve that question or discuss it in depth.

The Proper Influence of Parental Views

If schools should not make major decisions about the science curriculum exclusively on the basis of religious views, does it follow that such views should have no influence on curricular decisions? We know that these views have had a great influence—on text publishers, state educational authorities, school boards, and teachers. But is this influence wrong in some sense? I concentrate here exclusively on science, leaving for later chapters subjects for which religious views might have a greater role.

Educators should not rely on their own religious perspectives, or those of parents, to prevent the teaching of material that standards of a scientific discipline definitely indicate should be included. Whether religious views should play *any* role in choices about what science to teach is more debatable, but modest influence may be all right. Religion may figure as one reason among many for major curricular decisions, and it may play a more decisive part if the choice is between subjects of roughly comparable scientific importance for students. Very generally, the argument is that parental resistance, or positive interest, can be one factor in curricular choices, and that resistance or interest based on religious views should generally not be treated worse than attitudes based on other opinions formed from outside the discipline. Perhaps educators' own religious views also properly figure to some degree, but that is more doubtful.

The practical upshot of this analysis for the modern controversy about the history of life is this: In science courses, evolution should be presented as the dominant theory, with a clear indication about any gaps and uncertainties, and with a suggestion that some people believe evolution is perfectly compatible with a religious view of the origins of life and that other people believe religious sources provide a truer source of insight when the teachings of religion and the findings of science conflict. Any proposed alternative to neo-Darwinian theory should be taught in science as science, or as a perspective on the limits of science, *only* if the alternative has substantial support in scientific methodology. A teacher might comment that certain perplexities concerning the historical development of complex life and the way natural selection works may indicate that principles of order might help explain aspects of evolutionary processes; but that we now have no solid basis to assume that any such order will prove beyond scientific explanation and point decisively to intelligent design.

CONSTITUTIONAL LAW: JUDICIAL ENFORCEMENT

It remains to relate these conclusions to constitutional principles. I shall oversimplify the connection between what is acceptable constitutionally and judicial enforcement by assuming that courts here apply the full measure of constitutional law, that any discretion they accord to boards of education and teachers concerns constitutionally permissible choices by those determining what shall be taught.[11]

Our clearest indication of prevailing constitutional principles, and a helpful standpoint from which to develop a critical analysis, is what the Supreme Court has said. In 1968, it held invalid an Arkansas statute that forbade teaching of the theory that mankind descended from a lower order of animals.[12]

Justice Fortas's opinion indicated that courts should not often intervene in curricular decisions,[13] thus implicitly acknowledging that judges should not overturn every educational decision influenced by the religious views of parents or educators; but "the First Amendment does not permit the State to require that teaching and learning must be tailored to the principles or prohibitions of any religious sect or dogma."[14] The state law proscribed a segment of the body of knowledge "for the sole reason that it is deemed to conflict with . . . a particular interpretation of the Book of Genesis by a particular religious group."[15] Although *Epperson* directly addresses a state prohibition of teaching evolution, its principle also reaches a religious-based decision *not* to teach evolution or *not* to require its teaching.

Two decades later, the Supreme Court faced a more complex variant on the evolution problem. The Louisiana legislature required that *if* teachers were to teach evolution, they must also teach creation science.[16] Although proponents of creation science claimed that substantial scientific evidence supported that perspective, the Court concluded that the purpose was again a forbidden aim to advance religion.

Justice Brennan wrote for the Court that the law, which defined the theories of evolution and creation science as "the scientific evidences for [evolution or creation] and inferences from those scientific evidences,"[17] impermissibly promoted a religious point of view.[18] "The preeminent purpose of the Louisiana legislature was clearly to advance the religious viewpoint that a supernatural being created humankind."[19] During the legislative process, "creation science" was treated as including belief in a supernatural creator.[20] Since an improper purpose rendered the statute invalid, decision on the basis of summary judgment was appropriate.[21]

Justice Scalia's lengthy dissent was in two parts, the second of which was a sweeping attack on any "purpose" test that depends on the subjective motivations of legislators.[22] The first part of Scalia's opinion argued that even one who accepts a motivation test should reject the Court's conclusion.[23] The secular purpose required by *Lemon* has meant only *a* secular purpose, one that can be accompanied by religious purposes.[24] Examining the legislative history, Scalia found many claims in favor of the scientific evidence for creation science.

I have argued that at bottom creation science is a religious theory because inadequate scientific evidence supports it. If "scientists" do not have a literature explaining persuasively why their endeavors are scientific, and why their theory reaches a threshold of scientific plausibility, a court should not have to wait for oral evidence to conclude that their theory is essentially religious. Whatever legislators assumed, teaching creation science is teaching religious ideas, and a court rightly declared that unconstitutional on summary judgment.

But that is not quite the ground the Supreme Court gives. It relies on an impermissible purpose. Clearly, legislators could not permissibly seek to promote the Genesis account as true on religious grounds. Nor could they aim to satisfy zealous fundamentalist constituents who wished to promote the Genesis account. Suppose a legislator's attitude was this: "The possible truth of the Genesis account (or my constituents' belief in that truth) inclines me not to have evolution presented as the unvarnished scientific truth; therefore, it should be matched by instruction in scientific creationism, though I understand that the latter has extremely weak scientific credentials." That also should count as a religious purpose or forbidden motivation, even if the aim is not exactly to *promote* a religious view. The Court presents substantial evidence that the main proponents of the legislation inside and outside the state legislature had some variant of these attitudes.

Justice Scalia answers, in effect, "Ordinary legislators were told that creation science has strong scientific credentials. They may have been persuaded. Their decision in favor of equal treatment may have been based on their wish to avoid suppressing a theory with as much scientific merit as evolution."

Scalia has a point; legislators could have had a legitimate secular purpose even though, on analysis, creation science really amounts to religion. But the Scalia position is subject to these rejoinders: First, why were legislators satisfied with teachers instructing in neither evolution nor creation science if their ambition was to put a viable alternative theory before students? The law's allowing of a failure to teach either theory is hard to explain except by religious objections to evolution. Second, if many ordinary uninformed legislators were persuaded that creation science is powerful science, this very fact may suggest that the purposes of articulate proponents should carry greater intrinsic significance than the opinions of the inert, silent members of the legislature.[25] Third, to reiterate a point made earlier, whatever the possible misapprehensions of not very well informed legislators, teaching scientific creationism *is* teaching religion, and that is not permitted.

What are the implications of these cases, and of persuasive constitutional analysis, for "intelligent design"? The dominant neo-Darwinian account has enough conundrums for text writers, science teachers, and boards of education to conclude that teachers could usefully discuss them and, further, suggest that whether the dominant theory, and particularly the preeminent place it accords natural selection, may require substantial revision or supplementation is an open question. I do not claim that scientific evidence supports this qualified presentation of neo-Darwinism better than an unqualified account, only that the choice is within the range of constitutionally permissible judgment— something judges have to assess by the balance of scientific opinion *and* their own sense of the strength of arguments. Texts and teachers could further mention that some idea of order *might* be needed to fill in the gaps, although more standard explanations may well suffice; because any such order may well be explicable in scientific terms, intelligent design is only one conceivable possibility. Were educators to go further and insist that *intelligent design* is probably a needed supplement to natural selection and other aspects of neo-Darwinism, or that intelligent design is *the alternative* to unvarnished neo-Darwinian theory, they would step over the constitutional line, because such judgments could now be made only on religious grounds.

In explaining the reasons that support evolutionary theory, teachers cannot steer clear of all arguments that have some implications for religious propositions. But they should not advance religious arguments as sound or unsound. In particular, they should be careful about how they present the argument that imperfection supports evolution, avoiding assertions about what a divine creator would or would not do.

I have proposed a middle course somewhere between what evolutionists insist is the only sound scientific approach and what proponents of Genesis creation and intelligent design seek. This counsel of moderation may have little appeal for opposing camps who standardly accuse one another of dogmatism and dishonesty. The evolutionists suspect, with a good deal of justification, that intelligent design is supported by many as a device to sneak religious objections into the science curriculum. Proponents of intelligent design, with a good deal of justification, charge that their position is ruled out of court without a hearing. Each side often tries to make the arguments of the other look as ridiculous as possible, and neither seems much interested in a fair appraisal of, or even a candid debate about, how far teaching science should involve possible limits of science, and whether critics of evolutionary theory have any solid scientific basis to suppose that the history of life on earth may involve such limits. Nonetheless, the guidelines I have sketched make educational and constitutional sense.

History, Economics, and Literature

IN THIS CHAPTER, we will look at three subjects, two of which, along with mathematics and natural science, are part of the core of public school curricula. Literature is a central component of most English courses, and it is the primary focus of upper-level courses. Students learn history in most school years. Economics is less central, but is an important subtopic within the broader category of "social studies." In the next chapter we will take up education about government and good citizenship, as well as teaching about morality more generally.

We have seen that the natural sciences adopt a strategy of methodological naturalism, and that whatever difficulties philosophers may have in defining science, scientists themselves agree fairly widely about what counts as scientific evidence and what constitute persuasive scientific theories. This scientific perspective may be juxtaposed against other perspectives, including religious ones.

The standards for other areas of knowledge are less clear, and this complicates issues for public school teaching. History, for example, can be viewed from a religious, an atheistic, or an agnostic point of view. The particular religious approach to history with which Americans are most familiar is the Bible's; historical events carry forward God's plan and record the interrelationship of God with God's people. Marxism is one atheistic approach to history, explaining all religious phenomena in materialistic terms. Standard modern history as done in Western countries, whether mainly political or social, is neither religious nor atheistic.[1] It is agnostic, not in the sense of positively endorsing agnosticism as the correct stance on religious issues, but in declining to adopt a position on the validity of religious understandings and claims, rather treating those as outside the purview of their historical efforts, which focus on circumstances and causes and effects, without reference to claims about the supernatural. For instance, a historian recounts the Puritans' religious sense of their colony's historical significance, but without judging whether that sense corresponds with any transcendental truth.

Whatever historical scholars may regard as apt,[2] an agnostic approach is the right one for public schools. Teachers may describe various religious and atheist views of history, and they may criticize particular elements of such theories, but they should not present as either *true or false* the fundamental premise that God is involved in historical developments or that all religion is a figment of human projection. Thus, a teacher might say that social sciences strongly suggest that Marx and Engels were wrong to suppose that all human structures can be traced back to relations of production, but he should not say that their atheism was mistaken because history reveals the unfolding of God's will.

For history and literature, at least, a choice to exclude religion altogether as a subject of study does not flow naturally from modern conceptions of the discipline, as it does in math and natural science. Religious convictions and practices have mattered for historical events and ideas; and religious texts are part of our literary heritage. Choices to exclude or omit religion as a topic must be self-conscious; choices to include religious subjects generate questions about just *how* to teach them as aspects of a broader historical or literary inquiry.

HISTORY

Any history of humankind is woefully incomplete without serious attention to religion. A fair survey of world history must include consideration of the place of religions, including ones that are relatively unfamiliar to most Americans, such as Hinduism, Confucianism, and Taoism, as central aspects of diverse cultures. A history of the modern West cannot sensibly spend time on the Renaissance and omit the Reformation, and an account of the founding of the American colonies must explain what brought Puritans to the shores of Massachusetts with their "City on the Hill" vision for a new society. The religious understanding of Dr. Martin Luther King Jr. and many of his followers is a vital aspect of the civil rights movement, and an appraisal of modern social life in India, or Iran, or the United States—where almost 80 per-

127

cent of the population say religion is important in their lives[3]—should include an account of religious groups and practices. Although history texts and teachers do cover the Reformation and Puritan aspirations, most focus less on religion than any assessment of its historical significance warrants.[4] This inattention may lead students to underestimate the significance of religious groups and understandings in politics and culture.

Two arguments against greater attention to religion are that teachers and texts are likely to be inadequate or biased and that the subjects are too controversial. We may largely put aside the last worry. Perhaps textbook writers, school boards, and teachers generally choose to avoid controversy; among subjects of roughly equal significance, they may reasonably favor ones that will cause less controversy. But history teachers cannot avoid all controversial topics. If a subject has great intrinsic importance and teachers can present it fairly, students should learn about it.

The strength of the argument that teaching about religion will be biased or inept may depend partly on distance in time. Events that occurred centuries ago are likely to be less highly charged, and historians may have developed something approaching a consensus about their significance. Teachers may attain a more detached view of the influence of the Puritans in Massachusetts than of the religious Right during recent decades in the United States.[5]

Of course, many historical events continue to excite deep passions. Most teachers, and many students, will come to the Protestant Reformation with strong opinions about whether Protestants or Catholics were more faithful to the Christian tradition. A teacher has to work hard not to appear to be taking sides. If she teaches, as she should, that the spread of Protestantism contributed to the rise of individual liberty in Europe, she may appear to suggest that Protestant reformers had a more enlightened view of the relation of individuals to states than did the Roman Catholic Church. She might qualify this impression by noting that the main impetus to freedom of religion and other liberties was irreconcilable religious conflict, not enlightened Protestant views, and that only a small minority of early Protestants actually embraced religious liberty in principle.

Although teaching about religion in history carries a serious risk of bias or inadequate understanding, much teaching about other ideological influences, such as socialism and communism, creates similar dangers. The influences of religion, including influences on general "secular" thought,[6] have been so great that high school history courses should consider them in some depth, despite the risks involved.[7]

Just how deeply should texts and teachers probe religious views? Warren Nord and Charles Haynes suggest that teachers should make an effort to present religions from "the inside," using primary sources, as well as explaining from "the outside" how religions have related to each other and affected historical developments.[8] They also urge that if students are fully to comprehend religious perspectives, they need a sense of how history itself is understood from those perspectives, including notably the idea in Western religions that history is the unfolding of God's plan on earth.

These recommendations raise a set of questions about how far ordinary history texts and teachers should try to delve into religious perspectives. The most straightforward questions concern descriptive accuracy in the face of complex nuances.

Attempts to portray religions from the inside are undoubtedly desirable, and so are general presentations of their historical perspectives; but a teacher trained as a secular historian may not be well equipped to discuss these matters in depth. It is, for example, common ground among Jewish and Christian believers that God has been involved with human beings over the span of history. The Bible portrays Jews as a people specially chosen by God, but is being chosen mainly a matter of privilege or of obligation? Does any notion of a specially chosen people make sense for Christians? Many Christians would say "no," that either the Christian revelation indicates that all people are chosen or that individuals are chosen according to a grace of God that is not showered on any particular ethnic or national group. Yet part of the American tradition, influenced to a degree by Puritanism, is that God has "chosen" American society and that this involves some special blessings, material and other.[9]

What does it mean that history is a scene of interaction between God and people? Some Christians believe that the successes and failures of peoples and nations are revelatory of God's will. Others are highly skeptical. Some think that the true religious concept of history is one of progress; others that history shows the continuing, unabated power of human sin. Still others look for signs that the end of history is upon us, signaling the approach of the Judgment Day.

My crude sketch of these alternatives is not meant to pass as an adequate survey, but it does show how far we are from having one simple Christian, or Jewish, view of history. Teachers are not likely to do better if they try to explain a Hindu or Buddhist perspective on history.[10] A text writer or teacher who tries to go into those subjects deeply risks presenting an understanding of history that many people within the traditions he is explaining actually reject. And few high school teachers may be able to present a nuanced account of the range of possibilities. Teachers trained as secular historians have reasons to be cautious about undertaking a full explanation of religious perspectives toward history.

One way for teachers to respond to this problem is to concentrate on the historical perspectives of particular religious thinkers such as Jonathan Edwards.[11] One can fairly describe the views of such notables without claiming that they necessarily represent *the* Christian perspective.

Evaluative judgment raises a more complicated concern: how much should a text writer or teacher say about the religious subjects she introduces? This concern is most pervasive in courses directly devoted to comparative religion or another specifically religious subject—courses few public schools offer–but it also touches history, as well as other courses in which religious matters are considered.

Imagine that the topic is the Protestant Reformation. The teacher notes Martin Luther's objections to Catholic doctrine and practice. Should she go much beyond saying that Luther believed in justification by faith and assigned much less importance to good works than does the Catholic tradition? Should she explore biblical and theological arguments in favor of justification by faith, analyzing competing claims, but without declaring which are stronger, in the manner of law teachers who help students lay out opposing positions without tipping their hands as to which they accept? Should a teacher similarly explore the arguments about infant or adult baptism when she treats the rise of Baptist sects? Should she indicate what she herself believes, without suggesting that her position is official?

Dual questions about depth of coverage and teachers' freedom are posed well by a list Warren Nord has provided of stances that teachers might take when they approach religious topics in various areas of the curriculum.[12] Nord's first and third possibilities are ignoring religion and barely mentioning religion. Neither of these alternatives is a sound historical approach; "bare mention" should be adopted only if the hazards of deeper treatment appear too great. The eighth possibility that Nord mentions is arguing for a particular point of view and making that the official conclusion of the course. That is patently improper. The second possibility is treating religion reductively from a worldview hostile to religion, such as Freudianism or Marxism. A standpoint hostile to religion could not be the official position of the course, any more than the adoption of religious premises.[13] Nord's fourth possibility is conveying an understanding of religions from the inside; we may assume, subject to the caveats about descriptive accuracy, that one facet of historical understanding should be to convey such an appreciation.

Nord's remaining three possibilities pose the serious issues. His fifth possibility is the following: "The text or teacher might consider religious ways of understanding the world as live contenders for the truth, to be argued about and critically assessed," with the text or teacher refraining from drawing conclusions. The sixth possibility is that the teacher indicates his own *personal conclusion* but presents it as just that, saying something like, "Well, I happen to be a Roman Catholic, so my own belief is that good deeds matter more than Luther thought." The seventh possibility is that the text or teacher *argues* for particular conclusions but does not make them an official view. The teacher might say: "In my view, the letters of St. Paul place great emphasis on faith. Luther's stance is more consonant with the New Testament overall than is the Catholic position. As Christians are committed to the divine inspiration of the Bible, we should be persuaded by Luther. But you must consider for yourself the force of these arguments."

I believe teachers should rarely, if ever, argue for particular religious conclusions, and they should be cautious about in-class critical discussions of the merits of controverted religious claims.

How will students take arguments by teachers for particular conclusions, when teachers make clear their views are not official? This, of course, is what much university teaching is about; teachers express strong convictions that students know are not "official." One subject on which law teachers express opinions is statutory and constitutional literalism—the view that texts should be understood in accord with their literal meaning. Many regard the literalist position as insincere, incoherent, or, at best, foolish. Law students do not take long to pick up the idea that their teachers look down on literalism. What if each student had only one relevant teacher, a teacher who took a dim view of biblical literalism? What if the student were aged fifteen instead of twenty-five and had parents who believed that the words that might or might not be taken literally were words of God that God intended to be taken literally?[14] When the student relayed the teacher's view, perhaps in an approving way, to her parents, we can imagine their reaction. They might well prefer leaving religion outside the school to having teachers make critical assessments of their faith.

Similar dangers are presented by the fifth possibility, critical assessments and discussions, but with teachers withholding opinions. Children with minority and "bizarre" beliefs might feel ganged up on by their peers, whose approval they crave, and they might believe that the way the teacher puts crucial questions implies negative or positive views. The danger is particularly grave when most of the children in a class share a particular religious perspective. Critical discussion can work fairly well with a skilled teacher, and mature students who have diverse religious views and are respectful of each other's perspectives; but in other circumstances the risks are too great.

So long as the teacher makes clear that people in our society adhere to a wide variety of religious beliefs, his *stating* a position as a personal opinion—"I happen to believe that Christians are justified by faith"—seems to involve less risk than either the teacher's honest critical assessment, or an open critical discussion among students in which the teacher refrains from expressing his opinion.

The underlying problem is not just whether students will take a teacher's view as official. They must match their own (largely received) opinions against those of an individual who is more learned, more experienced, and perhaps more intelligent. The teacher is a figure of authority. Of course, teenagers are not noted for their taste for authority, but a student may rely on a teacher's status to resist the authority of a parent; and some high school teachers are greatly admired by some students. Fending off the powerful critical analysis of a respected teacher, or the strong opinions of peers, is not easy. And, as I have said, the teacher's guiding control of discussion may seem to point to conclusions even when the teacher refrains from expressing a view.

For all these reasons, I doubt that a critical discussion in school of the strengths and weaknesses of various religious perspectives is generally a good idea. Rather, the role of text and teacher should be largely to explain various perspectives, leaving it to students outside class to undertake whatever critical discussions they wish. I recognize that this is to assign the school a more modest role than it will take with many other ideological perspectives. But I believe that approach well reflects the fundamental idea that the state's responsibility in respect to religious ideas should be limited. Although students who reach universities should be prepared to deal with teachers who express their convictions on all matters that are relevant to a course—including religious convictions—teachers below the college level should usually not argue for religious positions in which they believe, even when those would otherwise be relevant to courses. Rather, they should restrict themselves to indicating what happen to be their personal affiliations and sets of beliefs.[15] Insofar as academic freedom includes expressing views about religious topics, the public school teacher's liberty to do so in the classroom is decidedly limited.[16]

A somewhat more subtle question is the proper locus of decision making about what teachers should say. Should higher educational authorities dictate what occurs in the classroom, or leave flexibility for individual teachers? Recent decisions grant extensive power to higher authorities, if they choose to exercise it;[17] but school boards and state officials should recognize that good teachers are most effective when they have some latitude to decide how to run their classes and that students may benefit from hearing teachers' views that dissent from those prevailing among educational authorities. Nevertheless, teachers should refrain from pressing religious views on their students.

Teachers are, of course, free to perform in religious roles separate from their school responsibilities—say, as a lay preacher for a church—but, ideally, a teacher who deals with his students away from school will remember that his teacher's coat is not shed completely when he steps outside the schoolhouse.[18]

ECONOMICS

The issues about economics texts and courses are an amalgam of those about science and history. If an "economics" course examines how societies may organize their economic life, it should consider religious, as well as secular, ideas about the economy.[19] Historically in the West, natural law notions connected with the Christian religion were highly influential in the Middle Ages, yielding such standards as the just price. Religious understandings continue to figure centrally in some cultures—one thinks particularly of strict Muslim societies. In the United States, churches and other religious organizations have been among the sharpest critics of an economic order that is materialistic, allows a striking discrepancy between rich and poor, and that undervalues meaningful work. A notable example was the Catholic bishops' pastoral letter "Economic Justice for All," issued in 1986.[20] To fail to mention religious understandings of economic life would be to understate their influence and to disregard their potential for the future—in short, implicitly to treat them as less relevant than a balanced appraisal would suggest.

Although some economics courses may touch briefly on varieties of economic organization, most, virtually exclusively, feature neoclassical economics, micro- and macro-economics studied from the assumptions of economic models with which we have become familiar—producers and sellers seeking to maximize profits, consumers furthering their own interests at minimum cost. Among the social sciences, this form of economics carries the greatest pretensions to being scientific, because its conclusions are thought to follow strictly from its premises.[21]

Just what is assumed about consumer preference by the standard economic model? Careful economists note that preferences need not be selfish or material; consumers could seek the welfare of the poor or spiritual wholeness. But these cautions tend to be neglected, and one never sees a model in which consumers want a higher price so that poor sellers can achieve a greater income without feeling they are receiving charity. For practical purposes, the economic model suggests primarily selfish consumers interested in material goods, and leaves scant room for religious understandings.

As with the natural scientist, the economist may say he is simply following the standards of his "science," not commenting on what people should value in life or even on how economies should be organized, taking all values into account. But we can see that if students study economics, understood in the narrower sense, without discussion of the broader subjects, they may easily slide into the assumption that neoclassical economics should be the guide to organizing an economy, and that the selfish pursuit of material welfare by individuals is, and properly is, at the heart of economic life. Even if the text or teacher does not explicitly teach the overall merit of organizing relations according to neoclassical assumptions, something that itself is common,[22] the course will convey the message that this is how to do things, implicitly favoring this secular approach to economic life over all competitors, religious and secular.

What should the teacher do? At a minimum, he should briefly place neoclassical economics within the framework of alternative approaches to economic life; he should stress that pure economic models do not tell us all that people actually value, much less what people should value; and he should emphasize that insofar as those models omit aspects of what people value, they cannot tell us what will necessarily occur in real life, much less what organizational forms would be desirable. The teacher should probably mention in these connections that spiritual values and perceived moral and social obligations that might come from a religious view, as well as some nonreligious approaches to value such as Marxism, are not easily captured by the models.

Again, we face the question of how deeply texts and teachers should probe. A teacher trained in secular economic theory may not be well suited to analyze debates about how far the principles of various religions should lead to a rejection or revision of the modified capitalist systems that prevail in Western countries and the global economy. To revert to the pastoral letter on the economy, which some prominent Catholic theorists criticized for undervaluing free economic enterprise,[23] a teacher should mention this disagreement and note differences in factual assess-

135

ments about how economies work, but should avoid detailed analysis of underlying theological divergences.

LITERATURE

The Bible and other religious texts properly enjoy a place in courses devoted substantially to literature.[24] In all literate cultures, religious writings have played a leading part; a succession of years of study that omits these writings gives a misleading picture of literature and culture.

How teachers should present such texts is more difficult. If teachers present them without regard to their religious significance, students may not understand their point. (It would be a little like assigning George Orwell's *Animal Farm* without explaining that it was an attack on Communism.) Teachers need to explain the basic religious understanding that underlies a religious text.

Teachers might undertake the more daunting effort to explain a culture's fundamental religious understandings about the nature of writings it takes as sacred; but this endeavor may exceed the competence of most present teachers of English. It creates the risk that the teacher's account may fail to provide adequate nuance and may be regarded as unacceptable by parents from the tradition the teacher describes. For example, we can say that traditional Christianity takes the Bible as the word of God, but the variations among Christians in just how that idea is understood are immense.

What religious literature an editor or teacher selects can create a problem, because a choice of material may convey approval of some religious views. In a subsequent chapter, I shall discuss a similar problem with comparative religion in more detail, but I believe compilers of readings and teachers should use three criteria for inclusion: (1) literary quality, (2) significance in terms of the world's religions, and (3) connection to the culture of the students. Biblical texts should be balanced with texts from other religious traditions. But a defensible choice may be made to emphasize texts that are part of the fabric of our culture, and the space occupied by Hindu texts need not be as great the space given to the Bible and other writings from the Christian and Jewish traditions.[25]

In deciding that a program of Bible instruction for fourth- and fifth-graders, which for forty years had been sponsored by Protestant churches that set the curriculum and hired the teachers, was an unacceptable religious exercise,[26] a federal district judge went on to indicate that a Bible course *would* be appropriate for elementary school students if it were taught by ordinary teachers under the supervision of the school board, and if students who chose not to take the course were offered a reasonable alternative.[27] Even if they allow students to opt out, schools should probably not offer courses devoted exclusively to the Bible, if that is the only treatment of religious texts for that age group.[28] No doubt, the Bible has affected our literature and broader culture far more than any other religious writing, but in a country that is increasingly diverse religiously, concentrating on the Bible alone may imply that we are really a Christian and Jewish nation. Of course, many school districts have very few non-Christians, but in one respect this makes the situation worse, since a Bible course reinforces the notion that Christianity is by far the most important religion.[29]

CHAPTER 12

Morals, Civics, and Comparative Religion

TEACHING MORALITY AND CIVICS

In this chapter, we focus first on the delicate subject of teaching morality and civic responsibility, both on general approaches and on how schools should deal with such controversial topics as sex education. In chapter 2, on educational purposes, we examined how far schools should teach morality, beyond what is relevant to good citizenship. We also asked whether students should be encouraged to deliberate about civic issues apart from their religious convictions, and whether schools should try to counter the negative effects on religious understandings of whatever they teach about civic morality and other aspects of the moral life.

Schools can hardly draw a sharp distinction between civic responsibilities and ordinary morality that concerns relations with other people. Many virtues have civic and noncivic applications. In theory, teachers might be able to distinguish honesty in one's life as a citizen[1] from honesty in personal relations and business dealings, but one cannot imagine that encouraging honesty could be very effective if it were limited to a single aspect of life. Much teaching about moral behavior and good citizenship is implicit, in the way classes are run. When a teacher treats boys and girls equally, that sends the message that men and women should not have a sharp division in responsibility and authority, inside civic life or outside.[2]

Teaching material in a way that suggests appropriate attitudes and actions is not limited to "political" subjects, like the American Revolution; *Othello* tells us about the dangers of mistrust and jealousy, and inventive geniuses like Thomas Edison are put forward as admirable exemplars.

A final reason why political morality may not be easily distinguished from much of the rest of morality is that we live within a society. How could it not be part of the school's role to teach us to live well together, even in parts of our lives that are not directly civic?

The two serious concerns about teaching morality are the comparative responsibility and authority of parents and schools and how schools should treat controversial aspects of morality that do not mainly concern our responsibilities to others—aspects of sexual morality being the prime representative.[3]

Although the main thrust of claims of parental rights has been that parents should enjoy an effective choice among kinds of schools,[4] the position also carries the implication that public school teaching about morality should be deferential to parents' judgments about how their own children should be taught, acknowledging that students come from different traditions and encouraging them to take seriously what their parents and other private authorities say about moral standards. Standard claims of parental rights vary from John Tomasi's argument, which we examined in chapter 2, that schools should counter negative effects on religion and should aid students in reintegrating public civic virtues with their own religious understandings. But the practical recommendation public schools might draw from the two positions may be similar—don't impose public perspectives in a manner that quashes a wide range of dissonant points of view. With both "parental rights" and "countering negative effects," we need to look at particular examples to see how these approaches might be implemented within public schools.

Values and How to Teach Them

In contrast to the subjects that science and history address, we have as a society no settled secular methodology to evaluate moral and political responsibilities.[5] If schools exclude religious perspectives from discussions of moral choice, that may seem to imply that the right way to go about resolving such questions is according to some nonreligious approach—despite the fact that for many citizens religion is at the center of their morality. Some ways of teaching about morality do more than neglect traditional religious approaches; they actively challenge them. For example, the theory that a morality of principle, according to which an individual employs a set of rational, general principles to make moral choices, constitutes a higher stage of development than a morality based on authority[6] treats reliance on reli-

139

gious authority, whether human authority or biblical passages, as implicitly inferior to more "enlightened" moral approaches.

Although "values clarification" has faded in popularity among school educators in favor of more "inculcative" teaching of morality,[7] that approach strongly illustrates the difficulties.[8] Texts suggested that students should clarify their values and make informed choices in terms of what they really value.[9] According to one summary, "Values clarification is a seven-step method for teaching students how to develop values. The child develops values by (1) choosing his values freely (2) from among alternatives, (3) after giving thoughtful consideration to the consequences of each alternative; the child should prize the choice by (4) being happy with the choice and (5) affirming his choice publicly; he should (6) act upon his value choice (7) repeatedly, developing it into a pattern in his life."[10]

One way a teacher *might* encourage students to clarify their values would be to ask them to consider whether they have a religious obligation to follow absolute values set by a transcendent being; but the gist of most "values clarification" has been to imply the absence of such values. Teachers have encouraged individual students to choose values as they might careers, based on their assessment of what suits them best. This "psychological" approach to values not only disregards religious conceptions of values, it strongly suggests that the best understanding varies from the traditional religious conviction that moral values, far from being a typical subject of choice, come from the outside in a sense.[11] Critics rightly have complained that such a "values clarification" approach is hardly neutral to religious points of view.

Does values clarification actually cross the line and take a forbidden position on fundamentally religious propositions? That is not so easy to say. The answer depends, I think, on whether a religious question is squarely faced and resolved, on whether a comment is dropped in passing or reflects a major theme, and on whether our society shares a consensus about the particular issue a text or teacher addresses.

Although a text might reasonably point out ways in which human beings develop values over time, suppose a text contained the following sentence: "Religions, such as Christianity, Judaism, and Islam, that claim that God is a source of absolute values are fundamentally mistaken; values are *purely* a human construction, having nothing to do with any divine being." This hypothetical statement is only about values, not about all aspects of religion, but it patently adopts a position on a fundamental religious question. If a school presented this passage as a correct appraisal, its offering of that view as part of the truth would violate the principle that schools should not teach the truth or falsity of religious propositions.

Actual passages in texts are less direct, leaving room for the possibility that they do not rule out religious approaches to values. A text may say that students should choose values, that values are "personal and subjective."[12] One might defend such formulations as covering only the human level, not what may be true from a transcendent perspective.[13] One might even argue that these terms encompass a thoughtful choice to accept absolute religious values and mean only that in our society no human institution can impose values on people from the outside.[14] A judgment about the overall aim or effect of passages that are less than direct in rejecting religious positions should depend partly on evaluation of whether they figure centrally or peripherally in the text.

It also matters whether the claim that a text makes is one backed by a social consensus or is the subject of sharp controversy. In a liberal democratic society, the idea that citizens, ideally, will consider carefully what they value is widely shared, although some religions may teach that young people should simply accept what their parents say about values.[15] Whether values are absolute or relative, to put the dichotomy roughly,[16] is highly controversial. Taking a clear position on that question is less neutral than recommending careful thought.

In any event, texts and teachers that discuss general perspectives on value questions should not, explicitly or implicitly, foreclose the appropriateness of religious approaches. More constructively, they should note major religious approaches, but without delving deeply into the premises that support them.

In respect to personal and political morality, a teacher cannot present any particular religious view as correct; but there are two ways in which a teacher may draw from religious morality to arrive at normative conclusions. The first way is to note ethical positions taken by the world's major religions, such as the idea that people should care about the welfare of their fellow human beings.[17] The teacher might suggest that if all these systems of belief and practice that include moral obligations have agreed (more or less) on certain moral duties,[18] that amounts to *some evidence* that such duties are part of a sound moral view.[19] This use of the moral aspects of various religions need not imply either that all, or any, of the religions are correct in the distinctively religious components of their beliefs or that the duties the religions posit could not be defended on other than religious grounds.

The second use of religious morality is peculiarly tied to religions that are influential in a particular country, or broader culture. Thus, it might be suggested that respect for the individual in ordinary life and in politics is part of *our* heritage, one influenced by our early Protestant settlers. In this mode, the argument in favor of a certain moral practice is neither universal (other countries may have different religious traditions) nor dependent on the truth of the underlying religious view; one points to the particular religious perspective only as part of our own tradition.

We need to acknowledge that both these ways of referring to religious morality, especially the second, flirt with claiming that the religious views are sound. Even if a teacher is careful not to assert the truth or falsity of any religious proposition, the teacher's comment about the ethics of major world religions or of our Puritan forebears may leave some students with the impression that religious perspectives are being endorsed. Nonetheless, this risk does not outweigh the inherent appropriateness of drawing from religious traditions to these limited extents. Avoiding any mention of world religions would be to impoverish references to moral practices as possible indicators of moral value; avoiding mention of moral strands of a culture that derive from religious understandings would impoverish representations of our historical traditions.[20]

In what teachers say about religious approaches, a significant difference in shading may be apt for civics concerns that would not be right for teaching morality generally. For most aspects of morality, the reasons why people behave in certain ways may diverge greatly, so long as they observe common, acceptable standards of behavior such as honesty in personal relations and business dealings. Here, religious bases compete with secular under-standings as perspectives students might adopt.

An important part of civic morality is the consideration and discussion of public issues. Many modern theorists of liberal democracy, the most prominent of whom has been John Rawls, believe citizens should address vital public issues from a shared perspective; that perspective cannot rest on specific religious or antireligious premises.[21] Thus, when citizens debate whether the law should require, forbid, or allow controversial forms of affir-mative action, they should rely upon shared ideas about equality in our liberal democracy, not a scattered variety of religious con-victions. Insofar as this view is sound, public schools have a rea-son to encourage students to consider public issues in a way that is detached from religious premises. In that context, teaching about religion would not aspire to be completely neutral be-tween nonreligious and religious approaches to civic issues[22] but would aim to help students understand and respect the variety of attitudes people have in a society.

Teaching Specific Moral Dilemmas and Choices

The questions that arise about a school's treatment of particular moral and religious issues can be particularly divisive. Schools often take definite positions—for example, that all people should be treated equally by government—that are powerfully supported by the great majority of religious views in the com-munity. On issues of morality about which religious convictions differ, such as the propriety of sexual intercourse between older high school students, a school may take no position, or it may teach as sound views that a number of the religious members of the community oppose.

When religious groups overwhelmingly support a position that the schools teach as a requisite of liberal democracy or as a component of a full and healthy life, teachers may say so, per-haps suggesting how religious ideas have influenced, and com-plement, secular ones, but without exploring the religious posi-tions in depth.

Teachers who tell students that they face a moral choice, and that the school takes no position about how they should act, should indicate that various religious traditions have different views about the choice, if that is the fact. Teachers should probably not undertake to explain exactly how the religions have arrived at their positions. Without going into the competing arguments, a teacher might say that the Roman Catholic Church and some Protestant and Jewish groups oppose premarital intercourse,[23] but that many Protestants and Jews consider it morally acceptable. This counsel of circumspection is not *just* a matter of teachers being inadequately trained. The issues can be so complex and controversial that almost anyone should be skeptical of his ability to present the religious perspectives in a detached and fair way.[24] If a school's judgment is that it would be better for students to engage in critical class discussion about various possibilities than to leave such discussions for outside class, teachers will have greater difficulty avoiding analysis of various religious points of view; but even then, they should probably not try to explain all the nuances of opposing positions.

Perhaps the hardest questions arise when religions in the community oppose norms that might be taught in school. Should schools ever teach as sound a moral view that faces significant community opposition,[25] and, if they do so, should they inform students about religious dissent? Two important variables are the degree of opposition and whether the matter concerns a good life or social justice (insofar as one can distinguish these).

I can illustrate these distinctions, and their tenuousness, in respect to homosexual relationships. A school considers teaching that gays warrant equal respect as citizens and that gay relationships are intrinsically as desirable as heterosexual ones. The first claim is one about social justice. Teachings about social justice typically concern premises on which liberal democracy rests. The prevailing view in American society is that gays deserve equal treatment as citizens.[26] That view is a central enough application of broader principles of nondiscrimination and equal respect so that schools should teach it,[27] even if substantial opposition exists within the community.[28] Suppose many members of the community belong to a church that teaches that gays should be punished or shunned if they engage in homosexual acts. When a teacher comments that some religions oppose a position she presents to her students as a demand of social justice, she risks diluting the force of the teaching or putting down the opposing religions as benighted; nonetheless, she should mention that the moral position is not embraced by religious traditions that are substantially represented in the community.

The claim that "gay" relationships are as beneficial as "straight" ones is about a good life, not social justice. That claim is opposed by a substantial number of religious citizens who believe that heterosexual relationships are "natural" and ordained by God in a way that is not true about homosexual relationships. Other people, who may believe that intrinsically (that is, apart from social structures) homosexual relations are as desirable as heterosexual ones, may think that in our society, given traditional family structures and remaining prejudice against gays, a person comfortable with each lifestyle would be more likely to be happy as a practicing heterosexual.[29]

Although many young people have powerful, unalterable homosexual inclinations, others may be subject to being influenced toward heterosexual or homosexual relationships; what is taught *could* make a difference for how some students lead their lives.[30] If public schools do take a stand on the comparative desirability of homosexual and heterosexual relations, they should certainly indicate that religious traditions significant in the community have a different view.[31] But should schools take a position at all?

This proves to be a complex question. If one puts aside the influence of religion, there is much to be said for the view that schools should not be teaching as sound moral conclusions about which the national and local communities are substantially divided. In contrast to natural science, no science of morality establishes what are correct and incorrect moral conclusions. When the community is divided, public schools probably should inform students about the options, without promoting any one position.

One possible objection to the schools not taking a stand goes like this. Adolescents with strong homosexual inclinations may feel isolated and not normal, and they may rightly understand that some other students have strong negative feelings about gays. If the school in its teaching does not affirm their making choices about sexual practice based on their inclinations, it will fail to counter all the influences that make them feel they are less than equal and are little respected (or would be little respected if they revealed their sexual preference).[32] Their identity is so strongly tied to their sexual preference, they will not feel they are potentially equal citizens unless that preference is positively endorsed. Thus, one cannot here divorce "the good life" from equal citizenship.[33]

There is much more than a grain of truth in this argument, and it helps us see a spectrum of possibilities about what schools should be teaching. The schools might teach that everyone should respect the sexual choices of gays; and they might teach that for mature individuals with confirmed homosexual preferences, sexual relations in accord with those preferences are preferable to a life of celibacy. These comments would go some distance toward affirming the sexuality of gays without tackling the complicated, highly controversial topic of comparative desirability. Despite its indirect relationship to equality of citizenship, and what it might do to help some gays through the difficult adolescent period, I think the schools should stay out of the topic of the comparative desirability of homosexual and heterosexual forms of voluntary sexual practice.[34]

If the general principle is that schools should not come down on one side or the other when there is deep controversy over how people should lead their lives, religion is a complicating factor. Let us suppose that the main opposition to homosexual relations is based on religious understandings. If schools *would* teach that homosexual relations are intrinsically not inferior to heterosexual ones, except for strong religious opposition, is their failure to do so the kind of surrender to religious understandings that I treated as unacceptable when considering evolution and creationism? I think not. Within the disciplines of natural science, practitioners have well-settled criteria for what counts as good science; according to these criteria, evolution would definitely be taught, were it not for religious opposition. For morality, no such settled criteria exist. In that context, religious opposition should not be treated worse than other, nonreligious, opposition to moral positions.[35]

A related point concerns the attitudes most religious people are likely to have on moral matters. Although much depends on the particular religious perspective, those opposed to homosexual relations on religious grounds commonly suppose they would reach the same position if they disregarded the religious grounds—the Roman Catholic view that natural law, not dependent on religious premises, condemns homosexual activity is a notable example. Thus, if we said that nonreligious opposition may count but religious opposition should not, one would either have to accept claims that opposing views could comfortably rest on nonreligious grounds, or discern that religious grounds are controlling despite what opponents sincerely claim. (By comparison, with natural science it is much easier to dismiss weak scientific claims as flimsy.) Thus, I conclude that schools should not teach as definitely sound claims of morality that fall outside the realm of social justice and are opposed by a large segment of the community.[36] Whether schools should relegate these claims to "outside the classroom" or should present alternatives to the students for critical evaluation and discussion may depend on the age of the students and their ability to discuss alternatives without rancor.

When we turn to positive moral teaching that reflects a controversial religious position and to religious objections to teaching that refrains from moral judgment, we face different considerations—ones well revealed by courses including sex education.[37] Some districts do not teach about use of condoms and use texts that teach that the only proper sexual relations are between married, heterosexual couples. Although community sentiments favoring abstinence could be a proper basis for not teaching opposing moral views as sound, it is hard at this stage of our culture to think that any community would unite behind this approach to sex education, except on religious bases. As Gary Simson and Erika Sussman argue, this approach to teaching should be regarded as religious.[38]

The religious underpinnings of the abstinence-only approach come out in the "Sex Respect" materials that are most commonly used,[39] but let us suppose all such references are deleted. Apart from religious conviction, someone might reasonably think teenagers should refrain from sexual intercourse, even that saving sex for marriage is generally desirable; but one would be unlikely to go further and preclude all teaching about the use of condoms.

Given statistics about the present level of sexual activity[40] and all the cultural cues teenagers receive, it is unrealistic to suppose that if schools omit comment about prophylactics, that will lower sexual activity very much (or, to put it differently, that teaching about prophylactics will raise the level of sexual activity very much). And, indeed, studies indicate that discussions about condoms do not hasten the onset of intercourse.[41] Sexually transmitted diseases, especially AIDS,[42] and unwanted pregnancies are serious social problems and (often) personal tragedies. Apart from religious objections, one can hardly imagine sex education for adolescents that said nothing about methods of safer sex, whatever people's views about desirability of adolescent sex.

Thus, an abstinence-only program that omits teaching about condoms could be justified only on religious grounds. If the objectives of those who decide in favor of such programs are limited to achieving the "correct" kind of sexual behavior, and do not include approving or promoting any general religious perspective, it is arguable whether the decision-makers are aiming to "promote" or "endorse" religion;[43] that they are imposing approaches that can only be justified on religious grounds is sufficient to make what they do improper.

Other controversies over sex education are whether to teach it, or aspects of it, at all; and whether to make participation in such instruction voluntary.[44] A fundamental aspect of most such education is to discourage students from unprotected sexual activities that could lead to unwanted pregnancies or the contraction of sexually transmitted diseases, including AIDS. This typically includes instruction about the use of condoms, and some schools hand out condoms to encourage sexually active students to protect themselves.[45] Instructors do not say that sexual activity among adolescents is desirable but, recognizing that much of it will take place, they aim to make it as safe as possible. Objectors argue that treating such activity as an option and telling students how to engage in it more or less safely will in fact encourage it and give it a kind of implicit approval. Of course, one would not expect schools to teach students how to rob so that the fewest people will be hurt, but given the frequency of sexual activity among young people and the degree of its acceptance, public schools have a strong rationale for teaching about safe sex that does not depend on any religious premise or controversial moral teaching; they should not be deflected even by substantial religious objections in the local community.[46]

Civics Instruction

Much of what I have written applies directly to civics courses. In these courses, teachers should trace major influences of religious ideas on civic understandings and the responsibilities of citizens. Students should learn about our tradition of religious liberty, about the basic ideas of free exercise of religion and separation of church and state, about religious pluralism and respect for people of different religious faiths, about religious organizations as important parts of civil society, and about religious perspectives or vantage points for evaluating the claims of secular governments.[47] As I have explained, the aim to build a common cultural discourse may mean that, as a topic for civics, religions should be presented *more* as a subject for "external" understanding and tolerance than as the basis for alternative perspectives from which to approach public issues.[48]

COMPARATIVE RELIGION

If students are to receive a full liberal education, they should understand major religious ideas. Throughout human history, what we call religion has provided a crucial way to understand life's meaning and has been an integral part of culture.[49] With the advent of discrete secular conceptions of many aspects of social and individual life, religious perspectives remain for many people a key to how they see themselves and their communities. Religious groups continue to play vital parts in most societies, including the United States. Especially when teachers of other subjects, such as history and English, are not familiar with covering religious points of view, a course about religions holds out the best hope for presenting religious understandings that compete with or supplement other perspectives.[50]

The troubling questions involve teachers' competence, the selection of subject matter, and depth of coverage. A dearth of high school teachers is now adequately trained to present such a course, but let us imagine that failing is met.

A major problem with selection of religions to teach is that it will be perceived as reflecting judgments about importance. Should the aim be to expose schoolchildren to the greatest range of religions possible, to those with the most significance world-wide, or to those heavily represented locally? No course could devote even an hour to every religious view that has figured importantly in human history or that matters to people now living on the globe. But a school might set out to fulfill the objective of exposure to diverse religions about as well as it could. A teacher would spend time on "early" religions, still accepted by many people on earth, as well as on more "developed" religions, and would examine atheism and agnosticism.[51] Christianity, in all its branches, would not receive significantly more time than Buddhism or Hinduism, in all their branches. In assigning time to Judaism, a teacher would have to weigh the religion's fertility in imagination, its influence, and its depth, against the relatively few people worldwide who embrace it.[52]

Few school districts in the United States would carry out anything like this program. Nor would they use worldwide significance as their guiding criterion. They would pay more attention than either of these approaches allows to the dominant religions in America. Many conservative Christians who complain about the absence of religion in the public schools would hardly be reassured by a program of instruction in which Christianity received 20 percent of the attention, and less than an hour was spent on evangelical Protestant conceptions. They might well suppose that such a course would be *more likely* to undermine their children's faith than the implicit secularism of other courses. Such feelings would constitute a strong reason not to make such a course mandatory.[53]

Could a greater concentration on Christianity than on other major religions be justified? A school could not do so on the basis that Christianity is probably the best religion; but it might aim to expose children to the religions that matter most in this society. Some mixing of criteria of worldwide and local importance is defensible. Children of minority religions, such as Hindus, might feel disadvantaged in the lesser attention paid to Hinduism, but *any attention* in school might help to dispel their neighbors' nearly complete ignorance of their beliefs and practices, and would be preferable to disregard of religion altogether.

The question of how to cover the religions that are chosen is also difficult. Students should be exposed to writings from each religious tradition that is studied;[54] they should develop a sense of the religion from the inside. Teachers should describe practices and basic understandings. They should make students aware of the many dimensions of religion—doctrines, sacred narratives, ethics and law, ritual, social institutions, and art and material culture, according to Ninian Smart's categorization.[55] And they should explain that among different religions (and among various branches of Christianity), those dimensions have different degrees of emphasis.

One valuable approach can be to have representatives of various traditions as visitors, although teachers need to be careful that explanations of these visitors (mainly clerics) do not turn into occasions for proselytizing.[56]

How far should teachers probe fundamental premises and understandings? These concerns have already been addressed in connection with history—can a teacher do justice to variations in understanding among adherents to each basic religious perspective,[57] and should a teacher argue for religious positions or at least allow critical discussions? What is said in chapter 10 has crucial application here, where the whole subject matter will touch religion. I believe teachers' offering "nonofficial" critical appraisals carries heavy risks, and that even critical discussions among students, supervised by a "neutral teacher," of what makes for sound religion is unwise in many schools.

CHAPTER 13

Constitutional Constraints and Other Legal Limits

In contrast to the chapters on evolution, creationism, and intelligent design, the discussions of history, economics, literature, morals, civics, and comparative religion do not clearly distinguish between what schools should do and the constitutional limits of what they may do. We now turn to those limits and to legal restraints on the expression of teachers that do not directly concern the curriculum—in particular, dress regulations.

Constitutional Constraints on Teaching

When a writer analyzes constitutional limits, he normally describes the relevant constitutional tests and suggests how they apply to the subject at hand. The broad constitutional tests for the Establishment Clause are now, as chapter 1 explains, in a kind of limbo. The threefold standard of *Lemon v. Kurtzman*[1]— secular purpose, no primary effect of promoting or inhibiting religion, no excessive entanglement—has not been abandoned in an opinion of the Court, yet most of the justices have expressed their dissatisfaction with its use as a comprehensive test for all establishment cases. Whether the state is or is not endorsing a religion has proved the critical inquiry for displays on public property,[2] and that approach has obvious relevance for whether teaching that purports to be *about* religion has become the teaching of religious truth. Subtle coercion figured as a central element when the Court has reviewed graduation prayers.[3]

Whatever the exact formulation of a constitutional test, the crucial issue for teaching about religion is whether or not the school or teachers are presenting religious propositions—positive or negative—as true or sound. This may well be viewed as an inquiry about endorsement and its opposite, condemnation or disapproval.[4] Schools can use individual books that take religious positions[5]—this indeed is implicit in the suggestion that they present religion from the inside—but they cannot endorse the positions. Although this point is more arguable, I think it is constitutionally impermissible for a schoolteacher to tell students that particular religious views are true,[6] even if she makes clear she is speaking only as an individual teacher and not as a representative of the school in that respect. Not only must the state refrain from endorsing religious propositions, it must not place individuals in roles as public school teachers who, in that capacity, endorse religious propositions.

Although *Lemon* as a comprehensive test may not have a long life expectancy, a majority of justices continues to suppose that either a purpose to promote religion or a direct effect of advancing religion may render a program unconstitutional. An otherwise acceptable program could be rendered invalid if a board of education or school superintendent were careless enough to make plain an impermissible purpose to promote or inhibit religion. To simplify our inquiry, we will assume in what follows that the purpose behind a program is no more vulnerable constitutionally than one would gather from observing the effects of the program in operation.

Everything that I have suggested is good educational practice is constitutionally permissible. Indeed, good educational practice in the United States should be substantially guided by the values of the religion clauses; religion should be treated fairly, but the state should have no position about religious propositions. But, when one asks about judicial enforcement, educators may do more or less about religion than I have recommended and remain within constitutional boundaries. What is appropriate depends partly on the nature of a local community, and any local community has a range of discretion.[7]

The point is easiest with "less." School boards may decide that, given the religious perspectives of parents in the community or the inadequacy of teacher training, or both, they should include much less treatment of religion than one would recommend for a full liberal education. If religion is *too* sticky or controversial, selective ignoring of religion is defensible. As Frank Manuel once said, "In some respects, avoiding may be the best thing we can do, because if we really gave the full blast of the religious traditions in all their complexity, we would be at each other's throats again."[8]

School boards or gifted teachers might also decide that mature students in communities can tolerate and benefit from instruction by teachers that engages critical assessment of religious ideas to a greater degree than I have suggested.[9] In principle, such an assessment may be all right, as it plainly is within state colleges and universities.

Judicial results cannot be finely calibrated to the qualities of individual communities. So long as schools and teachers scrupulously refrain from teaching particular religious propositions as true, they should have broad latitude to settle within a range that extends between comparative disregard of religion to critical scrutiny of religious propositions and practices.

What constitutional constraints can actually be imposed by courts? In any teaching *about* religion, some teachers, self-consciously or not, will indicate that particular religious views are sound or unsound. Inevitably, some students will understand teachers to have made such claims, or to have asserted that all religions are equally valid, although a teacher has avoided such judgments. How should a court respond to this reality?

If a teacher dominantly tries to convey a religious message or many students reasonably receive his teaching in that way, the constitutional border has been crossed. A court could say in an individual instance that what purports to be teaching *about* religion has become, in effect, teaching religion. But not too many parents will mount suits against individual teachers, and settling just what has taken place in a classroom will rarely be simple.[10] If these suits constituted the only protection against establishment, most teaching of religion, so long as it was labeled teaching *about* religion, would be unsanctioned, except by school authorities.

In some instances, claimants may be able to show that *many* teachers supposedly teaching about religion are crossing the constitutional threshold, or that the text they use as authoritative does so.[11] In that event, a court could declare a whole program unconstitutional, or it could decide that the program needs sufficient supervision and safeguards against teaching of religious truth.[12] When the courts deal with parochial schools, monitoring to avoid the promotion of religion with state funds may slide into impermissible entanglement between government authority and religious institutions, but that should not be a problem here. Public authorities are monitoring what occurs in public school classrooms. The judgments that supervising authorities make about texts and teaching are the same judgments that writers and teachers should make in the first instance. It is not entanglement for supervisory public authorities to make sure that public school teachers have not overstepped the constitutional line in their evaluations of religion and styles of presentation.

Courts can review texts more easily than teachers. So long as the texts stick to the discipline, say, science or economics, as commonly understood, their use as authoritative guides should not be regarded as unconstitutional, though we might hope for more references to religious understandings. For texts that deal with religion itself or with moral choice, isolated passages should not condemn them unless those passages involve direct endorsement or condemnation of religious perspectives. Texts about moral choice should be out of bounds only if they are explicit that widespread religious approaches to morality are misconceived. (Books or articles with this point of view could be used by teachers, if the teachers are careful to explain that this is only one approach, and the teachers present contrasting approaches as well.)

Finally, courts might consider whether available teachers are adequately trained to teach courses about religion.[13] Courts should defer to the judgments of educational authorities, but if it is obvious that teachers are far from adequately trained to teach courses about religion, a court could reasonably decide that the almost certain result will be an impermissible teaching of religion, and it could invalidate a program on that basis.

Teacher Expression, Including Garb and Title VII Accommodations That Affect Students

As we have seen in the last four chapters, public school teachers receiving instructions about how far they should analyze religious positions do not generally have rights of free speech and free exercise to act contrary to their directions, so long as these directions fall within the range of what is constitutionally permissible.[14]

Other constraints that do not concern curriculum can raise troublesome questions of wisdom and legality. Notable among these have been dress restrictions. One expression of religion by faculty members at public schools is the wearing of items with religious significance. Few cases involve jewelry with religious significance or yarmulkes, although some statutes seem broad enough to reach these, and apparently in Pennsylvania, at least, some teachers have been asked to remove such items.[15] Cases have arisen over more complete religious garb, clothing that clearly identifies the wearer as a member of a certain religion and that *may* further identify the wearer as occupying a particular position within the religion. A nun's habit is the most straightforward example; it identifies the wearer as a nun within the Roman Catholic religion.[16]

Whether schools should allow teachers to wear religious garb of this sort has proved to be an issue of some difficulty. On the one hand, if teachers generally are free to choose what to wear, why should not teachers be allowed to wear religious clothing, especially if doing so is meaningful for them or is even perceived to be a matter of religious obligation? On the other hand, if the students are continually exposed to a teacher wearing religious clothing, will that constitute a kind of encouragement or endorsement of her religion, improper for a public school?

The legal issues are more complex. The teachers who want to wear religious garb have a claim under the Free Exercise and Free Speech Clauses that they should be allowed to do so. They also have a claim that, as employees covered by Title VII of the 1964 Civil Rights Act, they have a right to have their religious needs accommodated, if that does not create an "undue hardship" on their employer.[17] Schools that wish to bar religious garb can argue that the Establishment Clause, and related state provisions, authorize them to do that.

Cases arise in two settings: (1) Parents or objecting taxpayers may seek to prevent teachers from wearing religious garb, although the schools have taken no action in that direction. (2) A state law, or local rule, forbids teachers from wearing religious garb; teachers seek to wear it despite the law.

One finds relatively few modern cases on this subject. Almost certainly one reason is that the Roman Catholic Church now permits priests and nuns to wear secular clothing and that a sharp decrease in religious vocations has left few nuns and priests teaching in public schools. Thus, the occasions of potential conflict have been sharply reduced. Further, the number of states with anti-garb laws may be less than it once was, and the laws that exist may not be rigorously enforced. An article about one case we shall consider notes that four states—Pennsylvania, Oregon, Nebraska, and North Dakota—have such laws,[18] and that a district court has called enforcement of the Pennsylvania law sporadic and inconsistent.[19]

What should be a state's or school's policy about religious garb? Officials should start with an initial disposition against regulation. If teachers are allowed to choose their own respectable clothing, they should be allowed to choose religious dress unless schools have a good reason to adopt a restriction. Although teachers are not free to dress just as they wish—a casual dresser could not successfully object if schools required male teachers to wear jackets and ties—singling out religious clothing for regulation amounts to a kind of discrimination against religious expression. If the state restricts dress because of the message it conveys, it engages in content discrimination and, after *Rosenberger*, probably what the Supreme Court regards as viewpoint discrimination. Regulation of that kind requires a powerful justification, if it is to be valid, and the reason obviously cannot be distaste for the religion whose members are most likely to wear religious dress.[20]

The reason for regulating religious dress concerns its likely effects on students. One possibility is that students will perceive that the school itself is somehow endorsing the religion of the teacher(s) wearing the religious garb. But even if students do not perceive such an endorsement, they may be influenced toward the religion. Schools have a reason to avoid such an influence, even if they do not fear that students will perceive an endorsement. The degree of each risk depends heavily on circumstances, yet a rule needs to be general with respect to all teachers or all teachers up to a particular grade level. First, imagine a locality in which 60 percent of the population is Roman Catholic and a number of nuns are teaching elementary school. Children will easily recognize the habits that their teachers are wearing. First and second graders, Catholics and non-Catholics, may not easily distinguish the religion of their teachers from the position of the school. Even if they do so, the habits are constant reminders that their teachers are committed Roman Catholics.[21] By contrast, imagine a substitute high-school math teacher in a district with few Roman Catholics. Students will not assume that the unusual sight of a teacher with a habit signifies school endorsement, and, seeing her one hour a day on a temporary basis, they probably will not be much influenced by her religious commitment.

States and school districts cannot easily engage in such particularized evaluations of individual circumstances. They must decide whether religious garb is a general enough problem to warrant regulation. My estimate is that it is now not such a problem statewide in any state. Perhaps in a few school districts, the problem is sufficiently widespread to warrant regulation of elementary school teachers, to whom children are exposed through the entire day.

The cases dealing with religious garb can be summarized fairly easily. Courts, with very few exceptions, have not declared that teachers in religious garb violate the Establishment Clause or state constitutional requirements against sectarian teaching. So long as the content of what is taught is appropriate, religious garb does not amount to teaching religion.[22] However, when state laws have forbidden religious garb, or officials have exercised discretionary authority to do so, courts have regarded these as appropriate means to assure a secular education.[23] They have not investigated whether a particular teacher's wearing of religious garb poses a serious risk by itself. It is highly doubtful whether broad laws against religious garb should be sustained in modern conditions.

United States v. Board of Education[24] posed the more complex question of whether a substitute teacher wanting to wear Muslim dress had a right to do so under the "reasonable accommodation" provision of Title VII, despite a Pennsylvania state law forbidding religious garb. The district court sustained her claim, stating, among other things, that her wearing of the attire of her religious faith would not cause students to perceive that the school district endorsed the Muslim religion. The court of appeals ruled that an accommodation would cause undue hardship on the employer by forcing the school board to violate the state law and to sacrifice a compelling interest in preserving the secular appearance of its public school system.

The relevance of the state law here is somewhat complicated. An invalid state law cannot justify a refusal to accommodate;

and this *should* be so even if educational officials reasonably thought that the law was valid. Title VII proceedings are mainly forward looking, not about penalties for past misbehavior. Unless the law was actually valid, a court should not say that "undue hardship" exists because officials relied on the law. However, if the law is valid and if it appropriately categorizes teachers in general, the district should be able to count violating the law as an "undue hardship," even if it cannot show any other hardship in the individual instance.

The state law's validity should be judged by the range of its applications. Because it is desirable to have a general policy that does not differentiate among teachers and among forms of religious garb, a school district should be able to show that there are good reasons for a rule against garb in the whole district or the whole state, taking all forms of religious garb into account. That is, a court should not ask, as one author proposes, what are the particular dangers of a substitute teacher wearing Muslim garb.[25] However, in order to succeed, the school district should have to make some showing of the number of public school teachers in Philadelphia or in the whole state who might wish to wear significantly religious garb.[26] If all it can produce are isolated instances, the district has failed to show a strong enough interest in its teachers maintaining a secular appearance, and the state law should no longer be considered valid as applied to Philadelphia.[27] In that event, accommodation to religious dress would not involve undue hardship under Title VII, and the teacher should be allowed to wear religious dress.

PART IV

RIGHTS OF STUDENTS

*

Student Rights to Religious Freedom and to Free Speech on Religious Topics

IN FULFILLING ASSIGNMENTS, responding to various school invitations, or acting on their own, public school students may wish to engage in speech that is religious or is about a religious topic. If teachers or school authorities do not allow the speech, the student's parents may claim that her rights to free speech and free exercise have been violated.[1] In this chapter we look at these issues—except for the activities of religious clubs and religious speech at graduation ceremonies, covered in previous chapters[2]—through the lens of some leading cases.

FULFILLING ASSIGNMENTS

A teacher gives students an assignment to write a paper or perform in class. A student chooses to respond with a presentation that is significantly religious. Told to write on an important historical figure, she decides to write about King David; or told to read a passage from a favorite book, she picks the verses from the Gospel of John that evangelical Christians often quote.

So long as the student's response falls within the assignment's subject matter, the teacher certainly *may* accept what the student has done, even if that involves a presentation to the class as a whole. Merely permitting a student to respond to an open-ended assignment in this way does not involve the state in sponsoring religion.[3]

The issue is more difficult if the teacher is trying to decide whether to accept the student's proposed response, or the teacher has decided not to allow the student's religious topic and has insisted on a different one, and the student's parents seek judicial review. May a school reasonably try to keep religious messages out of the classroom or do such restrictions violate the student's right to free speech or to the free exercise of religion?

In examining these questions, we need to assume that the assignment, fairly understood, either includes what the student wants to do or that the assignment would include that had the teacher not explicitly excluded religious topics—"Write an essay on what you care most about, except anything religious." No student has a right to respond with a religious message if an assignment cannot reasonably be fulfilled in that way. A teacher who instructs students to write on military strategies of World War II is justified in rejecting an essay on why true Christians are pacifists.

A student has a powerful argument that schools must aim to be neutral about religion and cannot exclude all religious topics. When a teacher rejects a religious subject, the student may claim that schools cannot, constitutionally, disfavor religious speech in comparison with all other forms of speech. Such negative treatment of religious speech is definitely a form of content discrimination; and the courts have followed the Supreme Court's lead in *Rosenberger v. Rector*[4] in regarding it as viewpoint discrimination.[5] Such discrimination can be justified under the Free Speech Clause only if the school has in this context wide latitude to decide what is written *or* if it has a very strong interest in excluding religion. Generally speaking, a teacher does have broad discretion to determine how students fulfill assignments.[6] Thus, a teacher may ask students to write about why democracy is a better form of government than traditional monarchy, although that undoubtedly is viewpoint discrimination. If a teacher opens up a "forum" in which students may freely express their opinions, however, he will need a more particular reason to exclude religious topics than his general discretion to direct his class.

The case that most pointedly raises these issues is *Settle v. Dickson County School Board*.[7] Dana Ramsey, a ninth-grade teacher, gave her students a research assignment whose purpose was "to learn how to research a topic, synthesize the information they gathered, and write a paper using that information."[8] Students had to use four research sources. Ramsey allowed students to select their topics, subject to her approval. Among the topics students chose were reincarnation (including its relation to Hinduism and Buddhism), witchcraft, spiritualism, and magic throughout history. Having initially picked another topic, Brittney Settle submitted an outline for a paper on "The Life of Jesus

Christ." Ramsey refused this topic, as well as a revised version entitled "A Scientific and Historical Approach to the Life of Jesus Christ." When Settle handed in a paper called "The Life of Jesus Christ," Ramsey graded it zero without reading it. Her reasons for refusing the topic were these: (1) Settle had not obtained permission for it by the deadline; (2) Settle's personal views would preclude her writing a dispassionate paper and would cause her to regard commentary as criticism of her religion; (3) "personal religion is just not an appropriate thing to do in a public school"; (4) Settle's knowledge of Jesus would prevent her from learning something new and discourage her from conducting significant research; (5) the law prohibits discussion of religious issues in the classroom; (6) Settle would rely on the Bible and could not meet the four-source requirement.

The district court, accepting Ramsey's idea about an objective research paper, also accepted her judgment that Settle might write more easily on Jesus than another topic and might be especially sensitive to criticism of her paper. The Sixth Circuit held that all six of Ramsey's justifications were within the "broad leeway of teachers to determine the nature of the curriculum and the grades to be awarded students."[9] For such classroom conflicts, it was sufficient that educators have legitimate pedagogical concerns.[10]

Perhaps the most crucial issue here is just how far courts will review teachers' decisions about assignments. Among Ramsey's six bases for decision, only some seem appropriate and constitutionally permissible.

(1) No doubt Ramsey *could* refuse a change of topic made too late. But, unless she is a very strict teacher, she would have accepted outlines for appropriate topics submitted after the deadline for picking a topic (especially if a student was switching from a topic chosen on time). If Ramsey would have accepted other changes in topic, her rejection of Settle's choice could not properly be based on untimeliness.

(2) If we assume that Brittney Settle is a committed Christian, as Ramsey probably knew or strongly suspected, Ramsey had good reason to think that she would have difficulty writing an "objective" paper on Jesus, and would take criticism as directed at her religion. Aiming to get students to write papers that are reasonably objective is definitely within a teacher's discretion.

165

(4, 6) Settle's religious convictions would not *necessarily* have prevented her from learning something new and doing significant research. She could have met the four-source requirement—many books and articles discuss the life of Jesus—but her heavy reliance on the already familiar Bible was a serious risk.[11]

(3, 5) Contrary to what Ramsey said, the law does not forbid all discussion of religious issues in classrooms, much less treatment of religion in a written paper. Even "personal religion" could be an appropriate way to fulfill some paper assignments. Personal religion would not be a good subject for an "objective" research paper, but Settle did not ever say she would write about her personal religion.[12]

We can sum up the crucial bases of Ramsey's decision as a mix of inappropriate reasons and responses to genuine risks, some of which Ramsey might have tried to meet in a different way. Had the case involved withdrawal of a basic benefit, a court, insisting that an administrator act for correct reasons, could have concluded that Ramsey's improper reasons may have affected the outcome. It could also have concluded that Ramsey might have reduced the risks by carefully explaining her requirements, exploring with Settle possible sources and perspectives, and asking Settle for an enriched outline of what she planned to cover.

But how much should we expect of a ninth-grade teacher giving an assignment to an entire class? Ramsey's disapproving a topic that she understandably perceived to be fraught with risk definitely fell within the range of reasonable pedagogical judgments. Ramsey knew Settle. She may have had a good sense of how hard it would be for Settle, even with further guidance, to write objectively about Jesus. If courts overturn such decisions because a teacher may also have relied on improper bases, what is to be the remedy? Will judicial efforts be expended so the teacher can reach her original judgment on a second try, this time stating only proper bases? In cases like this, it should be enough that teachers rely substantially on appropriate reasons, even if the mix also includes some misguided notions. The court was right to grant teachers fairly wide discretion over how assignments are fulfilled.[13]

In a case that was otherwise similar to *Settle*, very young students were to fulfill assignments with material other students would see or hear. In *C. H. v. Oliva*,[14] the Third Circuit Court of Appeals reviewed two complaints about a school's treatment of Z. H., the son of C. H. In kindergarten, Z. H. had been asked to make a Thanksgiving poster indicating what he was "thankful for." Z. H.'s poster was a picture of Jesus. The poster was displayed with others in the school building, was removed by some school employees because of its religious theme, and was later replaced by the kindergarten teacher in the hallway, but in a location less prominent than its original one. When Z. H.'s first-grade teacher invited students to bring a book to read to the class, Z. H. brought in *The Beginner's Bible* and planned to read an adaptation of the story of Jacob and Esau. The teacher told Z. H. he could not read the story to the entire class "because of its religious content," but could read it to her alone. In respect to this first-grade incident, the district court held that no constitutional violation had occurred,[15] because the teacher might reasonably have worried that classmates would think the teacher was endorsing the Bible. The Third Circuit panel affirmed.[16] Reviewing the panel decision, the judges en banc affirmed by an equally divided vote; according to standard practice for such votes, members of the full court wrote no opinions about the Bible story.

Teachers should not assume that *any* religious reading is automatically forbidden for public school classrooms, and even first graders can understand the idea that individual students who choose readings on their own do not represent the teacher or the school. However, in many circumstances, the teacher should exercise her judgment not to have the religious reading presented to the whole class. She might fear conflict over religion or the dominance of one view. (She might worry that if one student brings a Bible reading, others will begin to do so.) Or, given some connection the teacher has with a particular church, she might have a specific concern that the students would think she was endorsing the reading. So long as the teacher's judgment is not an automatic dismissal of any reading with religious content, a court should accept it.[17]

The en banc court disposed of the issue of the Thanksgiving poster in kindergarten on jurisdictional grounds. Plaintiff had failed to connect any of the defendants to whoever had removed the poster.[18] Judge Alito, dissenting, alone reached the merits of the complaint. He thought that relocating the poster because of its "religious theme" would violate the First Amendment. Public school students should have "the right to express religious views in class discussion or in assigned work, provided that their expression falls within the scope of the discussion or the assignment and provided that the school's restriction on expression does not satisfy strict scrutiny."[19] Even within closed forums, "viewpoint discrimination" must satisfy strict scrutiny. Judge Alito contrasted his approach with that of the panel, which said that schools may practice viewpoint discrimination in regulating what students say in class and how they fulfill assignments if the discrimination is "reasonably related to a legitimate pedagogical concern."[20]

If one focuses on viewpoint discrimination for school assignments, in general, the panel has the better of the argument.[21] Judge Alito's approach is much too broad. Consider the assignments to write about (1) "Why it is important to be honest," (2) "Respect for fellow citizens," and (3) "The value of religious liberty." Each of these topics is cast in terms of viewpoint discrimination, implicitly excluding essays that praise dishonesty, racial discrimination, and state-coerced religious orthodoxy. A school should not have to show a compelling interest in order for a teacher to reject an essay praising deceit or race-based slavery. Schools perform their educational purposes by aiming to instill some viewpoints to the exclusion of others, and this aim can be reflected in class assignments.

For Alito's position to be reasonably defensible, it requires a narrowing in terms of kinds of assignments and kinds of viewpoint discrimination. Alito is right that *real* viewpoint discrimination about religion should not be allowed—that is, promotion of one religious perspective at the expense of others. But, precluding religious topics, whatever the view expressed, is not real viewpoint discrimination.[22] Whether such an exclusion should be allowed depends on the religious makeup of the class and the nature of the assignment. For these inquiries, the panel's requirement of a reasonable relation to a legitimate pedagogical concern is apt. Whether, under that test, a school should be able to move a poster of Jesus to a less prominent position would depend on the religious attitudes of members of the student body, and, in particular, whether non-Christians might be offended.

Out-of-Class Activities

A variation on the subject of class assignments involves school-sponsored out-of-class activities. In *Gernetzke v. Kenosha Unified School District No. 1*,[23] student groups had been invited to paint murals for the main hallway of the school. The Bible Club submitted a sketch that included a large cross and an open Bible with a passage from the Gospel of John: "For God so loved the world that he gave his only Son, so that everyone who believes in him may not perish but may have eternal life."[24] The principal approved all but the cross, which he rejected on the ground that it might involve a lawsuit and might require him to approve murals of a Satanic or neo-Nazi character that would cause an uproar.

For the Seventh Circuit Court of Appeals, Judge Posner first rejected the argument that the decision about the mural discriminated against the religious club in violation of the Equal Access Act. The principal's discrimination was "against displays, religious or secular, that he reasonably believed likely to lead to litigation or disorder."[25] The act itself provides that it does not limit the authority of schools to maintain order and discipline, and First Amendment decisions give schools more control over the speech of students than the state has in regard to adults. Without quite resolving the club's First Amendment claim,[26] Judge Posner doubted that the First Amendment was relevantly broader than the Equal Access Act; and he expressed concern about litigation intended "to wrest the day-to-day control of our troubled public schools from school administrators and hand it over to judges and jurors who lack both knowledge of and responsibility for the operation of the public schools."[27]

This last thought may have been the main engine driving the court's decision, because the initial rationale under the Equal Access Act about fear of litigation and of disorder is curiously unsupported. The principal feared litigation because the cross is a very important religious symbol, which would have appeared in a mural on the school's walls. But the statute forbids discrimination against religious groups. School authorities cannot defend every disfavoring of the speech of religious clubs with the comment that they fear litigation.[28] To be justified, school officials must at least have a reasonable basis to believe that a legal chal-

169

lenge to their acceptance of a religious symbol might be sustained. Thus, insofar as the court relied on the principal's fear of litigation, it should have examined whether a legal challenge to a mural with a cross would have had a chance of success.[29]

The disorder point raises a different difficulty. Apparently, the principal did not worry that the mural with the cross would cause "an uproar" (although the opinion notes that the Bible Club mural was defaced with a witchcraft symbol), but that approval of it would "require him" to approve other murals that might cause an uproar, such as murals of a Satanic or neo-Nazi character. Why should one item be banned because other items might cause disorder? The court does not explain. One can imagine an analysis that the school should not distinguish among religious symbols, some of which might cause disorder. But then, what has a Nazi mural to do with that problem? In its Nazi manifestation, the swastika is overwhelmingly a political symbol, not a religious one. The relevant comparison for it is other political symbols. One doubts if the school would ban all murals with American flags or with themes related to political democracy, closer analogues to a neo-Nazi mural than a mural with a cross. Presumably, in respect to political symbols, the principal regarded himself as able to distinguish safe symbols from ones likely to cause disorder.

Why should not the same have been true about religious symbols? A court might respond that the state can favor some political symbols over others but cannot do that with powerful religious symbols. That is a reasonable position, but not one this court bothers to develop. In any event, the principal here did allow one of the best-known passages of the New Testament, with its powerful theological message. The court might have justified the distinction between what the principal allowed and what he forbade by claiming that written texts are less provocative than nonverbal symbols, but Judge Posner gives us no such analysis.

In sum, it appears that the court wished to avoid any close matching of the principal's logic against the Equal Access law and the First Amendment. Rather, it chose to leave school authorities a wide range of discretion, so long as they do not act arbitrarily. Here, the principal had gone a substantial distance to accommodate the Bible Club, and the court was not going to interfere. Perhaps it could have provided analysis of why this particular judgment was reasonable in light of concerns about disorder, but it did not do so.[30]

A similar case did not involve students alone, but parents of slain students and others associated with the terrible tragedy at Columbine High School, in which two students killed thirteen others and themselves and injured many more. Members of the community were invited to paint tiles for the renovated school. Initially, they were told not to make any reference to the attack, but this restraint was relaxed as time went by. Those making the tiles were also told not to use religious symbols, and tiles with religious symbols that had been mounted were taken down. The main subject of the lawsuit was the restriction on religious symbols.[31]

The district court regarded the point of the project as promoting the expression of private views.[32] The tiles represented a limited public forum. This allowed the school greater discretion as to subject matter than in a traditional public forum, but it did not permit the viewpoint discrimination of excluding religious expression. We see, again, how much work the oversimplification of the concept of viewpoint discrimination is doing. To say that someone can express nonreligious but not religious feelings is definitely not the same as saying they can favor Republicans but not Democrats or have a "pro-choice" sign but not a "pro-life" sign. So long as we understand religious expressions here *to include* atheist and agnostic expressions, the exclusion of religious expressions is typically very different from ordinary viewpoint discrimination; but since five justices of the Supreme Court conflated the two kinds of distinctions in *Rosenberger*, lower-court judges are accordingly applying the "viewpoint" label in the same loose way or are confused about what constitutes viewpoint discrimination.

The Tenth Circuit Court of Appeals reversed, deciding that because the tiles bear the imprimatur of the school and are related to pedagogical concerns, the school did not have to adopt viewpoint neutrality. School officials could reasonably think that religious references would lead to the walls becoming a situs of religious debate, disruptive to the learning environment.[33] That students would argue with one another, or that classes would be disrupted, because of tiles on the wall seems highly doubtful;

but I believe that the concern about apparent school endorsement when permanent fixtures are on the walls is a sufficient basis for officials to make a choice not to have tiles with religious messages. Also, apart from apparent endorsement, the school has a reason not to force its students to submit to continued exposure to religious messages they cannot easily avoid if they walk the halls.

STUDENT INITIATIVES

When students take the initiative to engage in religious speech, without any school assignment or invitation, the general principle is that schools cannot treat religious speech less favorably than other forms of speech. In *Muller v. Jefferson Lighthouse School*,[34] a school principal had refused to allow a fourth-grade student to hand out invitations to a religious meeting at church. The district court's conclusion that the handout could not be rejected just because it was religious was not challenged in the court of appeals.[35] Both courts approved most of the school's own rules for such handouts, including a requirement that the principal receive a copy one day in advance and an authorization for him to prevent distribution if the publication is insulting to any group or individual or he reasonably forecasts that the distribution will "greatly disrupt or materially interfere with school procedures and intrude into school affairs or the lives of others."[36] The district court held invalid a requirement that the publication indicate that any opinions expressed are not those of the school, but the court of appeals sustained that as well. That court regarded the school as a nonpublic forum, where restrictions on expression are permissible if they are "reasonably related to legitimate pedagogical concerns."[37]

Courts have consistently upheld dress codes for public schools against free speech challenges.[38] In *Vines v. Board of Education*,[39] the court did not resolve whether a student with religious reasons to violate a dress code would have constitutional rights greater than those of others who objected, because the dress code itself had an "opt out" clause based on religious beliefs.[40] In *Chalifoux v. New Caney Independent School District*,[41] the court did protect students' wearing of rosaries, which it characterized as religious speech. The school's basis for its prohibition was that rosaries were "gang-related apparel," since a few members of one gang had worn rosaries as an identifying symbol. The court found that the standard of gang-related apparel was too vague and that officials had failed to show the likelihood of substantial interference with school activities, required under *Tinker v. Des Moines Independent Community School Dist.*,[42] which upheld the right of students to wear black armbands protesting the Vietnam War. In a section of the opinion dealing with the free exercise of religion, the court noted that "the rosary is deeply rooted in orthodox Catholic beliefs." Because free exercise claims combined with free speech claims, the case was a hybrid according to the categorization of *Employment Division v. Smith*,[43] calling for heightened scrutiny and an inquiry whether the regulation places an "undue burden" on religious exercise and bears "more than a 'reasonable relation' to the . . . regulatory objective."[44] Under this approach the regulation of rosaries was invalid.

What the court does not address explicitly is whether free exercise actually provides any extra protection to the religious speech with which it is highly sympathetic. That seems doubtful. Once the court treats the religious speech as significant speech, the *Tinker* standard comes into play, and given *Widmar v. Vincent*, religious speech could not be treated more restrictively than other speech without strong reason. What is doubtful is whether free exercise scrutiny gives the wearers of the rosaries any extra protection that goes beyond *Tinker* and *Widmar*.[45]

The long-standing concern about head-scarves worn by Muslim girls in government schools in France provides an interesting point of comparison. Following a report by an independent commission, and a recommendation by the government, the National Assembly adopted a law banning the wearing of conspicuous religious symbols.[46] Such a law, singling out religious symbols, would be invalid in the United States, unless a state could present very powerful reasons on its behalf.[47]

Excusing Students When They or
Their Parents Object

In our final chapter, we will consider what schools should do when parents or students seek exceptions from standard requirements. Typically, parents with religious objections to aspects of the educational program want their children to be excused. In recent decades, most such complaints have been made by devoutly religious parents who worry that their children's faith will be undermined by forms of secular instruction. Religious objections to curriculums will almost certainly increase if schools deal more fully with religion; some parents will not want their children educated about other religions.

When responding to complaints of this sort, educators must evaluate the legitimate aims of their schools against the value of free exercise of religion for parents and for children. If courts are to declare that parents or children have constitutional rights to be excused, their primary locus will be the free exercise clauses of federal and state constitutions.[1] In some jurisdictions, parents may rely on statutory guarantees of free exercise.[2] I assume in what follows that parents and their children are in accord, although how courts should regard the wishes, or claims of conscience, of older teenagers who disagree with their parents about what instruction they should receive is itself a substantial question.

We can understand a great deal about the complex issues raised by parental claims to have their children excused by examining the notable case of *Mozert v. Hawkins County Board of Education*.[3]

PARENTAL OBJECTIONS

The controversy in Hawkins County, Tennessee, began when Vicki Frost was dismayed to learn that her daughter's sixth-grade reader contained a story, "A Visit to Mars," involving mental telepathy.[4] After inspecting more of the reader and conversing with like-minded neighbors, she quickly discovered other objectionable material. At a later time, she classified aspects of the reader to which she objected into categories including "futuristic supernaturalism, one-world government, situation ethics or values clarification, pacifism, rebellion against parents or self-authority, role reversal, animals are equal to humans, the skeptic's view of religion."[5]

Like virtually every adult in Hawkins County, Frost was a fundamentalist Christian, accepting the inerrancy of the Bible; the divinity of Jesus; his virgin birth (understood in a literal sense); "substitutionary atonement," according to which Jesus atoned for the sins of others by his crucifixion; resurrection of his body; and his future return to earth.[6]

The Holt, Reinhart and Winston Reader series, with stories from different traditions, was designed to stimulate imagination, critical understanding, and tolerance for diversity. The nature of the objections raised by Frost and the other complaining parents is suggested in the following examples. The version of the story of Goldilocks in the first-grade reader was flawed, they argued, because the bears did not punish her for her misbehavior.[7] A play based on *The Wizard of Oz* presented magic in a favorable light.[8] In the excerpt chosen from *The Diary of Anne Frank* for the eighth-grade reader, Anne says to her friend Peter, "I wish you had a religion. . . . [I]t doesn't matter what. Just believe in something."[9] The parents also objected to scant attention given to Protestant Christianity. Paul Vitz, a New York University professor of psychology, testified at the trial that none of the six hundred stories and poems in the readers depicted biblical Protestantism, whereas many stories presented non-Christian religions favorably.[10]

One way in which the protesters understood the Holt Reader series was as advocating secular humanism, loosely understood as promoting sexual permissiveness, gender equality, a decline in biblical morality, the diminution of religion in public life, acceptance of the theory of evolution, and laxity toward communism.[11] Although the parents had specific complaints about individual selections, their overarching objections concerned the cumulative effects of the readers' contents.[12]

At an initial school board meeting, the protesters asked for removal of the Holt books, one vocal critic insisting that they promoted secular humanism in violation of the Establishment Clause.[13] But the critical issue quickly became whether individual children would be excused from having to use the books. At the middle school, the principal agreed to let children of complaining parents leave class and read an alternate text in the library.[14] Two elementary schools refused to make any accommodations; another allowed a student to sit in the hallway while objectionable stories were read and discussed.[15] In response to continuing agitation by objecting parents, the school board resolved that the county schools would use only the Holt readers, thus blocking any further individual accommodations.[16] This set the stage for the parents' legal claim that they had a right under the Free Exercise Clause to have their children excused from using the Holt readers.

The trial judge summarized the plaintiffs' main objections in the following way:

1. teach[ing] witchcraft and other forms of magic and occult activities;

2. teach[ing] that some values are relative and vary from situation to situation;

3. teach[ing] attitudes, values, and concepts of disrespect and disobedience to parents;

4. teach[ing] that one does not need to believe in God in a specific way but that any type of faith in the supernatural is an acceptable method of salvation;

5. imply[ing] that Jesus was illiterate;

6. teach[ing] that man and apes evolved from a common ancestor; and

7. teach[ing] various humanistic values.[17]

Nomi Stolzenberg has discerned more general allegations, including:

1. The content of the readings in the Holt reading series is contradictory to the plaintiff's beliefs.

2. The content of the books is false; the readings teach schoolchildren false beliefs.

3. Permitting the children to read the Holt series contravenes the parents' duty, mandated by the Bible, to safeguard children from

"all influences of evil that might lead them away from the way of God."

4. The children will be punished with eternal damnation if they read the books.

5. The Holt readers contain "a pervasive bias against the religious beliefs of the parents."

6. By disparaging the parents' religion, the readings have the potential effect of making children feel embarrassed and ashamed of who they are, in much the same way that textbooks make black children feel inferior by omitting references to black culture.

7. The readings impart a skeptical view of religion and teach children to "view Scriptural truth as myth."

8. The readings pressure children "to accept the view that all religions lead to God and are equally valid."

9. By giving credence to alien philosophies, the reading program confuses the children and unfetters their imaginations when their imaginations ought to be bounded.[18]

Just what changes would have satisfied the complaining parents was not entirely clear—the appellate judges disagreed about the nub of the pleadings and testimony. Various objections evidently reached other collections of readings for English, as well as textbooks in other courses; but at a minimum, the parents insisted their children should not have to study from the Holt series, and that was the specific relief they demanded in their lawsuit.[19]

COMPETING STATE INTERESTS

The reasons educational officials of Hawkins County had for not granting the parents the requested accommodations connect closely to the preceding chapters, especially chapter 2 on purposes. Most obviously, the state has an important stake in the education of its children. Every state has a compulsory school attendance law. Although parents may provide alternate home education, they cannot decide to let their children do without schooling.

The proper locus of educational decisions and the value of uniformity constituted straightforward educational reasons not to accommodate the Hawkins County parents. People can always debate what texts to use; any text is bound to offend someone. Educational authorities assume they are better equipped to decide than are ad hoc collections of parents. Once texts are chosen, it makes sense to have all students use them. Teachers should not have to concern themselves with alternative texts for a few children. Even if teachers would not need to take positive measures to teach excused children from alternative texts, having children leave the classroom when the time rolls around for objectionable material is disrupting. And, in lower grades at least, class teachers often bridge subjects by references to what they have taught previously. A first-grade teacher who testified for the plaintiffs acknowledged on cross-examination that accommodating the plaintiffs would complicate teaching: "For one thing, I wouldn't know what they had been going over, the skills they had been taught, and I wouldn't be able to incorporate it into my other subjects that I would have to teach during the day."[20] Further, she wouldn't be able to introduce topics from the regular reading class that became relevant at other times.

More complex reasons not to excuse children concern choice among ways of life and democratic participation. Education enhances the ability of young people to choose among ways to live, and it also helps them understand how to participate actively in our democratic institutions. Part of the reason for education is to allow a liberal democratic order to reproduce itself. Children need to be taught tolerance, respect for others, critical thinking, and self-expression.

The Holt readers were selected because of their variety of stories and perspectives. The superintendent of schools testified, "These textbooks expose the student to varying values and religious backgrounds[;] neither the textbooks nor the teachers teach, indoctrinate, oppose or promote any particular value or religion."[21] Designed to teach tolerance and respect for many religions and ways of life, the readers were better suited for education in a pluralist democratic society than any text presenting a single perspective. Moreover, the experience of open class discussion is itself part of the education in critical thinking. Even were the children of the protesting parents to read other texts whose content could have served all the state objectives as well as the Holt series, they would lose the benefit of class exchanges.

Excusing Children of Christian Fundamentalists
from Using Readers to Which They Object

Hawkins County parents wanted their children to remain in school but to be excused from using the Holt readers for their English classes. Should they have been afforded an accommodation and, if so, what form should it have taken? Three preliminary points help focus our inquiry.

We need to assume that the education the state was providing did not itself constitute an endorsement of a particular religious view or a discrimination among religions. The Hawkins County parents did suggest that the Holt readers established the religion of secular humanism and discriminated against Protestant Christianity, especially conservative Protestant Christianity. Insofar as these complaints were valid, the proper remedy would have been to provide different reading materials for all students.[22] For purposes of this chapter, the issue is whether schools should accommodate parents who object to materials that themselves are intrinsically appropriate by excusing their children from using the materials.

One possible position is that the state should offer public education on a take-it-or-leave-it basis. Parents who do not like what goes on in public school can avail themselves of a private school or engage in home schooling. This position is unacceptably harsh.

Whether or not schools should insist that all students adhere to the same core curriculum, they should not require children to engage in military training,[23] pledges of loyalty,[24] and perhaps dancing[25] if they and their parents strongly object in conscience. To refuse to make *any* such accommodations would drive some students away from the public schools. Further, a strict "take it or leave it" policy would discriminate in effect against parents who are unable to do home schooling because of their own limited competence or their other responsibilities, and who either cannot afford private school tuition or live in an area without private schools they regard as suitable. An inflexible policy of never bending is not a sufficient basis to deny requests for accommodation.

This judgment is confirmed by the reality that the religious views of parents do influence curricular choice to some degree.[26]

Many textbooks are designed to avoid offense; and educational authorities aim to minimize antagonism toward their curriculum and texts by designing an acceptable curriculum and choosing inoffensive texts. If the majority (or a vocal minority) is able to achieve educational choices that do not cause religious offense to them, accommodating smaller minorities who are out of step cannot be misguided in principle.

Private schools figure in a more subtle way in an analysis of accommodation. All states allow parents to enroll children in private schools, including religious schools, and this right is constitutionally protected.[27] States also allow home schooling if the parents choose. In their regulation of private schools and home schooling, states do not concentrate on values education and on critical thinking; what they require is that major subjects be taught.[28] Parents have wide latitude to provide the positive religious instruction they want, and they need not expose their children to the kinds of nonreligious ideas the Hawkins County parents found so troubling. If parents who choose against public education need not expose their children to offensive ideas, that is *some* basis, though hardly a conclusive one, for believing that the state may also accommodate parents whose children are in public schools.[29]

Once we understand that educational authorities should sometimes accommodate when parents, and children, have religious objections to the children participating in aspects of the public school curriculum, the question arises of when schools should make such accommodations.[30] The strength of reasons to accommodate increases as the strength of the religious objections increases. The reasons against affording an accommodation increase as disruption of the curriculum, administrative costs, and loss to the students increase.

Disruption of the curriculum concerns adverse effects on the ordinary educational process. In elementary grades, where a teacher may weave subjects together, that effort is severely complicated if all students are not reading the same material. This particular problem diminishes in higher grades, in which teachers of one subject usually have little sense of what materials teachers use in other subjects.

Administrative costs, insofar as they differ from disruption of the curriculum, include the time, effort, and expense a school must make to reach an accommodation that satisfies parents. Will parents provide an alternative program or must teachers develop one? Is space available for children to study a separate set of materials? Must the school engage an extra teacher for the separate materials; if excused students are left to read on their own, will their educational experience be less valuable?

Educational loss to the students is viewed from the state's point of view. If parents succeed in exempting a child from a core part of the curriculum, such as history or science, and suggest no adequate substitute, the loss would be markedly greater than if parents had a child exempted from military training or square dancing.

The state's interest in developing adults competent to perform most roles in society was not seriously implicated in the Hawkins County dispute. A student using a different reader could acquire linguistic abilities to manage in a job and social activities, and the absence of some children from class would not much affect the progress of the remaining children. If it was too costly for the schools to devote extra resources because some parents objected to the curriculum, they might have made the students' being excused conditional on the provision of home schooling for one subject, English. Parents would then have had to see that their children maintained an appropriate level of competence in English. Schools should not have to make any accommodation that undermines the competence of students in basic subjects.[31]

The state could reasonably say that *if* the objections of fundamentalist parents are to opening up new areas of choice for students, that very exploration of possibilities enhances students' autonomy in a wide range of areas, including religion.[32] But the state's permission for parents to send children to private schools or to undertake home schooling reduces the strength of any argument that freedom of choice is so important that the school should override parental objections that materials threaten their children's religious welfare.[33] In any event, a child in a diverse public school who is excused from one course is likely to be exposed to a wider range of choice than a child schooled at home or at a doctrinaire religious school. Fundamentalist parents denied an accommodation may enroll their children in congenial Christian schools, as did many of the complaining parents in Hawkins County.

Perhaps the most troubling issues about the Hawkins County complaint concerned tolerance, equality, and participation in democratic institutions. Unlike the Amish, whose children were excused by *Wisconsin v. Yoder*[34] from standard schooling after the eighth grade, fundamentalist Christians are active in the political process. That process is damaged by participants who are rigid ideologues with little respect for the views of others. Of course, a person can be conservative, even rigid and authoritarian, in religious conviction and still recognize that for political purposes people should be treated equally and their misguided opinions taken seriously. (By the same token, people with liberal religious views can be harshly rigid and intolerant in politics.) But most people do not easily cabin domains of life. Those who are rigid and certain in their religious views are likely to adopt similarly fixed political attitudes. Too many uncompromising ideologues are unhealthy for liberal democracy. Thus, if the parental objection to exposure to diverse perspectives is validated, the consequence may be children less suited for active life in a liberal democracy. We can see that the argument here draws heavily on the idea that the development of civic virtue is a critical aspect of public education, and one's evaluation of the argument will depend partly on how one rates that purpose against the desirability of countering negative effects of public education on people's nonpublic moral and religious perspectives.

This argument about educating for democracy has some force; *but* it also runs into the reality that parents may choose private education with much less exposure to diverse perspectives than one finds in public schools, and that some parents whose objections are not met will actually choose that course. Given this parental option, denying an accommodation because it will interfere with democratic education becomes more doubtful as a matter of principle and potentially unpromising in its likely consequences.[35]

On balance, I believe that educational authorities should have accommodated the Hawkins County parents *if* (1) the schools did not have to undertake serious costs to develop alternative programs, (2) parents could assure that excused children would maintain an adequate level of competence, (3) students using the standard text would not suffer serious disruption or interference with their program, (4) the parents' objections were not so extensive that satisfying them would remove their children from most of the public school program (a public school is enough of a unified program so that parents should not be permitted to selectively pick and choose what subjects their children will take),[36] and (5) granting this exemption would not be likely to lead to a wide range of objections from parents with different views, satisfaction of which would be unmanageable in terms of space and a coherent program.[37]

Constitutional Principle

Mozert[38] has been the most important constitutional case on the topic of exemptions for public school students from parts of the curriculum. The decision was rendered against the background of *Wisconsin v. Yoder*,[39] in which the Supreme Court sustained the right of Amish parents to withdraw their children from school after the eighth grade. Because the *Mozert* decision preceded *Employment Division v. Smith*,[40] the judges comfortably assumed that if the parents established a constitutionally relevant burden on the exercise of their religion, the state could refuse an accommodation only if it had a compelling reason to do so. Whether such an approach remains valid federal constitutional interpretation after *Smith* is uncertain, but given what *Smith* says about hybrid cases, it probably does.[41]

Although the three judges in *Mozert* agreed about the result, their interpretations of the parents' objections and their own reasoning differed. All three judges agreed that the parents failed to state a relevant burden on free exercise, but one of them reached that conclusion with considerable hesitancy; all three judges were influenced by the difficulties educational authorities would face if a burden was recognized.

Chief Judge Lively wrote the majority opinion. Although he noted that the parents' overriding objection was to the Holt series as a whole, he doubted that their objections could be satisfied by any alternative that did not teach that religious views opposed to their own were in error. Suggesting that the Supreme Court had sustained claims only when children had to declare beliefs or to engage in practices offensive to them, Chief Judge Lively said that exposure to offensive materials did not create a burden on free exercise.[42] He wrote, "What is absent from this case is the critical element of compulsion to affirm or deny a religious belief or engage or refrain from engaging in a practice forbidden or required in the exercise of a plaintiff's religion."[43]

The holding that mere exposure cannot violate free exercise approaches the absurd, as Judge Boggs neatly demonstrated. Drawing from an earlier Roman Catholic view that the reading of books on an index of proscribed books could be a mortal sin, Boggs argued that forced exposure of children to materials that parents think might cause their damnation or lead them seriously astray could be a burden on their religion.[44] In any ordinary sense, forced exposure could itself burden someone's religious exercise,[45] as we can imagine were adults forced to witness religious ceremonies they abhor. The parents in Hawkins County believed that the Holt reading series seriously threatened the religious welfare of their children, and Judge Boggs persuasively argued that the less than explicit gist of their complaint was that their religious convictions forbade exposure of their children to the readers.[46]

The heart of the opinions of Judges Lively and Boggs concerns the burden state authorities would bear if they had to worry about accommodating various religious objections to course materials. The weight of this burden depends partly on the difficulty of satisfying complaining parents. Lively apparently believed that the only way to satisfy the *Mozert* parents was to violate the Establishment Clause, by using materials that adopted their particular religious perspectives.[47]

Judge Boggs thought that school authorities can often accommodate parents with religious objections to the curriculum, but, given the Supreme Court's failure to interfere with the prerogatives of school boards on free exercise grounds, and the importance of political control of those boards, he concluded that school authorities can set whatever curriculum they choose and impose it on all students, so long as their choices do not violate the Establishment Clause.[48] Boggs apparently favored some constitutionally required accommodation to free exercise claims of this sort. Although he said such an expansion of religious liberty should come from the Supreme Court,[49] it is not clear why he did not regard *Yoder* as having established such a principle.

Judge Kennedy joined the opinion of Chief Judge Lively, but

she also wrote separately to argue that even if the parents' free exercise rights were burdened, the state had a compelling interest in doing so. Mandatory participation in a compulsory reading program was the least restrictive means of helping students develop critical reading skills and discussing complex and controversial social and moral issues.[50] To let children opt out from aspects of the core curriculum was to disrupt the classroom and cause religious divisiveness.[51] Even granting that the free exercise compelling interest test has always been less stringent than the equal protection compelling interest test, Kennedy's conclusion about the state's strong interest in critical discussion is in some tension with the state's allowance of private schooling and home schooling (although the state can contend that it does have a strong interest in critical discussion, even if that interest gives way to basic parental choices about schooling).[52] The dangers of disruption and divisiveness would vary greatly with individual circumstances.

The constitutional issue posed by *Mozert* is difficult.[53] Without doubt, parents, who it has long been supposed have a basic right to raise their children in their religion faith, suffered an impingement on their exercise of religion. And constitutional relief from some mandatory school requirements is definitely appropriate. When students must declare beliefs, when students are not permitted to refer to their religious beliefs when they respond to questions about how they would handle problems, when students are forced to engage in activities they regard for religious reasons as abhorrent, religious claims should be reviewed by courts and often sustained. But it is arguable that objections to particular parts of the core curriculum are too complex for courts to evaluate in light of available alternatives. The unanimous conclusion of the three judges is defensible; but the majority opinion in *Mozert* is less empathetic to the plight of the parents than it should be, and I believe the judges should have recognized that parents have free exercise rights to have children excused even from parts of the core curriculum, if doing so will not cause substantial disruption and providing an acceptable alternative will not be costly.[54]

The one part of the curriculum from which parents and students are most commonly allowed to opt out involves sex education, but here the state's argument that it is not constitutionally required to grant exemptions is powerful.[55] Many parents object on religious grounds to their children learning about use of condoms, preferring that they be told that abstinence from sexual intercourse is the only proper behavior for unmarried adolescents. The instruction in condom use is aimed at preventing AIDS, other sexually transmitted diseases, and unwanted pregnancies. Of course, abstinence will do even better in this respect, but schools have no guarantee that all the children whose parents object to teaching about condoms will abstain from sexual relations. Thus, the state can offer a strong reason for requiring all students to attend sex education or health classes, one that should be sufficient to sustain such a requirement even if a court uses a "compelling interest" standard of review.[56]

This completes our analysis of religion and the public schools. Does God belong in those schools? Yes, but only in some respects. We have seen in this final chapter that schools can legally make some accommodations in their regular programs to satisfy special religious claims of parents, and, further, that doing so makes educational sense. I have argued that some few accommodations should be regarded as constitutionally required, but only if the school's general educational program does not suffer significantly. Other opportunities for religion to matter for individual students arise when they join religious clubs, which schools may not sponsor but must accept on the same basis as other clubs, and when they choose to fulfill general topic assignments with religious subjects.

The schools themselves cannot undertake devotional exercises or teach that religious propositions are true or false. A bar on oral school prayer and one on straightforward religious instruction are simple applications of the principle that public schools may not sponsor religion. More difficult issues are raised by moments of silence, implicitly accepted in their ordinary manifestations by a majority of the Supreme Court, and by the use of devotional music in Christmas concerts.

The most important concerns about religion and public schools involve teaching *about* religion. The wisest approach is for schools to make a greater effort to teach students about the role of religion in the lives of individuals and societies, at the same time avoiding the promotion of any religion. The content of courses, such as biology, should not be determined by religious opinions, even if all that is at issue is the omission of material. And students should not be told that perspectives such as scientific creationism, which may appear to be nonreligious but can be believed only on religious grounds, are plausible scientific options.

As virtually all our chapters illustrate, some issues are easy to settle from a constitutional point of view, but others are extremely difficult, calling on us to evaluate them with a fair and generous appreciation of the religious diversity of our society and the central place of religious liberty in our constitutional order. There is no last word on this subject. Complex circumstances will keep raising thorny problems that will require teachers, textbook writers, school administrators, legislators, and judges to determine what is wise education within constitutional bounds. These problems will continue to generate intense disagreements, but these are a small price to pay for the religious freedom we are fortunate to enjoy.

* *Notes* *

CHAPTER 1. A BRIEF HISTORY OF AMERICAN PUBLIC SCHOOLS AND RELIGION

1. Warren A. Nord, *Religion and American Education* 65 (Chapel Hill: Univ. of North Carolina Pr., 1995. William C. Bower, *Church and State in Education* 23–24 (Chicago: Univ. of Chicago Pr., 1944), wrote that the church controlled education in the middle and northern colonies. In the South, charity schools were sponsored by the English Society for the Propagation of the Gospel in Foreign Parts. *See also* Harry M. Ward, *Colonial America: 1607–1763* 325 (Englewood Cliffs, N.J.: Prentice Hall, 1991). According to Rosemary C. Salomone, *Visions of Schooling: Conscience, Community, and Common Education* 18 (New Haven: Yale Univ. Pr., 2000), schools generally were supported to some degree by tax revenues. *But see* Carl Kaestle, *Pillars of the Republic: Common Schools and American Society, 1780–1860*, at 4 (New York: Hill and Wang, 1983) ("Nowhere was schooling entirely tax supported or compulsory").

As Stephen Macedo has noted, "The vast majority of Americans throughout the eighteenth century worked on family farms and lived in rural areas." Stephen Macedo, *Diversity and Distrust: Civic Education in a Multicultural Democracy* 46 (Cambridge: Harvard Univ. Pr., 2002). New York and Boston each had fewer than fifteen thousand residents in 1755, and Philadelphia, the largest city, had only twenty thousand. *Id.*

2. Macedo, *Diversity and Distrust*, note 1 *supra*, at 47.

3. *Id.* at 47–48.

4. *Id.* at 48–49.

5. *Id.* at 51.

6. *Id.* at 52, quoting Kaestle, *Pillars of the Republic*, note 1 *supra*, at 55–56.

7. *Id.* at 52–53.

8. *Id.* at 53.

9. Rosemary Salomone, "Common Schools, Uncommon Values: Listening to the Voices of Dissent," 14 *Yale L. & Pol'y Rev.* 169, 174 (1996). For a summary of sources on Mann's life, *see* Robert Michaelson, *Piety in the Public School* 72–73 (New York: Macmillan, 1970). Not surprisingly, one consequence of the attempt to build a common culture for poor children of disparate heritages was to alienate students from the communal values of their parents. *See* Barbara Finkelstein, "Exploring Community in Urban Educational History," in Ronald K. Goodenow and Diane Ravitch, eds., *Schools in Cities: Consensus and Conflict in*

American Educational History 309 (New York: Holmes & Meier, 1983). *See also* Salomone, *Visions of Schooling*, note 1 *supra*, at 17.

10. Macedo, *Diversity and Distrust*, note 1 *supra*, at 60.

11. John C. Jeffries Jr., and James E. Ryan, "A Political History of the Establishment Clause," 100 *Mich. L. Rev.* 279, 303 (2001), have written, "[T]he shift in origin of nineteenth-century immigration from Ireland to central and southern Europe reinforced the racial element in anti-Catholic animosity." *See also* Richard Morgan, *The Supreme Court and Religion* 47 (New York: Free Press, 1972).

12. As Macedo puts it, *Diversity and Distrust*, note 1 *supra*, at 61, "Rome furnished ample grounds for many to wonder whether it was possible to be a good Catholic and a good republican." Pope Pius IX (1846–78) referred to freedom of conscience as "the liberty of perdition," *id.*, and he "published a list of condemned positions which fully comprehended the whole liberal agenda of a man like [Lord] Acton." Garry Wills, *Papal Sin: Structures of Deceit* 239 (New York: Doubleday, 2000). (Acton was a prominent liberal English Roman Catholic.) John Noonan, a leading Roman Catholic legal scholar, as well as judge on the Ninth Circuit Court of Appeals, briefly recounts nineteenth-century papal encyclicals opposed to religious liberty, in *The Lustre of Our Country: The American Experience of Religious Freedom* 26–27 (Berkeley and Los Angeles: Univ. of California Pr., 1998).

13. Joseph Viteritti, "Blaine's Wake: School Choice, the First Amendment, and State Constitutional Law," 21 *Harv. J. L. & Pub. Pol'y* 657, 666 (1998), writes, "The common-school curriculum promoted a religious orthodoxy of its own that was centered on the teachings of mainstream Protestantism and was intolerant of those who were non-believers." John Jeffries Jr. and James Ryan, "Political History,"note 11 *supra*, at 298, comment that "by promoting least-common-denominator Protestantism and rejecting particularistic influences," the advocates of common schools were able "to keep religion in the public schools but keep controversy out."

14. Nord, *Religion and American Education*, note 1 *supra*, at 71–72. As Rosemary Salomone writes, "Common Schools, Uncommon Values," note 9 *supra*, at 174, Mann's notion was that the schools "would inculcate a common core of values, a public philosophy, which intermingled religion, politics and economics in a vision of a 'redeemer nation.'"

15. Nord, *Religion and American Education*, note 1 *supra*, at 67.

16. *Id.*, relying on Ruth Miller Elson, *Guardians of Tradition: American Schoolbooks of the Nineteenth Century* 17–19, 21, 24 (Lincoln: Univ. of Nebraska Pr., 1964).

17. *Id.* at 61.

18. *Id.*

19. *Id.*, referring to a study by Dan Fleming, "Religion in American History Textbooks: Were the 'Good Old Days' of Textbooks Really So Good?" 18 *Religion and Public Education* 79, 85, 100 (1991).

20. Macedo, *Diversity and Distrust*, note 1 *supra*, at 57.

21. Horace Mann, Twelfth Annual Report 116–17 (1848), quoted in Raymond Culver, *Horace Mann and Religion in the Massachusetts Public Schools* 252 (New Haven: Yale Univ. Pr., 1929).

22. *See* Macedo, *Diversity and Distrust*, note 1 *supra*, at 68–69.

23. *See id.* at 67–72.

24. Such devotional practices can also have a differential effect among the very religions that countenance them. Few Protestants objected in principle to Bible reading without commentary. But some Protestants took the Bible as God's literal word, while others understood it as less authoritative and more figurative. When teachers read the Bible day after day without comment, this tended, in communities with diverse religious perspectives, to suggest that having the single correct interpretation was not essential to salvation. It is no coincidence that Horace Mann was a Unitarian who "waged fierce battle with conservative critics" wanting a "more pronounced religious content" in the schools. *See* Jeffries and Ryan, "Political History", note 11 *supra*, at 298. (In our time, reading of the Bible without commentary might favor more conservative religious groups who continue to assign the Bible particularly high authority.)

25. Nord, *Religion and American Education*, note 1 *supra*, at 63. Nord tells us, *id.* at 84, that higher education was also essentially secular by 1900, although in 1860, 262 out of 288 college presidents were clergymen.

26. According to Justice Brennan, concurring in Abington Township v. Schempp, 374 U.S. 203, 275 (1963): "The last quarter of the nineteenth century found the courts beginning to question the constitutionality of public school religious exercises." And in 1910 the Illinois Supreme Court said, "The truths of the Bible are the truths of religion, which do not come within the province of the public school." People ex rel. Ring v. Board of Education, 245 Ill. 334, 349, 92 N.E. 251, 256. But, prior to *Schempp*, most state courts continued to sustain Bible reading. *See* Donald E. Boles, *The Bible, Religion, and the Public Schools* 58–99 (Ames: Iowa State Univ. Pr., 1961); Joseph W. Harrison, "The Bible, the Constitution, and Public Education," 29 *Tenn. L. Rev.* 363, 381–85 (1962).

27. Nord well summarizes relevant elements in *Religion and American Education*, note 1 *supra*, at 16–39, stressing the contribution of Martin Luther.

28. *Id.* at 39.

29. Macedo, *Diversity and Distrust*, note 1 *supra*, at 58.

30. Nord, *Religion and American Education* note 1 *supra*, at 76–78.

31. *Id.* at 78.

32. *See* Salomone, "Common Schools, Uncommon Values", note 9 *supra*, at 178–79.

33. Salomone, *id.* at 178–79, describes the pendulum swinging back and forth in response to historical events and social movements.

34. Patricia Alberg Graham, "Educational Reform—Why Now?" 146, no. 3, *Proceedings of the American Philosophical Society* 256, 257–60 (2000). *A Nation at Risk* was a 1983 report of the U.S. Department of Education's National Commission on Excellence in Education. It strongly recommended greater concentration on academic subjects, accompanied by higher and measurable standards of academic performance. A similar emphasis is contained in the 'No Child Left Behind Act of 2001,' Public Law 110 of the 107th Cong., signed by President Bush on Jan. 8, 2002.

35. Meyer v. Nebraska, 262 U.S. 380 (1923).

36. Pierce v. Society of Sisters, 268 U.S. 510 (1925).

37. Everson v. Board of Education, 330 U.S. 1.

38. *Id.* at 16. In the 2002 decision upholding a voucher plan to provide tuition for private schools, including religious ones, the dissenters strongly asserted that *Everson*'s language plainly prohibited such extensive aid to religious schools. Zelman v. Simmons-Harris, 536 U.S. 639, 687–88 (Souter, J., dissenting). Justice O'Connor, concurring, responded that *Everson* permitted aid going to parents, which reached schools only according to voluntary parental choices, 536 U.S. at 669–70.

39. *See* Jeffries and Ryan, "Political History," note 11 *supra*, at 312–18.

40. McCollum v. Board of Education, 333 U.S. 203 (1948).

41. Zorach v. Clauson, 343 U.S. 306 (1952). My father, Kenneth W. Greenawalt, was counsel for Zorach.

42. Engel v. Vitale, 370 U.S. 421 (1962).

43. *Schempp*, 374 U.S. at 203.

44. Lee v. Weisman, 505 U.S. 577 (1992); Santa Fe Independent School Dist. v. Doe, 530 U.S. 290 (2000). John Jeffries Jr. and James Ryan explain that, in contrast to the breakdown of opposition to school aid among many Protestant groups, mainline Protestant clergy, as well as most Jews and secularists, remain opposed to public school prayer. Jeffries and Ryan, "Political History", note 11 *supra*, at 318–27, 352–68.

45. *Schempp*, 374 U.S. at 225. *See also id.* at 300 (Brennan, J., concurring), and *id.* at 306 (Goldberg, J., concurring).

46. *Id.* at 222.

47. The Court did not address the possibility that teaching "ordinary subjects" could advance or inhibit religion, an issue we shall address in chapter 5 and succeeding chapters.

48. Lemon v. Kurtzman, 403 U.S. 602, 612–13 (1971).

49. The *Lemon* opinion also suggested that a potential for political divisiveness could amount to a forbidden entanglement, *id.* at 622, but later opinions backed off from treating that factor as independently relevant.

50. Agostini v. Felton, 521 U.S. 203, 233 (1997). On at least one occasion, in Marsh v. Chambers, 463 U.S. 783 (1983), the Court relied heavily on practices when the Bill of Rights was adopted, to sustain prayers to begin legislative sessions, although the prayers would almost certainly have failed the *Lemon* test.

51. *Agostini*, 521 U.S. at 237. According to the justices' understanding, the Supreme Court has not abandoned a test until it does so in an opinion that represents a majority.

52. At least with older children, it *may* be enough if they object, whatever their parents believe.

53. West Virginia Board of Education v. Barnette, 319 U.S. 624 (1943). The case overruled a previous decision that rejected a free exercise claim to the same effect.

54. Wisconsin v. Yoder, 406 U.S. 208 (1972).

55. This general approach followed Sherbert v. Verner, 374 U.S. 398 (1963), a prior decision involving a refusal to work on Saturday.

56. Employment Decision v. Smith, 494 U.S. 872 (1990).

57. *Smith* creates two exceptions to its general rule, one of which covers the facts of *Yoder* and may cover other parental claims to have children excused.

58. *Smith*, 494 U.S. at 890.

59. In the cases the Supreme Court has actually considered, the free speech argument has been successfully made by people claiming that a state restriction on aid to religious speech is invalid; a state could rely on free speech as a reason *not* to impose a restriction that some private party claims that the Establishment Clause requires.

CHAPTER 2. PURPOSES OF PUBLIC SCHOOL EDUCATION

1. No doubt, education for certain occupations, such as driving trucks, has little to do with what are conceived as liberal educational objectives.

2. Amy Gutmann, *Democratic Education* 51 (Princeton: Princeton Univ. Pr., 1987).

3. *Id.* at 39. Stephen Macedo claims, "Liberal political institutions and public policies should be concerned to promote not simply freedom, order, and prosperity, but the preconditions of active citizenship: the capacities and dispositions conducive to thoughtful participation in

the activities of modern politics and civil society." Stephen Macedo, *Diversity and Distrust: Civic Education in a Multicultural Democracy* (Cambridge: Harvard Univ. Pr., 2000). The idea that public schools should teach civic virtues for democratic citizenship is sometimes linked to the notion that all citizens should participate actively (to some degree) in the political life of their societies. Given the variety of valuable and fulfilling lives that people can live, I do not believe some minimum of actual participation in political life is a requisite of every good life; but it turns out that this issue is not crucial for the educative one. Not only must *many* citizens participate actively for liberal democracy to work, every able citizen should have the opportunity to do so. Educators rightly emphasize the importance of participation and try to develop the capacity in all students.

4. Gutmann remarks, "In practice, the development of a deliberative character is essential to realizing the ideal of a democratically sovereign society." Gutmann, *Democratic Education*, note 2 *supra*, at 52. Macedo regards "a critical attitude toward contending political claims" as a core liberal virtue. Macedo, *Diversity and Distrust*, note 3 *supra*, at 179.

5. He writes, "There is no set of agreed-upon values for democratic citizens, except perhaps at a level of vagueness that ceases to be controversial because it ceases to be meaningful." Michael McConnell, "Education Disestablishment: Why Democratic Values Are Ill-Served by Democratic Control of Schooling," in Stephen Macedo and Yael Tamir, eds., *Moral and Political Education* 101 (New York: New York Univ. Pr., 2002).

Rosemary Salomone writes that debates about the public school curriculum are "tearing communities apart" and call "into question the inherently indoctrinative function of schooling." "Common Schools, Uncommon Values: Listening to the Voices of Dissent," 14 *Yale L. & Pol'y Rev.* 169, 170–71 (1996). *See also id.* at 184–85, describing and citing to various positions, and at 186–90, summarizing Supreme Court cases that support the educational authority of parents. James Bernard Murphy proposes an extremely limited role for public schools in teaching civic virtue and morality in "Good Students and Good Citizens," *N.Y. Times*, September 15, 2002 (op-ed). He argues that schools are "inept instruments for teaching good citizenship" and should concentrate on "intellectual virtues like thoroughness, perseverance and intellectual honesty."

6. McConnell, "Education Disestablishment," note 5 *supra*, at 87–97.

7. Thus, the regime he proposes differs in a crucial respect from the regime of disestablishment of religion. His acceptance of government-run schools is more than a concession to political reality. *Id.* at 135 n. 3.

8. McConnell assumes that private schools will educate for civic virtue in their own ways, and will actually do a better job than is done by public schools now. *Id.* at 120–28. If private schools are doing substantial education for civic virtue, one could hardly expect public schools to disregard that objective. *But see* the view of James Bernard Murphy, summarized in note 5 *supra*.

9. It is countered that the demand of neutrality concerns only government coercion, not instruction and encouragement. *See* Peter de Marneffe, "Liberalism, Neutrality, and Education," in Macedo and Tamir, *Moral and Political Education*, note 5 *supra*, at 221–24.

10. Salomone, "Common Schools, Uncommon Values," note 5 *supra*, at 225, offers a listing of common values including "character traits such as honesty, integrity, responsibility, delayed gratification, hard work, respect for authority."

11. Reviewing a debate between Amy Gutmann, who supports a robust civic education in public schools, and Stephen Gilles, who is taken as an example of a "civic minimalist," Christopher Eisgruber sees little to differentiate the kind of "deliberation" each believes teachers should encourage students to engage in. Christopher Eisgruber, "How Do Liberal Democracies Teach Values?" in Macedo and Tamir, *Moral and Political Education*, note 5 *supra*, at 74. Eisgruber concludes that the difference is not about kinds of deliberation but degrees of proficiency; "it is not the product of sharply differing moral perspectives about whether the state may teach values or whether it may instead teach only intellectual skills." *Id.* In a similar vein, Gutmann has said that "most (if not all) of the same skills that are necessary and sufficient for educating children for citizenship in a liberal democracy are those that are necessary and sufficient for educating children to deliberate about their way of life, more generally (and less politically) speaking." Amy Gutmann, in "Civic Education and Social Diversity," 105 *Ethics* 573 (April 1995). *See also* Eisgruber's quote of Eamonn Callan, *supra*, at 197.

12. Humphrey Taylor, "The Religious and Other Beliefs of Americans 2003," #11 The Harris Poll, February 26, 2003, *available at* http://www.harrisinteractive.com/harris_poll/index.asp?PID=359.

13. "Faith-Based Funding Backed, but Church-State Doubts Abound," Pew Research Center for the People & the Press, April 10, 2001, available at http://people-press.org/reports/display.php3?ReportID=15.

14. *Id.*

15. *See generally* Warren A. Nord, *Religion and American Education* (Chapel Hill: Univ. of North Carolina Pr., 1995); Warren A. Nord and Charles C. Haynes, *Taking Religion Seriously across the Curriculum* (Alexandria, Va.: ASCD; Association for Supervision and Curriculum Development; Nashville: First Amendment Center, 1998).

16. I say "in theory" because it may be that such a detached approach really is impossible.

17. Stephen Macedo, *Diversity and Distrust*, note 3 *supra*, at 121–22, urges that "maintaining an educational establishment that teaches children that important political issues can be deliberated without considering religious questions is itself part of the education for liberal democratic citizenship properly understood."

18. My opinions on that subject are in *Private Consciences and Public Reasons* (New York: Oxford Univ. Pr., 1995) and *Religious Convictions and Political Choice* (New York: Oxford Univ. Pr., 1988).

19. In theory, perhaps, one can discuss the issue of political philosophy without attending to particular religious views; in practice, the two are very hard to separate.

20. This is a point repeatedly emphasized by Nord, *Religion and American Education*, and Nord and Haynes, *Taking Religion Seriously*, note 15 *supra*.

21. Perhaps in a constitutional regime in which the government may not prefer one religion over another, it *may* either decide on a religion-blind basis or attempt to spread negative effects as equally as possible. If the government, when it builds roads, should take into account what the effects will be on neighborhoods and cultural institutions, it presumably should consider whether a proposed route will destroy religious sanctuaries, which can be important parts of lives of communities, but it *might* treat sanctuaries equally, regardless of particular affiliations. That approach would be "blind" about effects on particular groups.

22. *See generally* Sophie C. van Bijsterveld, "Church and State in Western Europe and the United States: Principles and Perspectives," 3 *Brigham Young Univ. L. Rev.* 989–95 (2000).

23. *See* Macedo, *Diversity and Distrust*, note 3 *supra*.

24. He says, "Some communities are outside the mainstream because of their resistance to basic civic values." *Id.* at 110. Clearly he thinks it desirable that these communities lose adherents or become transformed, but much of what he says goes further. In a paragraph that focuses on religious nonestablishment, he writes that "we must maintain political institutions and practices that work to transform the whole of the moral world in the image of our most basic political values." *Id.* at 151. Elsewhere, he worries that those who argue for greater "fairness" toward religious people in our public life "might cripple the subtle and indirect means of turning religious and other systems of private belief in directions that support the regime." *Id.* at 137–38. Even among groups that do not "resist" basic civic values, some will have beliefs, ways of thought, and organizational practices that are more

conducive to healthy political life than will others; and I take Macedo to consider any indirect, unintended favoring of those groups as a good thing.

Macedo attributes the transformation of the Roman Catholic Church toward religious liberty and liberal democracy in part to the influence of American political culture, and he regards that transformation as having been highly desirable. *Id.* at 132–33.

25. John Tomasi, "Civic Education and Ethical Subservience: From *Mozert* and *Santa Fe* and Beyond," in Macedo and Tamir, *Moral and Political Education*, note 5 *supra*, at 193–220.

26. *Id.* at 193.

27. These "cultural spillovers," largely the consequence of liberal programs of civic education, may *alienate* some citizens, disaffecting them and threatening the breadth of consent to the political order, and may *colonize* other citizens, weakening the freedom of their assent. *Id.* at 194–95, 198.

28. *Id.* at 195.

29. *Id.* at 198.

30. *Id.* "[C]ivic education, for political liberals, must address issues that lie deep in the moral worlds of individual citizens." *Id.* at 200. Some religious perspectives are directly at odds with core notions of civic virtue. The Amish do not believe in participating in politics. No full reconciliation of their religious perspectives to broad notions of civic virtue is possible. For the Amish, countering spillover effects cannot amount to reconciling explanations; the issues must be whether to make concessions to their nonpublic convictions out of respect for their intrinsic importance and whether to achieve the degree of political acceptance that is possible for the Amish.

31. *Id.* at 210.

32. Tomasi puts forward his thesis as covering moral perspectives in general, including religious ones, but we may usefully distinguish spillover effects in respect to religious belief, practice, and affiliation from effects on other moral perspectives. Even if we found Tomasi's legitimacy claims, note 27 *supra*, to be less than persuasive in their general form, demanding too pure an assent to the political order, we can recognize that neutrality *as to religion*, in some sense, is a well-established aspect of our liberal democratic order.

33. *Id.* at 206–13. A question for some chapters of this book is whether a particular practice can reasonably be justified as countering negative spillover effects—and I will return to comments Tomasi makes about practical issues in those contexts.

34. In 1989, the Ayatollah Khomeini issued a fatwa calling for the death of Salman Rushdie for his satirical novel *The Satanic Verses*. For

his reaction, see Salman Rushdie, *Step across This Line: Collected Nonfiction, 1992–2002* (New York: Random House, 2002). More recently, the governor of a Nigerian state issued a similar fatwa (later rescinded) against a journalist for her suggestion that Mohammed might have chosen a wife among the contestants in a Miss World pageant. *See* Katha Pollit, "As Miss World Turns," *The Nation*, December 22, 2002, 9.

35. We can imagine an attempt at a fuller accommodation of the two approaches. In general, educators would regret negative spillover effects; their failure to fulfill a neutral approach as fully as would be ideal would constitute a reason to counter them. On the other hand, spillover effects that promote civic virtue would be welcomed as positively valuable. When spillovers negatively affect particular religions *and* promote civic virtue, educators would first examine whether the effects could be countered without sacrificing the benefits for civic virtue. If not, they would have to decide whether the negative effects on religion or the positive benefits for civic virtue were more important in context. That judgment would dictate whether they would try to counter the negative effects or let them be.

Although this approach is theoretically coherent, it introduces unacceptable difficulties. Public officials responsible for education would have to assess whether negative effects on particular religions are desirable from a civic point of view, and whether they are desirable enough to outweigh a loss from the objective of neutrality. This creates too much risk of bias and misjudgment in evaluations of particular religions; such evaluations themselves violate the principle of neutrality.

36. This is the sort of reconciling effort that Tomasi mainly suggests; if effective, it would tend to enhance benefits to civic virtue, because students would see how democratic values can fit with their own religions.

37. Gutmann, *Democratic Education*, note 2 *supra*, at 22–41.

38. *Id.* at 41–47, 71–126.

39. *Id.* at 108.

40. The parental approach need not assert that children are completely within the control of parents. (No one believes that the state should fail to step in and prevent grosser forms of parental abuse.) But it assigns authority to sane parents who are acting conscientiously in what they perceive to be their children's interests and are not exposing their children to serious physical or mental harm (as by refusing a needed blood transfusion); parental judgments should then prevail over those of political authorities.

41. If families were once regarded as prepolitical units, with parents (or fathers, in our paternalistic past) enjoying substantial authority against society as a whole, that is no longer the view.

42. Salomone, "Common Schools, Uncommon Values," note 5 *supra*, at 178, 224–29, focuses attention on the respective authority of the state and local communities.

43. In some instances, judges ask what questions juries can decide.

44. Eisgruber, "Liberal Democracies Teach Values," note 11 *supra*, argues this point forcefully.

CHAPTER 3. DEVOTIONAL PRACTICES: PRAYER AND BIBLE READING

1. Engel v. Vitale, 370 U.S. 421, 422 (1962).

2. Abington Township v. Schempp, 374 U.S. 203 (1963). In the Abington, Pennsylvania, high school, this was done by a broadcast over the loudspeaker to the entire school of a child's reading passages she chose from the version of the Bible she preferred. The 1905 Baltimore rule required Bible reading or recitation of the Lord's Prayer, or both; the practice was to read the Bible.

3. Justices Frankfurter and White did not participate in *Engel*.

4. Marjorie Silver, "Rethinking Religion and Public School Education," 15 *Quinnipiac L. Rev.* 213, 215 (1995).

5. *See id.* at 216–17. An amendment proposed by Representative Ernest Istook, H.J. Res. 81, referred to the House Subcommittee on the Constitution, January 14, 2002, provided that "the people's right to pray and to recognize their religious beliefs, heritage, and traditions on public property, including schools, shall not be infringed." For an account of the defeat of a much earlier proposal, *see* Karl E. Campbell, "Senator Sam Ervin and School Prayer: Faith, Politics, and the Constitution," 45 *J. Church and State* 443 (2003).

6. Everson v. Board of Education, 330 U.S. 1.

7. Exactly what aids to religion amounted to an establishment of one or more religions is debatable, but Leonard Levy, *The Establishment Clause: Religion and the First Amendment* 76 (New York: Macmillan, 1986), puts the number of states with establishments when the Bill of Rights was ratified at seven—exactly half the states in existence, Vermont having joined the original thirteen.

8. *See, e.g.,* Steven D. Smith, *Foreordained Failure: The Quest for a Constitutional Principle of Religious Freedom* 17–18 (New York, Oxford Univ. Pr., 1995).

9. The most extensive discussion in a Supreme Court opinion is in Justice Brennan's concurring opinion in *Schempp*, 374 U.S. at 254–58.

10. *Everson,* 330 U.S. at 16.

11. *Id.*

12. Zorach v. Clauson, 343 U.S. 306 (1952).

13. *Engel,* 429, 431.

14. *Id.* at 425.

15. *Schempp*, 374 U.S. at 223.

16. *Id.* at 222.

17. *Id.* He explained that an Establishment Clause violation, unlike a free exercise violation, need not be predicated on coercion. *Id.* at 223.

18. *Id.* at 222.

19. *Id.* at 225.

20. *Id.* quoting 330 U.S. at 23–24. In the other *Everson* dissent, Justice Rutledge had written that our "constitutional policy" denies that the state can undertake "religious training, teaching, or observance" in "any form or degree." *Id.* at 218, quoting 330 U.S. at 52.

21. Jackson himself raised a doubt about its realism.

22. *Schempp*, 374 U.S. at 231. Countering the argument that religious exercises to start the school day may serve the secular purposes of fostering harmony, tolerance, and discipline, Brennan wrote that religious means could not be used to achieve secular ends when nonreligious means will suffice. *Id.* at 280–81. Brennan was unwilling to give great weight to the historical pedigree of the practices; what mattered was whether the practices were at odds with the broad purposes underlying the religion clauses. *Id.* at 236, 241.

23. *Id.* at 242. Reviewing the history of Bible reading in schools, Brennan suggested that statutory requirements to this effect are relatively recent. *Id.* at 269. (Of course, education would have been regarded as mainly a local function.) He also discussed a few state cases that had struck down required devotional exercises under state constitutional provisions. *Id.* at 275–77. In the majority of state cases, Bible reading had been sustained. *See* Donald E. Boles, *The Bible, Religion, and the Public Schools* 58–59 (Ames: Iowa State Univ. Pr., 1961), indicating that Bible reading had increased steadily since the beginning of the twentieth century, and that thirteen of the twenty-one highest state courts facing the issue (including cases in the nineteenth century) had ruled favorably. Joseph W. Harrison, "The Bible, the Constitution, and Public Education," 29 *Tenn. L. Rev.* 363, 381–85 (1962); David Fellman, "Separation of Church and State in the United States: A Summary View," 1950 *Wis. L. Rev.* 427, 450–52; "Note, Bible Reading in Public Schools," 9 *Vand. L. Rev.* 849, 854–59 (1956); "Note, Nineteenth Century Judicial Thought Concerning Church-State Relations," 40 *Minn. L. Rev.* 672, 675–78 (1956); Robert E. Cushman, "The Holy Bible and the Public Schools," 40 *Cornell L.Q.* 475, 477 (1955).

24. *Engel*, 370 U.S. at 444; *Schempp*, 374 U.S. at 308.

25. *Engel*, 370 U.S. at 445. He relied heavily on the history of our traditions, in which countless similar practices involving official occasions were deemed acceptable. *Id.* at 446–50.

26. *Schempp*, 374 U.S. at 313.

27. *Id.* at 312.

28. *Id.* at 316–18. The state must not coerce those who do not wish to participate.

29. *See* Michael J. Klarman, "Rethinking the Civil Rights and Civil Liberties Revolutions," 82 *Va. L. Rev.* 1, 15 (1996) (indicating that polls showed that 60 to 80 percent favored prayer and Bible reading in schools).

30. For arguments that the original intent was only to forbid preferential aid, see Wallace v. Jaffree, 472 U.S. 38, 91–114 (1988) (Rehnquist, J., dissenting); Robert Cord, *Separation of Church and State: Historical Fact and Current Fiction* (Grand Rapids, Mich.: Baker Book House, 1982); Michael J. Malbin, *Religion and Politics: The Intentions of the Authors of the First Amendment* (Washington, D.C.: American Enterprise Institute, 1978). The Court's position is defended in Douglas Laycock, "The Origins of the Religion Clauses of the Constitution: Nonpreferential Aid to Religion: A False Claim about Original Intent," 27 *Wm. & Mary L. Rev.* 875 (1986).

31. *See* E. R. Norman, *The Conscience of the State in North America* 4 (Cambridge: Cambridge Univ. Pr., 1968); John F. Wilson, *Public Religion in American Culture* 7–9 (Philadelphia: Temple Univ. Pr., 1979); John Witte Jr., *Religion and the American Constitutional Experiment: Essential Rights and Liberties* 97–100 (Boulder, Colo.: Westview, 2000). In Wallace v. Jaffree, 472 U.S. 38, 104–14 (1985), Justice Rehnquist in dissent appears to accept Joseph Story's assertion that the religion clauses were not meant to preclude favoritism for Christianity, but Rehnquist does not defend that as a principle for modern law.

32. Pub. L. No. 89–239, 79 Stat. 911, codified in scattered sections of 8 U.S.C. 1101–1351 (1995); *see* Hiroshi Motomura, "Law and Equality: Whose Alien Nation?; Two Models of Constitutional Immigration Law," 94 *Mich. L. Rev.* 1927, 1932 (1996).

33. The crucial issue is significantly different for students who believe (or whose parents believe) they must pray orally at particular times in the day. Devout Muslims, for example, believe they should pray five times a day; *see* John Alden Williams, ed., *The Word of Islam* 71–72 (Austin: Univ. of Texas Pr., 1994), including one or two times when students will be in school. Such beliefs are not a basis for the schools themselves to undertake prayers, but they are a basis to excuse these students briefly from ordinary school activities. *See* Samina Quddos, "Accommodating Religion in Public Schools: Must, May, or Never?" 6 *J. Islamic L. & Culture*, 67, 93–94 (2001); Anjali Sakaria, "Note, Worshipping Substantive Equality over Formal Neutrality: Applying the Endorsement Test to Sect-Specific Legislative Accommodations,"

37 *Harv. C.R.-C.L. L. Rev.* 483 (2002). *See also* "Schools to Allow Ramadan Prayer," *N.Y. Times*, November 17, 2001, D2, col. 6 (Muslim students in New York City public schools permitted to withdraw from class to pray during Ramadan). Whether the matter is regarded as within the discretion of school authorities, or controlled by a broad statutory or state constitutional standard (a problem discussed in more depth in chapters 13 and 14), students should be excused to pray, unless doing so is seriously disruptive of their education or that of classmates. Quddos, *supra*, uses the hypothetical of a Muslim high school student who wants to be allowed to leave school for one and a half hours every Friday to go to Jum'ah congregational prayers that men are required to attend. In many schools, excusing a small percentage of students for such a long period every Friday could create a substantial educational burden. *See* Commonwealth v. Bey, 70 A.2d 693 (Pa. Super. 1950).Quddos relies partly on *Zorach* to conclude that an accommodation to the student may be required and is certainly permitted; but in that case most students took advantage of "released time," so that teachers did not present new material in that period.

Because any disruption will be minimized if students excused to pray stay within the school building, allowing them to pray in an empty schoolroom should not be regarded as an advancement or endorsement of their religious views. When New York City Schools chancellor Harold O. Levy directed schools to accommodate individual students wishing to pray during the holy month of Ramadan, he directed that schools not set aside rooms for prayer, perhaps in response to a communication from the Catholic League asking parity for Christians and Jews. *See* "Chancellor's Statement on the Religious Accommodation of Students," November 15, 2001, available at http://www.nycenet.edu/press/01-02/n6902.htm (accessed June 22, 2003); *see also* Press Releases, Catholic League (Nov. 15–16, 2001), available at http://www.catholicleague.org/01press_releases/pr0401/htm (accessed June 20, 2003). Whatever may have been the politics of the situation, Christians and Jews ordinarily do not believe they have a religious requirement to pray orally during the school day. Making a room available for members of religion who believe they have such an obligation would not reflect any absence of parity.

On the related topic of students who wanted more than the prescribed maximum number of religious holidays, *see* Church of God v. Amarillo Independent School Dist., 511 F. Supp. 613 (N.D. Tex. 1981), aff'd, 670 F.2d 46 (5th Cir. 1982) (per curiam).

34. So-called originalists (because they rely on original intent) are divided among those who think what is crucial is the understanding of

the enactors of a provision and those who think the sense of the people to whom a provision applies is what counts.

35. My own thoughts on this topic are summarized in Greenawalt, "Constitutional and Statutory Interpretation," in Jules Coleman and Scott Shapiro, eds., *The Oxford Handbook of Jurisprudence and Philosophy of Law* 268–310 (New York: Oxford Univ. Pr., 2002).

36. Philip Hamburger, in *Separation of Church and State* (Cambridge: Harvard Univ. Pr., 2002), has suggested that the original notion of "disestablishment" was stretched to an idea of "separation" that lacks constitutional warrant. I do not think the governing metaphor matters for prayer and Bible reading. Other reflections on Hamburger's thesis are in Kent Greenawalt, "History as Ideology: Philip Hamburger's Separation of Church and State," to be published in the *California Law Review*.

37. *See* note 35, *supra*.

38. For an explanation in terms of the alignment of political forces for why the Court has become more permissive about aid to parochial education but not about religion in public school education, *see* John C. Jeffries, Jr. and James E. Ryan, "A Political History of the Establishment Clause," 100 *Mich. L. Rev.* 279, 303 (2001).

39. Lee v. Weisman, 505 U.S. 577.

40. *Id.* at 631.

41. *Id.* at 602–4 (Blackman, J., concurring); 609, 618–19, 623 (Souter, J., concurring).

42. *See* County of Allegheny v. American Civil Liberties Union, 492 U.S. 573, 655–56 (1989) (concurring in part and dissenting in part).

43. *Lee*, 505 U.S. at 586, 595.

44. *Id.* at 593.

45. *Id.* at 637–38.

46. *Id.* at 629.

47. *Id.*

48. *Id.* at 630.

49. Of course, some parents and students who agree with the content of graduation prayers are indifferent about whether they are offered, and some who do not agree with the content will not mind their being said.

50. Santa Fe Independent School District v. Doe, 530 U.S. 290 (2000).

51. *Id.* at 312.

52. *Id.* at 308.

53. Chief Justice Rehnquist and Justices Scalia and Thomas are firmly committed to a much more permissive reading of the Establishment Clause in this respect. Two more justices with their views could turn the constitutional law on school prayer upside down.

54. *See generally* Alan E. Brownstein, "Prayer and Religious Expression at High School Graduations: Constitutional Etiquette in a Pluralist Society," 5 *Nexus* 61 (Fall 2000).

55. *See* ACLU of New Jersey v. Black Horse Pike Regional Bd. of Educ., 84 F.3d 1471 (3d Cir.) (en banc); Hans v. Joint School Dist. No. 241, 41 F.3d 44 (9th Cir. 1994), vacated as moot, 515 U.S. 1154 (1995); Deveney v. Board of Education, 231 F. Supp. 2d 483 (S.D. W.Va. 2002).

56. However, many students and other members of the audience may not understand just how much review school officials have undertaken.

57. Of course, if a speaker spontaneously invites prayer on an isolated occasion, courts are unlikely ever to pass what he has done.

58. *See* Gearon v. Loudoun County School Bd., 844 F. Supp. 1097 (E.D. Va. 1993). *But see* Doe v. Madison School Dist., 7 Supp. 2d 1110 (D. Idaho 1997), vacated as moot, 177 F.3d 789 (9th Cir. 1999).

59. In *Lee*, 505 U.S. at 630 n. 8, Justice Souter, concurring, wrote, "If the state had chosen its graduation day speakers according to wholly secular criteria, and if one of those speakers (not a state actor) had individually chosen to deliver a religious message, it would have been harder to attribute an endorsement of religion to the state."

60. Alan Brownstein, "Prayer and Religious Expression," note 54 *supra*, at 77 writes, "Each of the graduates and their families deserve to hear remarks that are respectful to them and appropriate to the occasion." I agree with Brownstein that a speech advocating commitment to a particular faith is inappropriate; but audiences tolerate political messages that many of them reject, and a comment that a spiritual dimension enhances life seemed proper to me the one time I spoke at a (nonpublic) school graduation.

61. *See* Adler v. Duval County School Board, 206 F.3d 1070 (11th Cir. 2000). However, officials *may* exercise more control over content if the speaker is a student, and the school's supervision is seen as part of the educational enterprise. In Cole v. Oroville Union High School, 228 F.3d 1092 (9th Cir. 2000), the court said that officials could properly prohibit sectarian content in valedictory graduation addresses. In Lassonde v. Pleasanton Unified Sch. Dist., 320 F.3d 979 (9th Cir. 2003), the court sustained a principal's insistence that a student speaker (though he could refer to his religious faith) not proselytize in his graduation speech; such supervision was necessary to avoid apparent sponsorship and undue coercion.

62. It is hard to imagine any such objective criterion for someone who is neither a student nor a school official, such as the principal.

63. It is a common form of speech to say, "I pray that . . ." That is not to offer a prayer in the usual sense.

64. Chandler v. Siegelman, 230 F.3d 1313 (2000).

65. U.S. Department of Education, *Guidance on Constitutionally Protected Prayer in Elementary and Secondary Schools* (Feb. 7, 2003), available at http://ed.gov/policy/gen/guid/religionandschools/prayer_guidance .html (accessed Feb. 10, 2003).

66. *Id.,* "Student Assemblies and Extracurricular Events."

67. *See Lassonde,* 320 F.3d 979.

68. Stone v. Graham, 449 U.S. 39.

69. In those days, the Edgemont school ended after tenth grade, and all grades were in the same building. Within a few years of my graduation, the district built a high school, and elementary grades are now distributed among a number of schools.

70. However, in my school, all members of the tenth-grade music class were expected to participate.

71. *See* John M. Hartenstein, "Comment, A Christmas Issue: Christian Holiday Celebration in the Public Elementary Schools Is an Establishment of Religion," 80 *Cal. L. Rev.* 981 (1992).

72. Skarin v. Woodbine Community School Dist., 204 F. Supp. 2d 1195 (S.D. Ia. 2002). *See also* Doe v. Aldine Independent School Dist., 563 F. Supp. 883 (S.D. Tex. 1982) (holding invalid recitation and singing of a school prayer).

73. *See* Doe v. Duncanville Independent School Dist., 70 F.3d 402, 407 (5th Cir. 1995).

74. There are a few nonreligious "carols," such as "Jingle Bells" and "White Christmas."

75. Faith D. Kasparain, "Note, The Constitutionality of Teaching and Performing Sacred Choral Music in Public Schools," 46 *Duke L.J.* 1111, 1117 (1997). Interestingly, in communities in which almost everyone is a practicing Christian, it is hard to think of carol singing as performing an educational function.

76. Communion is *the* central event in Roman Catholic worship, and it is a vital element of Anglican and Episcopalian services. Many Protestant groups do not include Communion as an aspect of most Sunday services, but Communion remains a profound religious moment for Protestants.

77. *See* Brian A. Whitaker, "Note & Comment, Religious Music in the Public Schools: A Guide for School Districts," 2003 *B.Y.U. Educ. & L.J.* 339, 356–57. Whitaker summarizes policies of four school districts that are more restrictive in various respects, *id.,* at 353–56; he also proposes his own model policy, *id.* at 358–61.

78. Much popular religious music refers to God but is not specifically Christian.

79. *Doe,* 70 F.3d 402.

80. *Id.* at 411 n. 1 (Mahon, D. J., dissenting in part). According to the case report, the song, in this version, omits the "up" that follows "lift" in the biblical text.

81. Bauchman v. West High School, 132 F.3d 542 (1997). The opinion of the district court, 900 F. Supp. 254, 260 (D. U. 1995), leaves it unclear whether the entire choir participated as a group in Christian worship services.

82. Florey v. Sioux Falls School Dist., 619 F.2d 1311 (8th Cir. 1980), cert. denied, 449 U.S. 987 (1980).

83. *Id.* at 1316–17 n. 5.

84. Non-Christians may "learn" more from singing carols than Christians, but many non-Christians will feel uncomfortable singing songs that so explicitly acknowledge Jesus as "Christ the Lord," at one of the two times of year (Easter is the other) when most of their fellow citizens specially celebrate that claim.

85. However, any teacher must take care to avoid that some children receive many cards and others none.

86. They do differ from Valentine's Day cards in being strongly associated with a holiday that remains powerfully Christian.

87. Episcopalians and Lutherans adopt intermediate positions between "symbolic" and transubstantiation; the former refer to the "real presence," the latter "consubstantiation." Eastern Orthodox Christians, with Catholics, believe in transubstantiation.

88. I say "avoidable harm" because, as chapter 5 explains, some school teaching inevitably gives a negative impression of some religions. Schools can do without simulated devotional exercises.

89. *See, e.g.,* Clever v. Cherry Hill Township Bd. of Educ., 838 F. Supp. 929 (D.N.J. 1993).

90. For an argument that Christmas celebrations impose unconstitutionally on religious minorities, *see* Hartenstein, "A Christmas Issue," note 71 *supra*.

91. Elk Grove Unified Sch. Dist. v. Newdow, 124 S. Ct. 2301 (2004).

92. The right of students not to be compelled to take the pledge had been established in West Virginia Board of Education v. Barnette, 319 U.S. 624 (1943).

93. Newdow v. U.S. Congress, 292 F.3d 597 (9th Cir. 2002).

94. One report of the oral argument before the Supreme Court is Linda Greenhouse, "Atheist Presents Case for Taking God From Pledge," *N.Y. Times*, March 25, 2004, p. A1, col. 1. Excerpts from the argument itself are on *id.* at p. A22, col. 1.

95. *Newdow*, 124 S. Ct. at 2321–27.

96. Another suggestion has been that giving students an option to say the pledge with or without the "under God" language would not

meet constitutional objections. *See* Robert Stern, "Princeton Prof Offers Pledge Compromise," *The Times* (Princeton Metro), March 27, 2004, p. A1, col. 1.

97. See John Tomasi's ambivalent comments about the Santa Fe case, in "Civic Education and Ethical Subservience: From *Mozert* and *Santa Fe* and Beyond, in Stephen Macedo and Yael Tamir, eds., *Moral and Political Education* 213–15 (New York: New York Univ. Pr., 2002).

Chapter 4. Moments of Silence

1. In Wallace v. Jaffree, 472 U.S. 38, 70–71 (1985), Justice O'Connor, concurring, cited twenty-five state laws that permit or require moments of silence. Apparently thirty-two states now have such statutes. *See* Derek H. Davis, "Editorial: Moments of Silence in America's Public Schools: Constitutional and Ethical Considerations," 45 *J. Church and State* 429, 432 (2003). *See also* Debbie Kaminer, "Barring Organized Prayer through the Back Door: How Moment-of-Silence Legislation for Public Schools Violates the Establishment Clause," 13 *Stan. L. & Pol'y Rev.* 267, 268 (2002) (at least twenty-nine states have moment-of-silence legislation).

2. However, Davis, "Moments of Silence," at 440, comments that moments of silence "often carry little meaning for some religious traditions," and he summarizes forms of Muslim prayer.

3. I attended Swarthmore College, a private college founded by the Society of Friends. Assemblies began with a moment of silence. In that context, one could speak of a moment of silence showing respect for and reflecting the value of Quaker traditions and practices.

4. This is not true if the moment of silence is set aside for a specific mental exercise that is not prayer—a coach might tell her team to reflect silently for a moment on how they plan to defend their opponents.

5. Marjorie Silver, "Rethinking Religion and Public School Education," 15 *Quinnipiac L. Rev.* 213, 225–26 (1995), recounts her experience during moments of silence at the Meeting House of a Quaker school her children attended. She felt "individual peace and community harmony." *Id.* at 226. Silver remarks that the virtue of the moment of silence "is that there is no orthodoxy on how it will be used." *Id.* But whether anyone would actually say so now, I think there is a tradition according to which some uses are misuses.

6. That is, I believe such a moment of silence is proper in light of the values of disestablishment. However, concerns that such a mandatory "moment" may trivialize prayer or disturb non-Christian minorities are reasons for states and localities not to initiate moments of silence. *See* Douglas Laycock, "Equal Access and Moments of Silence: The Equal Status of Religious Speech by Private Speakers," 81 *Northwestern*

U. L. Rev. 1 (1986); Davis, "Moments of Silence," note 1 *supra*, at 435–37, 439–41.

7. According to Kaminer, "Barring Organized Prayer," note 1 *supra*, at 304, "[A] ritualized daily school-sponsored moment of silence is itself a very powerful form of government expression, which is clearly understood as a time set aside for voluntary prayer."

8. Wallace v. Jaffree, 472 U.S. 38 (1985).

9. *Id.* at 56–60.

10. *Id.* at 60.

11. *Id.* at 61.

12. *Id.* at 62 (Powell, J., concurring); *id.* at 70–78 (O'Connor, J., concurring).

13. *Id.* at 78. However, out of twenty-nine statutes, eighteen now do not mention prayer, a contrast with the situation prior to *Wallace v. Jaffree.* Kaminer, "Barring Organized Prayer," note 1 *supra*, at 301.

14. *Wallace*, 472 U.S. at 59. See also Justice Powell's statement (overstatement), *id.* at 62, that the suggestion that some moment-of-silence statutes may be constitutional "is set forth in the Court's opinion as well."

15. In Brown v. Gilmore, 2000 U.S. Dist. LEXIS 21623 (E.D. Va. Oct. 26, 2000), cert. denied, 534 U.S. 996 (2001), the Court declined to review acceptance of a statute specifically including "prayer" as one possible use of silence. For a compilation of cases in lower courts, see "Annotation, Constitutionality of Regulation or Policy Governing Prayer, Meditation, or 'Moment of Silence' in Public Schools," 110 A.L.R. Fed. 211, § 6.

16. *Wallace*, 472 U.S. at 72.

17. *Id.* at 73.

18. *Id.*

19. Three negative views about moments of silence are in David Z. Seide, "Note, Daily Moments of Silence in Public Schools: A Constitutional Analysis," 58 *N.Y.U. L. Rev.* 364, 406 (1983) (stating that they are analytically no different from oral prayers); "Note, The Unconstitutionality of State Statutes Authorizing Moments of Silence in the Public Schools," 96 *Harv. L. Rev.* 1874 (1983); Kaminer, "Barring Organized Prayer," note 1 *supra. See also* Davis, "Moments of Silence," note 1 *supra*, on ethical considerations. Most courts have found secular purposes for moments of silence; "see Annotation," note 15 *supra*.

20. O'Connor remarked that the solution to conflicts between free exercise and nonestablishment is not "neutrality." *Wallace*, 472 U.S. at 83.

21. *Id.* at 68–70, 76. O'Connor also rejected a free exercise accommodation argument in favor of the Alabama law. She wrote that accom-

modation must lift a government-imposed burden on the free exercise of religion, and that protecting silent prayer does not lift any state-imposed burden on religious activity. I believe O'Connor's approach to permissible accommodation is too rigid. It may be appropriate to accommodate a desire for religious observance, even when that accommodation is not in response to an impediment imposed by the government, *if* there is no pressure on minorities or offense to them. Moments of silence qualify in this respect. *See* George W. Dent Jr., "Of God and Caesar: The Free Exercise Rights of Public School Students," 43 *Case Western L. Rev.* 707, 747 (1993), arguing that students have an interest in "associational aspects of free exercise."

22. She seems to assume that endorsement or disapproval will *always* be the issue about aiding or inhibiting religion, apparently disregarding instances in which public officials try secretly to aid one or more religions.

23. *Wallace*, 472 U.S. at 76, 83.

24. O'Connor is explicit that the issue is a mixed question of law and fact in which appellate judges do not give great deference to determinations by trial judges and juries. *Id.*

25. The reason is not *only* that a majority of the Supreme Court *might* use that approach; Justice O'Connor's vote is crucial in many Establishment Clause cases.

26. Perhaps she thought that for most statutes a court could not tell whether legislators were completely indifferent between prayer and other possibilities, but one need not know much about any particular legislature to imagine that a moment of silence is largely designed to allow prayer.

CHAPTER 5. TEACHING RELIGIOUS PROPOSITIONS

1. Teaching that any particular religious ideas are true is one way to prefer that religion over others.

2. Abington Township v. Schempp, 374 U.S. 203, 218.

3. Epperson v. Arkansas, 393 U.S. 97, 103–4 (1968). One may think of Stone v. Graham, 449 U.S. 39 (1980), which held invalid a Kentucky statute that required posting the Ten Commandments in each school classroom, on grounds that the law lacked a secular purpose, as based on a principle that the government cannot implicitly assert the religious truth of the Ten Commandments.

4. *See* Berger v. Rensselaer Cent. School Corp., 982 F.2d 1160 (7th Cir. 1993), cert. denied, 508 U.S. 911 (1993), deciding that a school cannot allow the Gideons to distribute Bibles in public schools during school hours.

5. In her concurring opinion in Wallace v. Jaffree, 472 U.S. 38, 68–70, 76 (1985), Justice O'Connor presented her endorsement approach as an interpretation of the purpose and effect aspects of the *Lemon* test. That approach is now usually conceived as an alternative to *Lemon*.

6. *See* Nicholas Wolterstorff, "Neutrality and Impartiality," in Theodore Sizer, ed., *Religion and Public Education* 3–21 (Boston: Houghton Mifflin, 1967). I comment on this problem in more detail in "Religion and the Public School Teacher," in *Religion in the Liberal Polity*, ed. Terence Cuneo (South Bend: University of Notre Dame Press, 2004).

7. At a distant time in the West, theology was regarded as the queen of the sciences, the keystone into which all other knowledge fits. In the late seventeenth and early eighteenth centuries, figures as diverse as Isaac Newton and Jonathan Edwards still understood what we call natural science as clearly connected to religious truth. *See* James Gleick, *Isaac Newton* 8, 148 (New York: Pantheon 2003); George M. Marsden, *Jonathan Edwards: A Life* 64–81 (New Haven: Yale Univ. Pr. 2003).

8. One might say that religion per se is healthy or good for people, but even that would be odd, given the diverse practices in which religious people have engaged throughout history. To take one extreme example, in devotion to the dual-natured Hindu goddess Kali, a group of marauding Thugees in nineteenth-century India emphasized her dark side and strangled strangers from behind in sacrifice to her.

9. It is theoretically possible for some claims about life after death to be based on scientific studies or personal observations, such as the "white light" recollections of people who have been resuscitated, or communications during seances or psychic readings from those who have "crossed over." I would not count these claims as religious.

CHAPTER 6. EQUAL FACILITIES

1. Widmar v. Vincent, 454 U.S. 263.

2. *Id.* at 265.

3. Against Justice White's argument in dissent that religious worship differs distinctly from other speech acts, *id.* at 282–87, Justice Powell answered that the distinction may have no intelligible content, would be impossible for courts to administer, and is not relevant. *Id.* at 270 n. 6.

4. *Id.* at 271–72.

5. *Id.* at 273–75. Rather, any benefit to Cornerstone is only "incidental"—and therefore permissible.

6. The Court also rejected an argument that Missouri could employ its policy to satisfy the state constitution's antiestablishment provisions. *Id.* at 275–76.

7. 20 U.S.C. § 4071–74.

8. Westside Community Board of Education v. Mergens, 496 U.S. 226 (1990). The Court did not need to decide whether the school's policy directly violated the Constitution.

9. According to Justice O'Connor, for the majority, a school creates a limited open forum under the statute when it allows "noncurriculum related student groups" to meet on school premises. *Id.* at 235.

10. Justice O'Connor said that a curriculum-related student group had to have more than a tangential relation to school courses. In this sense, the chess club and community service club were "noncurriculum related." In dissent, Justice Stevens, *id.* at 276, argued for a narrower sense of noncurriculum-related groups that covered only advocacy of partisan theological, political, or ethical views.

11. *Id.* at 247–50. In this part of her opinion, Justice O'Connor wrote only for herself and three other Justices. Justice Kennedy, joined by Justice Scalia, rejected an endorsement approach in favor of one that focuses on coercion.

An issue of sponsorship arose when someone challenged the creation of a gospel choir run by a school secretary. The court said the school should not have allowed the choir, since her leadership violated a specific provision of the Equal Access Act. Sease v. School District of Philadelphia, 811 F. Supp. 183 (E.D. Pa. 1993).

12. Justice Stevens dissented on the statutory issue. *See* note 10 *supra.*

13. *Widmar*, 454 U.S. at 265–70 (Marshall, J., concurring in the judgment).

14. Hsu v. Roslyn Union Free School Dist., No. 3, 85 F.3d 839 (2nd Cir. 1996). One federal court of appeals held that a school must make facilities available at lunchtime for religious groups if it does so for other groups, Ceniceros v. Board of Trustees, 106 F. 3d 878 (9th Cir. 1997).

15. The Equal Access Act has proved something of a two-edged sword for some conservative Christians. They have used it to establish school groups, but have been dismayed to find gay and lesbian organizations relying on the law to establish their right to use school facilities. *See* Michael Winerip, "Tolerance and Hypocrisy on Gay-Straight Club," *N.Y. Times*, January 29, 2003, B10, col. 5; David R. Parkinson, "H. Utah Senate Bill 1003: Prohibiting Specified School Clubs," 23 *J. Contemp. L.* 268 (1997).

16. Good News Club v. Milford Central School, 533 U.S. 98 (2001). Previously one federal court of appeals held that a school must make facilities available at lunchtime for religious groups if it does so for other groups. *Ceniceros*, 106 F.3d 878.

17. *Good News Club*, 533 U.S. at 103.

18. *Id.*

19. *Id.* at 106–10.

20. *Id.* at 2112–17. Courts have held, however, that schools can restrict advertising for proselytizing activities, Rusk v. Crestview Local Schools, 220 F. Supp. 2d 854 (N.D. Ohio 2002), and the distribution of religious gifts, Walz v. Egg Harbor Twp. Bd. of Educ., 187 F. Supp. 2d 232 (D.N.J. 2002).

21. *Good News Club*, 533 U.S. at 118.

22. *Id.* at 115.

23. *Id.* at 130.

24. *Id.* at 138.

25. On worship services and other religious meetings, see Campbell v. St. Tammany Sch. Bd., 206 F.3d 482 (5th Cir. 2000), vacated and remanded, 533 U.S. 913 (2001); Moore v. City of Van, 238 F. Supp.2d 837 (E.D. Tex. 2003).

26. According to this approach, the government may have powerful enough reasons to engage in viewpoint discrimination. Thus, a public school could presumably refuse to permit a club devoted to the peaceful realization of racial apartheid (although citizens at large are free to express that idea). By and large, the courts have failed to recognize that many acceptable criminal prohibitions of expression involve forms of viewpoint discrimination. I may urge a willing listener to treat someone generously but not to kill that person.

27. Lamb's Chapel v. Center Moriches Union Free School District, 508 U.S. 384 (1993).

28. For recent decisions, *see* DeBoer v. Village of Oak Park, 267 F.3d 558 (7th Cir. 2001); Amandola v. Town of Babylon, 251 F.3d 339 (2d Cir. 2001); Culbertson v. Oakridge Sch. Dist. No. 76, 258 F.3d 1061 (9th Cir. 2001); Bronx Household of Faith v. Bd. of Educ. of N.Y., 226 F. Supp. 2d 401 (S.D.N.Y. 2002); Daily v. N.Y. City Housing Authority, 221 F. Supp. 2d 390 (E.D.N.Y. 2002).

The Second Circuit Court of Appeals has held that school officials cannot condition approval of an antiabortion protest on its being cast in nonreligious terms. Orin v. Barclay, 272 F.3d 1207 (9th Cir. 2001). However, when something permanent is being built out of segments made by students or parents, schools have been allowed to foreclose religious messages. Fleming v. Jefferson County School Dist., R-1, 298 F.3d 918 (10th Cir. 2002); Gernetzke v. Kenesher Unified School Dist. No. 1, 274 F.3d 464 (7th Cir. 2001); Anderson v. Mex. Acad. & Cent. Sch., 186 F. Supp. 2 193 (N.D.N.Y. 2002).

29. Rosenberger v. Rector and Visitors of the University of Virginia, 515 U.S. 819 (1995).

30. *Id.* at 830–35.

31. *Id.* at 893–99.

32. *See* Greenawalt, "Viewpoints from Olympus," 96 *Colum. L. Rev.* 697 (1996).

33. *Rosenberger*, 515 U.S. at 868–76.

34. *Id.* at 840–44; *id.* at 849–52 (O'Connor, J., concurring).

35. The possibility has been largely foreclosed by Board of Regents v. Southworth, 529 U.S. 217 (2000).

36. *Rosenberger*, 515 U.S. at 842–44.

37. *Id.* at 847.

38. *Id.*

39. Prince v. Jacoby, 303 F.3d 1074 (9th Cir. 2002).

CHAPTER 7. TEACHING AND RELIGION IN THE PUBLIC SCHOOL

1. I am not here relying mainly on the limited capacity of courts to scrutinize what is *really* happening if a program is presented as satisfying valid educational objectives—the practical freedom teachers have, because few parents will sue over what individual teachers say, and because judges and juries will find it hard to determine just what has transpired in the classroom. The problem is not only replicating the actual words a teacher has used, but capturing the teacher's tone of voice, expressions, and gestures.

2. As Justice Fortas wrote in Epperson v. Arkansas, 393 U.S. 97, 104 (1968), "By and large, public education in our Nation is committed to the control of state and local authorities."

3. Abington Township v. Schempp, 374 U.S. at 225. *See also id.* at 300 (Brennan, J., concurring), and *id.* at 306 (Goldberg, J., concurring).

4. In his concurring opinion, however, Justice Goldberg, *id.*, wrote, "Government must inevitably take cognizance of the existence of religion, and, indeed, under certain circumstances, the First Amendment may require that it do so."

5. Nor should they say what is the correct understanding of a particular religion, when that is debated. *See* Presbyterian Church v. Mary Elizabeth Blue Hull Mem'l Presbyterian Church, 393 U.S. 440 (1969); Kent Greenawalt, "Hands Off! Civil Court Involvement in Conflicts over Religious Property," 98 *Colum. L. Rev.* 1843 (1998).

6. When, if ever, schools should excuse children whose parents have religious objections to appropriate material, or courts should require such exemptions under free exercise guarantees, are topics I reserve for the last part of the book.

7. In his recent article "Preparing for the Clothed Public Square: Teaching about Religion, Civic Education, and the Constitution," 43 *Wm. & Mary L. Rev.* 1159, 1172–91 (2002), Jay Wexler provides a helpful

historical account of developments since the *Schempp* decision in 1963. He concludes that, thanks largely to the efforts of reformers like Charles Haynes, Warren Nord, and Oliver Thomas, "the movement to encourage public schools to teach about religion is at its strongest point in the last forty years." *Id*. at 1191.

8. 330 U.S. 1, 23–24 (1947), quoted in *Schempp*, 374 U.S. at 218. Justice Jackson went on to express some doubt whether such a disjunction was possible or wise.

9. Warren A. Nord, *Religion and American Education* 244 (Chapel Hill: Univ. of North Carolina Pr., 1995).

10. One account of secular humanism as seen by its opponents is in Christopher P. Toumey, *God's Own Scientists* 77–99 (New Brunswick, N.J.: Rutgers Univ. Pr., 1994). He analyzes two styles for expressing its meaning, one in terms of negation of a writer's personal beliefs and the other emphasizing human autonomy.

11. Nord, *Religion and American Education*, note 9 *supra*, at 60–84, and the brief discussion in chapter 1.

12. An exception, a very important exception, in this respect was John Dewey, who did propound a complete worldview that rejected traditional religion. His "civic totalism" is summarized and criticized in Stephen Macedo, *Diversity and Distrust: Civic Education in a Multicultural Democracy* (Cambridge: Harvard University Press, 2000), at 139–47.

13. Nord, *Religion and American Education*, note 9 *supra*, at 160. Nord concludes that "at least in its textbooks and formal curriculum students are indoctrinated into the modern (secular) worldview and against religion." *Id*.

14. Smith v. Board of School Commissioners, 827 F.2d 684 (1987). *See also* Grove v. Mead School Dist. No. 354, 753 F.2d 1528 (9th Cir.) cert. denied, 474 U.S. 826 (1985). The claim had succeeded in the district court in *Smith*, but with a judge, Brevard Hand, who has shown himself to be extremely unsympathetic with the Supreme Court's establishment jurisprudence, refusing at an early stage of the moment-of-silence case, *Wallace v. Jaffree*, to accept the application of the Establishment Clause to the states. Jaffree v. Board of School Commissioners, 554 F. Supp. 1104, 1119 (S.D. Ala. 1983).

15. Smith, F.2d 684 at 689, 690. *See also* William v. Board of Education, 388 F. Supp. 93, 94–95 (S.D. W.Va.), aff'd without opinion, 530 F.2d 972 (4th Cir. 1975).

16. *See* Greenawalt, "Five Questions about Religion Judges Are Afraid to Ask," in Nancy Rosenblum, ed., *The Obligations of Citizenship and Demands of Faith* 196, 206–24 (Princeton: Princeton Univ. Pr., 1999); Greenawalt, "Religion as a Constitutional Concept," 72 *Cal. L. Rev*. 753 (1984). For cases that exemplify an approach very close to the one I en-

dorse, *see* Malnak v. Yogi, 92 F.2d 197, 200 (3d Cir. 1979) (concurring opinion of Adams, J.) (analyzing transcendental meditation taught in public schools); Africa v. Commonwealth, 662 F.2d 1025 (3d Cir. 1981) (rejecting claim by members of MOVE for a special diet in prison), cert. denied, 456 U.S. 908 (1982).

17. *See* Torcaso v. Watkins, 367 U.S. 488, 495 n. 11 (1961), including secular humanism in a list of religions that do not maintain a belief in God, and referring to cases in which people were organized to carry on activities like those in standard religions.

18. I believe that agreement on negative propositions about religion is not sufficient to make a religion if there is no analogy to devotional practices and no organization of like-minded people.

19. In its formulations of the Establishment Clause test of Lemon v. Kurtzman, 403 U.S. 602 (1971), the Supreme Court has treated inhibiting religion as it does promoting religion; and Justice O'Connor's endorsement approach treats disapproval like approval.

20. I explore this issue in "Diverse Perspectives and the Religion Clauses: An Examination of Justifications and Qualifying Beliefs," 74 *Notre Dame L. Rev.* 1433, 1456–73 (1999).

21. This is Nord's ultimate conclusion, *Religion and American Education*, note 9 *supra*, at 190.

22. *See* Winton E. Yerby III, "Toward Religious Neutrality in the Public School Curriculum," 56 *U. Chi. L. Rev.* 899, 933 (1989). One could think that the idea of "choice" leaves open a judgment that one is bound to absolute moral standards set by God, but the texts do not encourage that way of thinking.

23. Sir Walter Hamilton Moberly, *The Crisis in the University* 55–56 (London: SCM Press, 1949).

24. What matters for this answer is not historical causation but present understanding. Thus, Nord's point that the main historical explanation for the secularity of public schools lies in the general secularization of learning rather than in constitutional understandings is hardly relevant.

25. One might defend neglect of religion as promoting civic virtues. As chapter 2 explains, Stephen Macedo does suggest that a negative effect of public education on some religions is actually to be welcomed, *see* Macedo, *Diversity and Distrust*, note 12 *supra*, at 141–42, but he recognizes that many religious perspectives are fully compatible with democratic citizenship. One could not defend a negative effect on all religions as worthwhile because a negative effect on a few religions is wholesome.

26. I say this suggestion is less strong because one might consistently believe that (1) most subjects can be understood with reference

to religion, and that (2) public schools must steer clear of religion, but that (3) any life without religion is impoverished.

27. *See, e.g.,* George M. Marsden, *Jonathan Edwards: A Life,* 150–238 (New Haven: Yale Univ. Pr. 2003).

28. I do not establish priorities among all the legitimate reasons to teach about religion, although resolution of some issues may depend on such judgments. Jay Wexler, "Clothed Public Square," note 7 *supra,* at 1168–71, does undertake to prioritize the reasons, concluding that civic education is the most important one. My own hesitancy is based on the premises that the comparative importance of reasons may differ for different subject matters and that people can often agree more easily on practical action than on abstract priorities.

CHAPTER 8. TEACHING NATURAL SCIENCE I: RELATION BETWEEN
SCIENCE AND RELIGION

1. *See* Heinz Pagels, *The Cosmic Code* 290, 304 (New York: Simon & Schuster, 1982).

2. *See* Warren A. Nord, *Religion and American Education* 164 (Chapel Hill: Univ. of North Carolina Pr., 1995). Various religions may find special significance in certain numbers; but no one contends that these conventions should be taught in mathematics courses.

3. One can engage in modern scientific analysis of nature *and* appreciate nature as part of God's creation, but the scientific view commonly pushes aside the religious one.

4. Jeffrie Murphy, *Evolution, Morality, and the Meaning of Life* 47 (Totowa, N.J.: Rowman and Littlefield, 1982); the primary contribution of *The Origin of Species* was "to organize and synthesize a set of ideas that had pervaded the scientific literature for more than fifty years."

5. Philip Kitcher, *Abusing Science: The Case against Creationism* (Cambridge: MIT Pr., 1982). *See also* Robert T. Pennock, *Tower of Babel* 55 (Cambridge: MIT Pr., 1999).

6. Although Darwin's account covers both plants and animals, I shall largely restrict myself to animals. *See* Dorothy Nelkin, *The Creation Controversy* 26 (New York: W. W. Norton, 1982). Darwin's approach contrasted with the earlier theory of Chevalier de Lamarck, who assumed that animals developed progressively as members of one generation passed on adjustments they had made during their lives. *See* Edward J. Larson, *Summer for the Gods* 14 (Cambridge: Harvard Univ. Pr., 1998).

7. *See* John Horgan, "Life against the Odds, from The Riddle in the Skies: Cosmos, God, and Us," *UNESCO Courier* (May 2001; accessed

Jan. 3, 2002), *at* http://unesco/org/courier/2001_05/uk/doss21.htm, part 2.

8. Kitcher, *Abusing Science*, note 5 *supra*, at 16–21.

9. In a population in which half the people had two blue genes for eye color and half had two brown genes, the number of brown-eyed people would increase with intermarriages, because the brown-eye gene is dominant.

10. Kitcher, *Abusing Science* note 5 *supra*, at 21, 55.

11. *Id.* at 26–27.

12. Some modern evolutionists have offered a punctuated-equilibrium model, according to which evolution is jerky rather than continuous—with periods of stability followed by ones of substantial change. *See* N. Eldredge, *Time Frames: The Rethinking of Darwinian Evolution and the Theory of Punctuated Equilibrium* (New York: Simon & Schuster, 1985); Stephen Jay Gould, "The Meaning of Punctuated Equilibrium, and Its Role in Validating a Hierarchical Approach to Macroevolution," in R. Milkman, ed., *Perspectives on Evolution* 83–104 (Sunderland, Mass.: Sinauer, 1982). Richard Dawkins, in *The Blind Watchmaker* 223–52 (New York: W. W. Norton, 1987), suggests that the difference between a standard neo-Darwinian view and the theory of punctuated equilibrium is slight. *See also* Kenneth R. Miller, *Finding Darwin's God* 111–15 (New York: HarperCollins, 1999). H. Allen Orr describes changes in Stephen Jay Gould's understanding of punctuated equilibrium and notes the theory's decline in the 1990s. "A Critic at Large: The Descent of Gould," *New Yorker*, September 9, 2002, 134–36.

A few theorists claim that not only the timing of evolution but also its mode differs from the gradualist account; major changes may occur from macromutations rather than from a succession of unnoticeable alterations. Kitcher, *Abusing Science*, note 5 *supra*, at 148–49.

13. *See generally* Ernan McMullin, "Plantinga's Defense of Special Creation," in Robert T. Pennock, ed., *Intelligent Design Creationism and Its Critics* 178 (Cambridge: MIT Pr., 2001).

14. In perhaps the best-known, but now controversial, example, the great majority of peppered moths became darker, and thus less conspicuous to predators, where pollution had darkened the trunks of trees. Kitcher, *Abusing Science*, note 5 *supra*, at 25. Critics have disputed the reliability of claims about peppered moths, *see, e.g.,* Jonathan Wells, *Icons of Evolution—Science or Myth? Why Much of What We Teach about Evolution Is Wrong* 137–58 (Washington, D.C.: Regnery, 2000), for a chapter debunking the "myth" of the peppered moth, whose evidentiary role in respect to evolution survives a close examination by Michael E. N. Majerus, *Melanism: Evolution in Action* 97–156 (New York:

Oxford Univ. Pr., 1998). Judith Hooper, *Of Moths and Men: An Evolutionary Tale* (New York: Norton 2002), provides a narrative of events. The principle that natural selection can work changes *within* species is not doubted by most creationists.

15. The precise objections have varied, and their intensity has waxed and waned. *See, e.g.*, Larson, *Summer for the Gods*, note 6 *supra*, at 22–27; Christopher P. Toumey, *God's Own Scientists: Creationists in a Secular World* 31–146 (New Brunswick, N.J.: Rutgers Univ. Pr., 1999).

16. In the passages with which Genesis begins, Genesis 1:1–31, God created plant life on the third day, bird and water life on the fifth day, and land animals and human beings on the sixth day. (Genesis 2:4–24 also contains an account of creation, one that is variously interpreted as a separate creation story or as supplementing the first account.) Many creationists accept the idea that the days of the creation represent ages.

17. John C. Whitcomb Jr. and Henry M. Morris, *The Genesis Flood* (Phillipsburg, N.J.: Presbyterian and Reformed Pub., 1961). *See* Toumey, *God's Own Scientists*, note 15 *supra*, at 31–35.

18. According to one recent summary, "Today most 'scientific' creationists hedge or disavow the claim that dinosaurs and humans coexisted on the Paluxy." Rich Fox, in "Debunking the Paluxy River Claims" (University of South Dakota Department of Anthropology, last modified Apr. 13, 1996; accessed Jan. 8, 2002), presenting a list of references, both creationist and noncreationist, compiled by Paul V. Heinrich, *at* http://www.usd.edu/anth/cultarch/paluxybib.html. Robert Pennock provides a summary of events, *Tower of Babel*, note 5 *supra*, at 216–21, and also rebuts positive creationist evidence based on the scarcity of moon dust and on human population growth, *id.* at 221–26.

19. Access Research Network "FAQ" about intelligent design (2001; accessed Jan. 3, 2002) *at* http://www.arn.org/id_faq.htm. Intelligent-design claims fall within a wider ambit of creationist approaches, but I shall contrast "intelligent design" theory with creationism to avoid any confusion with Genesis creationism.

20. The term *fundamentalist* is drawn from a series of essays published from 1905 to 1915 called "The Fundamentals," which were opposed to modernism in religion. The label *fundamentalist* is itself now somewhat controversial, and critics use it more frequently than do the people whose views fall within the designation. But terms such as *conservative Christian* or *evangelical Christian* are less precise for our purposes, because many people within those designations do not accept biblical literalism.

21. The Tennessee Supreme Court sustained one of these in 1925 when it reviewed a teacher's conviction in the famous Scopes trial (the "Monkey Trial"). *See* Larson, *Summer for the Gods*, note 6 *supra*.

22. Nelkin, *The Creation Controversy, supra* note 6, at 33, writes, "A scholarly survey of the content of biology texts up to 1960 found the influence of antievolutionist sentiment to be persistent, if undramatic, and showed the teaching of evolution actually declined after 1925."

23. *Id.* at 39–53.

24. Epperson v. Arkansas, 393 U.S. 97.

25. *Id.* at 103.

26. McLean v. Arkansas Board of Education, 529 F.Supp. 1255 (E.D. Ark. 1982).

27. Edwards v. Aguillard, 482 U.S. 578 (1987).

28. *See* Steve Benen, "Evolution Evasion," *Church & State*, October 1999, 4. Although local school districts were free to teach evolution, the subject was to have been omitted from statewide tests for evaluating students. For a caustic evaluation, *see* Stephen Jay Gould, "Dorothy, It's Really Oz," Viewpoint, *Time*, August 23, 1999, 59. The board's reversal, following a change in membership, is recounted in Kate Beem, "Emphasis on Evolution Adopted by Kansas Board," *Kansas City Star*, Feb. 15, 2001, A1.

29. Whatever its religious status, the Bible may be *a* source of historical truth, for example, supporting the assertion that Israel had a king named David, but it obviously lacks that nonreligious authority about the moment of the earth's creation.

30. As Stephen Jay Gould has put it, they have "nonoverlapping magisteria," science dealing with facts about the world, religion concerning itself with matters of the spirit and morality. Stephen Jay Gould, "Nonoverlapping Magisteria," in *Intelligent Design Creationism*, Pennock, note 13 *supra*, at 737–49. See generally Stephen Jay Gould, *Rocks of Ages: Science and Religion in the Fullness of Life* (New York: Ballantine, 2001).

31. Because religions typically include perspectives on human nature that could coincide or conflict with what social scientists assert, few believers suppose that religion has *no* overlap with the human sciences. *See* McMullin, "Plantinga's Defense," note 13 *supra*, at 173.

32. Philip Kitcher, in *Science, Truth, and Democracy* 11–82 (New York: Oxford Univ. Pr., 2001) provides a persuasive defense of scientific realism.

33. These two possibilities may be viewed as aspects of traditional Christian faith. According to some passages in the antievolution literature, belief in these two forms of divine control might be sufficient to qualify one as a creationist. *See*, for example, Phillip Johnson, in *Darwin on Trial* 113 (Washington, D.C.: Regnery Gateway, 1991). I am considering as creationist and intelligent-design theories only those claims that to some degree, at least, conflict with a neo-Darwinian account.

34. The relations between the findings of science and two other common religious ideas—an afterlife and divine inspiration of human beings—is less straightforward. Besides noting them here, I do not discuss these relations. Science cannot rule out the possibility of a personal afterlife or reincarnation, although many skeptics think that what science does establish suggests strongly that death is the end of personal existence. Science, as of now, cannot explain all aspects of human behavior, and thus cannot foreclose the possibility that a divine spirit inspires human understanding and behavior on some occasions.

35. Kenneth Miller, *Finding Darwin's God*, note 12 *supra*, at 19, says that over years of teaching in science he has "come to realize that a presumption of atheism or agnosticism is universal in academic life."

36. These people typically believe that perfect scientific and perfect religious understanding will coincide—that is, they do not think that God has created the natural world in a way to deceive our natural reason and test our faith—but that present understandings are fallible.

37. The attitudes of some religious critics of evolutionary theory are illustrative. *See* Alvin Plantinga, "When Faith and Reason Clash: Evolution and the Bible," in Pennock, *Intelligent Design Creationism*, note 13 *supra*, at 136–39. They believe that if one gave no credence to the existence of a divine creator, the neo-Darwinian explanation, as uncertain as they say it is, would be the best we could do to account for the origins of life. But when one considers a divine creator, another explanation, involving God's creative action, seems much more likely.

38. Such arguments are countered by religious arguments that a creator would be likely to create a universe with "functional integrity," not intervening from time to time to violate its natural laws, Howard J. Van Till, "When Faith and Reason Cooperate," in Pennock, *Intelligent Design Creationism*, note 13 *supra*, at 158–59, and that evolution, in all its contingency, fits well with a dynamic creation in which new life comes into being through natural processes, and human beings enjoy true freedom. Arthur Peacocke, "Welcoming the 'Disguised Friend'— Darwinism and Divinity," in Pennock, *supra* at 472–81; Miller, *Finding Darwin's God*, note 12 *supra*, at 270–75.

39. Stephen Jay Gould has highlighted the panda's thumb, which is not like other digits in structure but which functions moderately well. The explanation for its development must be the historical link of modern pandas with prior species, not the hand of God. *See* Stephen Jay Gould, "The Panda's Thumb," in Pennock, *Intelligent Design Creationism*, note 13 *supra*, at 669–76. Another author suggests that an even more powerful example is the laryngeal nerve in mammals, which is

much longer than would be ideal and reaches a ridiculous length in giraffes. Kelly C. Smith, "Appealing to Ignorance behind the Cloak of Ambiguity," in Pennock, *supra* at 724–25.

40. According to one formulation of this central idea: "The methodological naturalist is the person who assumes that the world runs according to unbroken law; and that science involves just such understanding without reference to any extra or supernatural forces like God." Michael Ruse, "Methodological Naturalism under Attack," in Pennock, *Intelligent Design Creationism*, note 13 *supra*, at 365.

41. However, Matthew J. Braver and Daniel R. Brumbaugh, "Biology Remystified: The Scientific Claims of the New Creationists," in Pennock, *Intelligent Design Creationism*, note 13 *supra*, at 32, suggest, "[W]hen it comes to unraveling scientific problems, most practicing scientists, regardless of their religious beliefs, refuse to invoke the existence of unknown supernatural forces—even in the absence of known naturalist mechanisms. This suspended judgment is accompanied by the hope that human minds will eventually find a crack in the apparently impenetrable surface of the mystery." For a suggestion that most scientists are committed to a more far-reaching naturalism, one that denies the existence of any supernatural reality, *see* Phillip Johnson, "Evolution as Dogma: The Establishment of Religion," in Pennock, *supra* at 72.

Logically, it is possible that some physical events in the universe are beyond conceivable human explanation but are nonetheless purely natural.

42. Plantinga, "When Faith and Reason Clash," note 37 *supra*, at 139–41; Plantinga, "Methodological Naturalism?" in Pennock, *Intelligent Design Creationism*, note 13 *supra*, at 355–56. *See also* Phillip Johnson's support of "theistic realism," in *Reason in the Balance* 107 (Downers Grove, Ill.: InterVarsity Pr., 1995), and Nicholas Wolterstorff's assertion, that "one's authentic Christian commitment ought to function *internally* to scholarship." *Reason within the Bounds of Religion* 77 (Grand Rapids, Mich.: Eerdmans, 1976).

43. Richard Dawkins, *The Blind Watchmaker*, note 12 *supra*, at 5, has commented, "I could not imagine being an atheist before 1859." "Darwin made it possible to be an intellectually fulfilled atheist." *Id.* at 6. He subsequently suggests that beliefs about God are superfluous and assume the existence of the main thing we want to explain, organized complexity. *Id.* at 316.

44. This problem is a variant in the pervasive problem of natural evil, which Christians have always found hard to explain. Evils caused by human actions can plausibly be attributed to a freedom of choice

given human beings. Although some have said human sin is also responsible for natural evil, the connection is much less obvious, *and* natural evil existed long before human beings appeared on earth, if evolutionists are right about history.

45. Sheila Anne Feeny, "Is Prayer Good Medicine?" (Medscape Health, 2002) http://health.medscape.com/cx/viewarticle/405270 (accessed Feb. 21, 2002). *See also* Eric Nagourney, "A Study Links Prayer and Pregnancy," *N.Y. Times*, October 2, 2001, F6; and Jim Holt, "Prayer Works," *N.Y. Times*, December 9, 2001, § 6 (Magazine), at 92. According to reports, the women received identical medical procedures—in vitro fertilization and embryo transfer. American researchers did not inform either the women or the medical personnel assisting them that they were engaging in a prayer experiment. Groups in the United States, Canada, and Australia, with pictures of the women for whom they prayed, prayed for half the women. Other groups prayed that these prayers might be effective.

46. Neil Shanks, *God, the Devil, and Darwin* 145–53 (New York: Oxford Univ. Pr., 2004), summarizes some earlier prayer experiments and sharp criticisms of their methodologies.

47. Non-Catholics may be surprised to discover just how rigorous the church is about distinguishing the unusual but possibly explicable from the truly miraculous. The Congregation for the Causes of Saints has a body of medical consultants who must "determine that the extraordinary healing—these days virtually all accepted miracles are medical cures—is inexplicable by science." Kenneth L. Woodward, *Making Saints* 192 (New York: Simon & Schuster, 1990). The doctors review the medical records of the person whose cure is claimed to be miraculous, as well as the written testimony of witnesses and other scientific evidence. The cure must be complete and lasting, and "inexplicable by all known scientific means." *Id.* at 195. A similar process is employed by local and international medical bureaus that certify cures at the Grotto of Lourdes. To qualify, a cure must be "certain, definitive and medically inexplicable." Lourdes Sanctuary lists the criteria for a cure on its web site (created Feb. 11, 1996; accessed Jan. 10, 2002), *at* http://www.lourdes-france.org/gb/gbsb0027.htm.

48. An explication of David Hume's skeptical discussion of miracles is in Robert J. Fogelin, *A Defense of Hume on Miracles* (Princeton: Princeton Univ. Pr., 2003). Contrary to what is sometimes assumed, Hume did not contend that no testimony could ever be sufficient to establish a miracle; rather, no testimony has come close to being strong enough to providing persuasive evidence that a miracle has occurred.

49. *See* McMullin, "Plantinga's Defense," note 13 *supra*, at 185–89.

CHAPTER 9. TEACHING NATURAL SCIENCE II: EVOLUTIONISM, CREATIONISM,
AND INTELLIGENT DESIGN

1. *See* Alvin Plantinga, "Evolution, Neutrality, and Antecedent Reality: A Reply to McMullin and Van Till," in Robert T. Pennock, ed., *Intelligent Design Creationism and Its Critics* 212–13 (Cambridge: MIT Pr., 2001).

2. Jeffrie Murphy, ed., *Evolution, Morality, and the Meaning of Life* 24, 35 (Totowa, N.J.: Rowman and Littlefield, 1982).

3. A teacher discussing the *history* of a science may, of course, comment on theories overtaken by time, and explain the power of a dominant theory by comparison with rejected competitors. Bernard Williams, in *Truth and Truthfulness* 217 (Princeton: Princeton Univ. Pr., 2002), comments on how orderly scientific inquiry deals with crank views.

4. Philip Kitcher, *Abusing Science: The Case against Creationism* 72, 98 (Cambridge: MIT Pr., 1982). The theory does not clash with the second law of thermodynamics—that systems increase entropy or disorder—which applies only to closed systems, not to the development of life on earth, an open system with new energy continually supplied by the sun. *Id.* at 91–92.

5. As Robert T. Pennock, *Tower of Babel* 99–100 (Cambridge: MIT Pr., 1999), explains, the famous philosopher of science Karl Popper once expressed this view but later abandoned it. The theory would be unfalsifiable in this way if it were unable to predict any changes and it declared that the survival of a characteristic proves that the characteristic was fitted for survival—however difficult it may be for us to see that the characteristic is competitively advantageous—or that the characteristic flows from a gene that confers a competitive advantage in some other respect.

The theory of descent of complex life from simple common ancestors is more easily subject to disconfirmation. If fossils showed that animals that must have appeared later, according to the theory, actually appeared earlier, that would be a serious blow to the theory. *See* Richard Dawkins in *The Blind Watchmaker* 225 (New York: W. W. Norton, 1987).

6. *See* Phillip Johnson, "Evolution as Dogma: The Establishment of Religion," in Pennock, *Intelligent Design Creationism*, note 1 *supra*, at 73.

7. Imre Lakatos defended what he called sophisticated methodological falsificationism, according to which "no experiment, experimental report, observational statement or well-corroborated low-level falsifying hypothesis alone can lead to falsification. There is no falsification before the emergence of a better theory." "Falsification and the Meth-

odology of Scientific Research Programmes," in Imre Lakatos and Alan Musgrave, eds., *Criticism and the Growth of Knowledge* 91, 109 (Cambridge: Cambridge U. Pr., 1970). *See also* Imre Lakatos, "II—Criticism and the Methodology of Scientific Research Programmes," *lXIX Proceedings of the Aristotelian Society* 149, 163 (1969).

8. Michael J. Behe, *Darwin's Black Box: The Biochemical Challenge to Evolution* x (New York: Touchstone Books, 1998); *see also* Michael J. Behe, "Molecular Machines: Experimental Support for the Design Inference," in Pennock, *Intelligent Design Creationism*, note 1 *supra*, at 241–56. When one looks at cilia, bacterial flagella, the mechanism for blood clotting, and other microsystems, one finds "irreducibly complex systems," which are "composed of several well-matched, intersecting parts that contribute to the basic function, wherein the removal of any one of the parts causes the system to effectively cease functioning." Behe, *Darwin's Black Box*, at 39. It is fair to say that this is not a precise definition. As Professor Behe's responses at a debate over intelligent design, at the American Museum of Natural History on April 23, 2002, made clear, a system could qualify if it had some redundant parts, or if the elimination of one (nonredundant) part would still permit the function to be served fairly well. An example, discussed in Kenneth Miller, *Finding Darwin's God* 152–61 (New York: HarperCollins, 1999), is animals whose blood clots without every aspect of the full clotting systems. This clarification undercuts Behe's basic argument only insofar as it indicates a greater possibility than he acknowledges of development from simple to highly complex systems.

9. Behe notes that attempted explanations of how such systems could have developed by natural selection are few and far between. *Darwin's Black Box*, note 8 *supra*, at 176. Miller, *Finding Darwin's God*, note 8 *supra*, at 147–52, responds that there have been such articles written after Behe's book and that the main reason more has not been done is that scientists do not yet know just how these biochemical systems work. Franklin M. Harold, *The Way of the Cell: Molecules, Organisms, and the Order of Life* 189–215 (New York: Oxford Univ. Pr., 2001), offers a general evolutionary theory for the development of complex cells. See also Neil Shanks, *God, the Devil, and Darwin* 176–90 (New York: Oxford Univ. Pr., 2004). For a caustic appraisal of Behe's theory, see Philip Kitcher, "Born Again Creationism," in Pennock, *Intelligent Design Creationism*, note 1 *supra*, at 257, 262–68.

10. *See, e.g.*, Dawkins, *The Blind Watchmaker*, note 5 *supra*, at 77–86.

11. Kauffman, *At Home in the Universe* vii (New York: Oxford Univ. Pr., 1995). *See also id.* at 23–25. In defending a neo-Darwinian approach,

Robert Pennock, *Tower of Babel*, note 5 *supra*, at 103, comments, "There might also turn out to be underlying patterns of order that emerge because of the self-organizing properties of non-equilibrium systems, or because of limits imposed on evolutionary change by developmental constraints." Apparently, one might consider the built-in constraints of which Kauffman writes as being a feature of neo-Darwinian evolutionary theory rather than a partial alternative to natural selection. Conversation with Philip Kitcher, September 26, 2003.

Gordon Rattray Taylor asserted that, in order to explain *all* aspects of evolution, we should imagine "some directive force or process [that] works in conjunction with it. I do not mean by that a force of a mystical kind, but rather some property of the genetic mechanism the existence of which is at present unsuspected." Taylor, *The Great Evolution Mystery* 137 (New York: Harper & Row, 1983). On this page, Taylor asserts only that the evidence he has presented makes "it necessary to consider" this possibility "quite seriously"; but the remainder of the book makes clear that Taylor believes this explanation is probably correct.

12. However, Behe, *Darwin's Black Box*, note 11 *supra*, argues that the same features that show the implausibility of a Darwinian explanation also establish the great likelihood of intelligent design. *See also* William A. Dembski, *The Design Inference* (Cambridge: Cambridge Univ. Pr., 1998), adopting a mathematical approach to complexity. Providing a detailed analysis of probability theory, Dembski argues that when the improbability of a patterned outcome is very high, one can rule out regularity and chance in favor of intelligent design.

13. It is now common currency among philosophers of science that individual anomalies, instances in which observations do not comport with what a theory predicts (or "retrodicts"), do not undermine scientific theories; but a very powerful criticism of a theory *should* be taken seriously whether or not the critic offers a substitute.

14. If other alternatives are already in the field, see Karl Popper, "Natural Science and Its Dangers," in Lakatos and Musgrave, *Criticism*, note 7 *supra*, at 51, 54–56, scientists might give them renewed attention. If there is a dominant paradigm of the sort described by Thomas Kuhn, *The Structure of Scientific Revolutions* (Chicago: Univ. of Chicago Pr., 1962), at least some scientists might devote their efforts to trying to imagine new possibilities that would significantly revise or overthrow crucial aspects of the dominant theory. However, since scientists require some theoretical framework to guide their work, it is understandable that most scientists will continue to use the prevailing theory until an alternative is put forward.

15. I am supposing, contrary to what Richard Dawkins has claimed, *The Blind Watchmaker*, note 5 *supra*, at 223–52, that the disagreement is substantial and not mainly terminological.

16. Addressing two competing suggestions about how cilia might have developed according to standard evolutionary theory, Michael Behe concludes, "Each points out the enormous problems with the other's model, and each is correct." *Darwin's Black Box*, note 8 *supra*, at 69.

17. In *id.*, at 29, Behe remarks, "Mathematicians over the years have complained that Darwinism's numbers just do not add up."

18. I am passing over the argument that the physical conditions necessary to sustain separate suns and planets were themselves highly improbable.

19. *See* Mochary v. Caputo, 100 N.J. 119, 494 A.2d 1028 (1985) (a civil case seeking a reform of procedures). The state supreme court evinced no doubt that the procedure had not consistently been fair. The case is discussed in Dembski, *The Design Inference*, note 12 *supra*, at 9–20, 162–67, and Branden Fitchen, Christopher Stephens, and Elliott Sober, "How Not to Detect Design—Critical Notice: William A. Dembski, *The Design Inference*," in Pennock, *Intelligent Design Creationism*, note 1 *supra*, at 599–600.

20. In his deservedly popular defense of dominant evolutionary theory, Richard Dawkins accepts the relevance of probability arguments, *The Blind Watchmaker*, note 5 *supra*, at 41, but he adopts an unwarranted assumption that is highly favorable to evolutionary theory. *Id.* at 139–47. Assuming that the likelihood that a planet would develop life with the degree of complexity of life on earth is extremely slight, *id.* at 141–42, he says that the relevant probability for judging evolutionary theory, the "luck" we can postulate, is correlated to the number of suitable planets for life in the universe—roughly 100 billion billion. It is quite consistent with highly improbable odds that complex life might have developed on one planet; that has to be ours, since we are highly complex life, able to understand what has happened.

Dawkins persuasively establishes four propositions. (1) If the universe has 100 billion billion suitable planets, we would expect complex life to develop on at least one if the odds for each suitable planet were more favorable than one in 100 billion billion. (2) The existence of life on our planet does not necessarily establish a high likelihood of life on other planets; ours may be the single instance in which an incredibly long shot paid off. (3) There is nothing paradoxical about that planet being ours. (4) If the odds against any life beginning are extremely high, although more favorable than one in 100 billion billion, we should not be surprised that no one has yet figured out just how life arose from nonlife.

But Dawkins's central question is "how much luck are we allowed to assume in a theory of the origin of life on Earth?" *Id.* at 143. He implicitly acknowledges that if complex life has arisen often, say on one out of every thousand suitable planets, a theory according to which complex life arises only once in nearly 100 billion billion times is in trouble. Dawkins says that since we are entitled for the sake of argument to assume that "life has originated only once in the universe, it follows that we are *allowed* to postulate a very large amount of luck in a theory, because there are so many planets in the universe where life *could* have originated." *Id.* at 144.

The fly in the ointment is that we do not know about complex life on most other planets. We do know that within our solar system complex life is limited to earth, and we can draw negative inferences about life as complex as ours for a few neighboring solar systems, based on an absence of radio communication from them. We have not a clue about the vast majority of planets in the universe. If someone asserts that a design explanation is more plausible than that provided by dominant evolutionary theory, I do not see why we should assume, *in making that comparison*, that life exists only rarely or not at all on all those planets. The opponent of evolution offers some form of design or creative intervention as an explanation for much of the history of life's development, arguing that occurrence of complex life by ordinary natural causes is so unlikely that his theory is more persuasive than neo-Darwinism. For this purpose, the existence of planets about which we know nothing hardly seems relevant.

21. Kitcher, *Abusing Science*, note 4 *supra*, at 106–15.

22. *Id.* at 144–55.

23. Strictly speaking, how life developed from nonlife is not an aspect of evolutionary biology, Pennock, *Tower of Babel*, note 5 *supra*, at 161, but in discussions of evolution and creationism, it is usually included.

24. The history of science, as Thomas Kuhn has shown, *Structure of Scientific Revolutions*, note 14 *supra*, does reveal instances in which scientists have clung to existing "paradigms" for reasons other than scientific evidence; but scientists did shift from a Newtonian view of physical laws when Einstein presented powerful arguments for special and general relativity, and scientists subsequently accepted a quantum theory that was highly counterintuitive and rejected in part by Einstein. *See* Heinz Pagels, *The Cosmic Code* 60–65, 96–97, 160–65 (New York: Simon & Schuster, 1982).

25. Kitcher, *Abusing Science*, note 4 *supra*, at 63.

26. *Id.* at 159. See *id.* at 155–64.

27. Conversation with Philip Kitcher, September 26, 2003.

28. The results, as chapter 8 suggests, might be explained by a natural power of mental telepathy no one yet understands.

29. Many people believe that the Big Bang theory of the beginning of the universe fits more comfortably with the idea of a God who creates ex nihilo than the steady-state view of the universe, which used to be popular, *see* Robert John Russell, "T = O: Is It Theologically Significant?" in W. Mark Richardson and Wesley J. Wildman, eds., *Religion and Science* 201–24 (New York: Routledge, 1996), but that does not make the Big Bang theory religious.

30. Behe, in *Darwin's Black Box*, note 8 *supra*, at 203–4, puts it this way: "No one would be foolish enough to categorically deny the possibility" of an "as-yet-undiscovered natural process that would explain biochemical complexity," but "no one has a clue how it would work" and "it would go against all human experience."

31. McLean *v.* Arkansas Board of Education, 529 F. Supp. 1255, 1267 (E.D.Ark. 1982). Judge Overton wrote that the "essential characteristics of science are (1) It is guided by natural law; (2) It has to be explained by reference to natural law; (3) It is testable against the empirical world; (4) Its conclusions are tentative, i.e., are not necessarily the final word, and (5) It is falsifiable."

32. Laudan, "Science at the Bar: Causes for Concern," in Murphy, *Evolution, Morality*, note 2 *supra*, at 149, 152–53, taken from Laudan, "Commentary on Ruse: Science at the Bar—Causes for Concern," in M. LaFollette, ed., *Creationism, Science, and the Law: The Arkansas Case*, at 161–66 (Cambridge: MIT Pr., 1983). As of 1982, this was true about the theory of plate tectonics, and at the time of Darwin's *Origin of Species*, it was true about major aspects of his own theory.

33. What now seem miraculous medical cures may later become explicable scientifically, and a chemist may discover how life could naturally have developed from nonlife three billion years ago.

34. As a terminological matter, such theories might or might not be classed among *scientific* theories.

35. In his famous argument for design, William Paley said that if he finds a watch in a heath, he knows it has been designed. William Paley, *Natural Theology* (1802) 9–10 (New York: American Tract Society, n.d.). Had we traced the origin of two thousand watches randomly chosen and found that all were designed by human beings, we might call this a scientific conclusion. As it is, we know that many watches have been designed, and we can't imagine how else they would be generated. Ordinary common sense tells us the watch in the field is designed. Nicholas Wolterstorff, *Reason within the Bounds of Religion* 60 (Grand Rapids, Mich.: Eerdmans, 1976), remarks that a fisherman who says that fish won't bite after heavy rains is "propounding a theory"; "scien-

tific activity is not to be differentiated from other human activities on the ground that it deals with theories, not even . . . theories of a special kind."

36. For the view that science cannot accommodate supernatural explanations, *see* Pennock, *Tower of Babel*, note 5 *supra*, at 189–94.

37. On the ambiguity of the term *explanation*, *see id.* at 185–89.

38. Of course, one might say that lurking in the background of any such causal explanation is the implicit idea that similar conditions would produce similar actions by similar individuals; but, whatever merit this view may have for ordinary historical explanations, it seems inapt as applied to an omnipotent God.

39. Francis X. Clines, "Ohio Board Hears Debate on an Alternative to Darwinism," *N.Y. Times*, March 12, 2002, A16, col. 1. A further discussion, including comment on the resolution of the Ohio board, took place on *Talk of the Nation: Science Friday*, National Public Radio, on November 8, 2002. This archived program can be heard at http:/www .sciencefriday.com/pages/2002/Nov/hour1_110802.htmll.

40. Science might explain why people have come to value what they do, and it might show that ethical behavior helps preserve the species; but any such explanations fall short of providing reasons why people otherwise inclined, and caring more about their own satisfaction than human survival, should act ethically.

41. Because these subjects deal mainly with contemporary phenomena, and the limits concern human behavior, it is easier to design research that can establish the limited effectiveness of models for prediction than can be the case for possible interventions by God millions of years ago.

42. I do not mean that every detail could be explained, but that the outlines of the process could be fully explained.

43. I am not suggesting that these very words are the right ones to speak to ninth or tenth graders, but I am confident the ideas they express can be communicated to high school students. Here is how Philip Kitcher put the views of a thoughtful evolutionist: "The evidence for the universal relatedness of life is compelling. Further, we know of a number of natural processes that have produced evolutionary change. We can't always say for sure which of these has been operative at which stage of life, nor do we know that our inventory of possible mechanisms is complete, but, on the evidence we have, there's no reason to think that any supernatural process was needed in the evolution of organisms." Kitcher, *Abusing Science*, note 4 *supra*, at 272.

44. Dorothy Nelkin, *The Creation Controversy* 79–81 (New York: W.W. Norton, 1982).

45. It is also true that one reason many evolutionists think intelligent

design in any form is *not* plausible is because they reject its religious assumptions.

46. Kitcher, *Abusing Science*, note 4 *supra*, at 174.

47. This sentence implicitly rejects the conclusion of Michael Behe and others that an inference from complexity to *intelligent design* is very powerful. In part, this rejection is based on my own sense that one cannot move so easily from the complexity that signals intelligent design in ordinary life to what signals such design in basic life processes. In part, the rejection is based on the limited degree of acceptance the theory has among scientists, and the fact that the kinds of uncertainties that characterize theorizing about evolution are far from unique within science.

CHAPTER 10. TEACHING NATURAL SCIENCE III: WHAT AMOUNTS TO TEACHING RELIGION?

1. Douglas Futuyma has called the work of creation scientists a "caricature of science [based on] no evidence." Douglas J. Futuyma, *Science on Trial: The Case for Evolution* 21 (Sunderland, Mass.: Sinauer, 1995). Philip Kitcher has remarked that they "have constructed a glorious fake" useful "to illustrate differences between science and pseudoscience." Philip Kitcher, *Abusing Science: The Case Against Creationism* 5 (Cambridge: MIT Pr., 1982).

2. In McLean v. Arkansas Board of Educ., 529 Supp. 1255, 1267, 1269 (E.D. Ark. 1982). Judge Overton commented that creationists "do not take data, weigh it against the opposing scientific data, and therefore reach . . . conclusions. . . . Instead, they take the literal wording of the Book of Genesis and attempt to find scientific support for it." Stephen L. Carter, "Evolutionism, Creationism, and Treating Religion as a Hobby," 1987 *Duke L. J.* 980–82, and Warren A. Nord and Charles C. Haynes, *Taking Religion Seriously across the Curriculum* 134–42 (Alexandria, Va.: ASCD Nashville First Amendment Center, 1988), assume that creationism is a religious, not a scientific, theory, despite their substantial empathy with the basic perspectives that underlie creationism.

3. David K. DeWolf, Stephen Meyer, and Mark Edward DeForest develop the argument that teaching intelligent design is not teaching religion in "Teaching the Origins Controversy: Science, or Religion, or Speech," 2000 *Utah L. Rev.* 39. *See also* by the same authors *Intelligent Design in Public School Science Curricula: A Legal Guidebook* (Foundation for Thought and Ethics, 1999), available at http://arn.org/docs/dewolf/guidebook.htm. Jay Wexler takes a contrary view in "Note, Of Pandas, People, and the First Amendment: The Constitutionality of Teaching Intelligent Design in the Public Schools," 49 *Stan. L. Rev.* 439 (1997).

4. *See* Marjorie George, "Comment: And Then God Created Kansas? The Evolution/Creationism Debate in American Public Schools," 149 *U. Pa. L. Rev.* 843, 868–71 (2001); Eric P. Martin, "Note, The Evolutionary Threat of Creationism: The Kansas Board of Education's Omission of Evolution from Public School Curricula," 27 *J. Legis.* 167, 176–78 (2001).

5. See the requirement adopted by the Cobb County School District, Georgia, that texts covering evolution have a sticker with a disclaimer on their covers: Cobb County Board of Education, Approval Purchase of Science Health and Physical Education Textbook Adoption, Discussion Agenda of Board Meeting March 28, 2002, *available at* http://boarddocs.cobbk12.org/Board.nsf/Public?OpenFrameSet (Apr. 17, 2002).

Compare Freiler v. Tangipahoa Parish Bd. of Educ. 185 F.3d 337 (5th Cir. 1999), cert. denied, 530 U.S. 1251 (2000), holding that a disclaimer that teaching of evolution was "not intended to influence or dissuade the Biblical version of Creation" had no secular purpose.

Among aspects of evolutionary theory, an "old earth" and "descent with modification" are established to a greater degree of certainty than the exact role of natural selection. Kenneth Miller, *Finding Darwin's God* 53 (New York: HarperCollins, 1999) writes that descent with modification "is as much a fact as anything we know in science."

6. *See* Nord and Haynes, *Taking Religion Seriously*, note 2 *supra*, at 134–35.

7. On sonograms and similar devices, people can observe what they are told are their own hearts doing what seems to be pumping blood.

8. Nord and Haynes, *Taking Religion Seriously*, note 2 *supra*, at 154, suggesting that studying religious accounts of origins and nature could serve a valid secular purpose of liberal education. *See also* Jay Wexler, "Darwin, Design, and Disestablishment: Teaching the Evolution Controversy in Public Schools," 56 *Vand. L. Rev.* 751 (2003). In such a study, one would not restrict the religious accounts to those of Christians and Jews.

9. Notice that an argument that evolution and theism are compatible can be employed to defend evolution against creationism *and* to defend theism against atheism.

10. See Robert T. Pennock, *Tower of Babel*, 246–47 (Cambridge: MIT Pr., 1999).

11. An alternative conceptualization is that the educators really are bound constitutionally to do certain things but that courts will not declare invalid decisions that are within a certain range, even if the decisions may exceed constitutional limits.

12. Epperson v. Arkansas, 393 U.S. 97. There was no record of prosecutions under the statute, but a science teacher challenged the law. The

Arkansas Supreme Court had sustained the law, finding it unnecessary to resolve whether the statute "prohibits any explanation of the theory of evolution or merely prohibits teaching that the theory is true." *Id.* at 101 n. 7. The U.S. Supreme Court decided that the law was unconstitutional in either event.

13. *Id.* at 104.

14. *Id.* at 106.

15. *Id.* at 103. In a concurring opinion relying on the statute's vagueness, Justice Black made the suggestion that removing evolution from the curriculum might leave the state in a neutral position between religious and antireligious doctrines (*id.* at 113). I have indicated why I do not think it is "neutral" to wipe from the curriculum an otherwise essential topic because its theories conflict with some religious views.

16. Edwards v. Aguillard, 482 U.S. 578 (1987).

17. *Id.* at 581.

18. Officials claimed that the act's purpose was academic freedom, but Justice Brennan wrote that it furthered neither the goal of providing a more comprehensive science curriculum nor the goal of freeing individual teachers to instruct as they thought best. *Id.* at 586–87.

19. *Id.* at 591.

20. Various efforts after the law was adopted to define "creation science" without reference to a supernatural creator were not relevant to what the legislature's purpose had been. *Id.* at 595–96.

21. Justice Brennan also urged that the statute discriminated in favor of creation science as against evolution because it provided curriculum guides and resource services (supplied by a panel of creation scientists) for the former, but not the latter. The easy answer to this contention is that the legislature understood that science teachers in the main believed in evolution, and since plenty of teaching materials were available, no curriculum guides or resource services were needed for evolution. See Justice Scalia's dissent at *id.* 630–31.

22. *Id.* at 636–39.

23. *Id.* at 613.

24. *Id.* at 614.

25. I explore this issue in *Statutory Interpretation: Twenty Questions* 145–59 (New York: Foundation Pr., 1999).

CHAPTER 11. HISTORY, ECONOMICS, AND LITERATURE

1. A brief overview of changing approaches to history is in "History," in Paul Lagassé, ed., *Columbia Encyclopedia*, 6th ed. 1295–96 (New York: Columbia Univ. Pr., 2000). *See also* R. G. Collingwood, *The Idea of History* (New York: Oxford Univ. Pr., 1956).

2. I see no reason why a historian so inclined should not write from a religious or atheist point of view, although such approaches are rare among modern American historians.

3. *See* Warren A. Nord and Charles C. Haynes, *Taking Religion Seriously across the Curriculum* 1 (Alexandria, Va.: ASCD; Nashville: First Amendment Center, 1998).

4. One reason for this comparative neglect may be uncertainty about what judicial decisions under the Establishment Clause may allow. *See* Marjorie A. Silver, "Rethinking Religion and Public School Education," 15 *Quinnipiac L. Rev.* 200, 220 (1995). The situation has improved in the last decade and a half. *See id.* at 78; Gilbert T. Sewall, "Religion in the Textbooks," in James T. Sears and James C. Carper, eds., *Curriculum, Religion, and Public Education: Conversations for an Enlarging Public Square* 73, 80 (New York: Teachers College Pr., 1998).

5. Whether we *really* have a more objective view of distant than modern events is debatable. Perhaps it is only that "history written by the victors" has become solidly entrenched, that our sense of "objectivity" is blindness to suppressed alternative understandings. The challenge of "multiculturalists" to dominant white European perspectives rests substantially on this insight.

6. The connection between Puritan thought and ideas of democratic government is one example.

7. *See* Philip C. Kissam, "Let's Bring Religion into the Public Schools and Respect the Religion Clauses," 49 *Kan. L. Rev.* 593, 604–7 (2001). For less central matters regarding religion, a judgment about whether to teach them should include an assessment of whether available teachers can do so competently and fairly.

8. Nord and Haynes, *Taking Religion Seriously*, note 3 *supra*, at 50–53, 85–87. Charles Haynes has developed a very interesting guide for high school teachers that contains important documents about religion in American history, explains their relation to crucial issues, and provides bibliographic sources. *Religion in American History* (Alexandria, Va.: Association for Supervision and Curricular Development, 1990).

9. For a highly critical appraisal of the view that American society is distinctively innocent, *see* Reinhold Niebuhr, *The Irony of American History* (New York: Scribner's 1952).

10. Jay D. Wexler, "Preparing for the Clothed Public Square: Teaching about Religion, Civic Education, and the Constitution," 43 *Wm. & Mary L. Rev.* 1159 (2002), provides examples of sharply divergent views within the Buddhist and Confucian traditions.

11. *See* George M. Marsden, *Jonathan Edwards: A Life* 193–200 (New Haven: Yale Univ. Pr., 2003). Edwards saw the events of political his-

tory as revelations of God's will. He also looked for signs that Christ's reign on earth was approaching.

12. Warren A. Nord, *Religion and American Public Education* 249–51 (Chapel Hill: Univ. of North Carolina Pr., 1995).

13. If all that were involved was critical analysis hostile to some or all religions, my comments about Nord's possibilities 5 through 7, discussed below, would apply.

I am assuming that covert inculcation of ideas the teacher does not candidly acknowledge is never justified in school. Given religious beliefs in the United States, not too many high school teachers will teach consistent Marxism or Freudianism.

14. Of course, no one thinks *every* phrase in the Bible is to be taken literally; there are some obvious metaphors.

15. In Moore v. Gaston County Bd. of Educ., 357 F. Supp. 1037 (W.D. N.C. 1973), a student teacher was wrongly discharged for answering students' questions about his personal beliefs.

16. Among cases sustaining instructions to teachers not to discuss religious beliefs are Marchi v. Board of Cooperative Educational Services, 173 F.3d 469 (2d Cir. 1999); Peloza v. Capistrano Unified School Dist., 37 F.3d 517 (9th Cir. 1994). *See also* Bishop v. Aronov, 926 F.2d 1066 (8th Cir. 1991) (professor of health in university); Downing v. West Haven Bd. of Ed., 162 F.Supp.2d 19 (D. Conn. 2001) (wearing of Christian T-shirt). The *Bishop* decision is criticized, in part, for using high school cases to mark the permissible restraints on teachers in universities. John W. Hamilton, "*Bishop v. Aronov*: Religion-Tainted Viewpoints Are Banned from the Marketplace of Ideas," 49 *Wash. & Lee L. Rev.* 1557 (1992).

17. In addition to the cases cited in note 16 *supra*, the Court of Appeals of Minnesota upheld a class reassignment for a biology teacher who insisted he wanted to challenge dominant evolutionary theory in his class, LeVake v. Independent School Dist. 625 N.W. 502 (2001); and the Fourth Circuit, en banc, upheld the transfer of a drama teacher who had put on a controversial play, on the theory that choices of plays are curricular decisions that teachers have no right to control. Boring v. Buncombe County Board of Educ., 136 F. 3d 364, cert. denied 525 U.S. 813 (1998). For criticisms of the contraction of teacher authority, *see* Karen C. Daly, "Balancing Act: Teachers' Classroom Speech and the First Amendment," 30 *J. Law & Education* 1 (2001); Kara Lynn Grice, "Striking an Unequal Balance: The Fourth Circuit Holds That Public School Teachers Do Not Have First Amendment Right to Set Curriculum in *Boring v. Buncombe Co. Board of Education*," 77 *N.C. L. Rev.* 1960 (1999).

18. In Marchi v. Board of Cooperative Educational Services, 173 F.3d 469 (2d Cir. 1999), the court ruled that a supervisor properly treated a

letter to a parent about his child as falling within the writer's responsibilities as a teacher.

19. If a course spends substantial time on Marxist communism, for example, it should devote some time to Christian Socialist movements.

20. National Conference of Catholic Bishops, Economic Justice for All, in 5 *Pastoral Letters of the United Catholic Bishops* 371 (Hugh J. Nolan, ed., 1988).

21. This alone would not make economics *a science* rather than an exercise in logic; one needs to add that its premises, and therefore its conclusions, bear a significant relation to what happens in the outside world—isolating crucial factors as one would in the calculation of how fast a physical body falls in the absence of friction.

22. To be somewhat more precise, there is in the West a substantial consensus since the fall of Communism that production and distribution should occur according to a model of free enterprise, with some regulation. No consensus exists about how redistributive a system of taxation and government expenditures should be.

23. Lay Commission on Catholic Social Teaching and the U.S. Economy, "Liberty and Justice for All," 4 *Crisis* 4–16 (1986).

24. Upper-level courses may be labeled courses in literature, and study of literature plays a role in lower-level English courses. Many foreign language courses include reading and discussion of literature in those languages.

25. However, at some stages of the educational process, educators might decide that materials should emphasize exposure to less familiar traditions.

26. Crockett v. Sorenson, 568 F. Supp. 1422 (W.D. Va. 1983). A recent case to similar effect is Doe v. Porter, 188 F. Supp. 2d 904 U.S. Dist. LEXIS (E.D. Tenn. 2002); without supervision from public school officials, students from a religious college taught Bible classes to elementary school pupils. In this instance, the court found that the Bible was being taught as literally true.

27. *See also* Gibson v. Lee County School Board, 1 F. Supp. 2d 1426 (M.D. Fla. 1998). In Vaughn v. Reed, 313 F. Supp. 431 (W.D. Va. 1970), the court reached a similar conclusion, but said that a constitutionally acceptable Bible course should be appropriate for all students and should be mandatory.

28. Wexler, "Clothed Public Square," note 10 *supra*, at 64, suggests that such a course "would not bring the civic benefits that a fuller religious studies program offers" but that it is, nonetheless, constitutionally permissible.

29. If, at a high school level, students have the opportunity to study other religious texts, an elective course in the Bible may be all right.

CHAPTER 12. MORALS, CIVICS, AND COMPARATIVE RELIGION

1. Despite its disregard by many who are powerful politically—one who reads Robert Caro's biographies of Robert Moses, *The Power Broker: Robert Moses and the Fall of New York* (New York: Vintage Books 1975), and Lyndon Johnson, *The Path to Power*, vol. 1 of *The Years of Lyndon Johnson* (New York: Knopf 1982), *Means of Ascent*, vol. 2 of *The Years of Lyndon Johnson* (New York, Knopf 1990), and *Master of the Senate*, vol. 3 of *The Years of Lyndon Johnson* (New York, Knopf 2002), cannot fail to be struck by the extent to which deceit of various kinds contributed to their immense power—honesty *is* valuable in the life of liberal democracies.

2. When I was a student, boys took "shop" and girls took "home economics." In places where I have lived, it would now be unthinkable to routinely assign boys to shop and girls to home economics.

3. *See* Amy Gutmann, *Democratic Education* 107–11 (Princeton: Princeton Univ. Pr., 1987), suggesting that schools may legitimately decide to undertake sex education or not. Of course, much of sexual morality *does* involve responsibilities to others, but the primary reasons why some people object to homosexual activity, premarital intercourse, and particular varieties of sexual activity do not concern such responsibilities.

4. *See*, e.g., Andrew A. Cheng, "The Inherent Hostility of Secular Public Education toward Religion: Why Parental Choice Best Serves the Core Values of the Religion Clauses," 19 *Hawaii L. Rev.* 697 (1997).

5. I do not mean to imply that there is a settled methodology about teaching science and history, only that agreement is fairly wide about how to do science and, to a lesser extent, history.

6. *See* Rosemary Salomone, "Common Schools, Uncommon Values: Listening to the Voices of Dissent," 14 *Yale L. & Pol'y Rev.* 169, 181 (1996), on the "cognitive moral development movement" of the 1970s. *See* Lawrence Kohlberg, "The Philosophy of Moral Development," in *Essays on Moral Development*, vol. 1 (San Francisco: Harper & Row, 1981).

7. *See* James Davison Hunter, *The Death of Character: Moral Education in an Age without Good or Evil* 107–28 (New York: Basic Books, 2000) (describing a neoclassical and a communitarian backlash to psychological approaches); Jeffrey J. Pyle, "Socrates, the Schools, and Civility: The Continuing War between Inculcation and Inquiry," 26 *J. L. & Education* 65 (1997); Christina Hoff Sommers, "How Moral Education Is Finding Its Way Back into Schools," in William Damon, ed., *Bringing in a New Era in Character Education* 24–41 (Stanford, Calif.: Hoover Institution

Pr., 2002); Thomas Lickona, *Educating for Character: How Our Schools Can Teach Respect and Responsibility* (New York: Bantam Books, 1991).

8. Warren A. Nord, *Religion and American Education* 89 (Chapel Hill: Univ. of North Carolina Pr., 1995), places values clarification within a broader movement of "expressive education." "Expressivists are more likely to use the language of self-actualization and modern psychology than the language of morality or religion. They believe teachers should be nonjudgmental." Nord also quotes Karl Rogers to the effect that education should "free curiosity; . . . permit individuals to go charging off into new directions dictated by their own interest." *Id.* at 90.

9. *Id.* at 326–28.

10. B. Douglas Hayes, "Secular Humanism in Public School Textbooks: Thou Shalt Have No Other God (Except Thyself)," 63 *Notre Dame L. Rev.* 358, 372 n. 100 (1988), citing L. Raths, M. Harmin, and S. Simon, *Values and Teaching* 28–30 (1966). *See also* Hunter, *The Death of Character*, note 7 *supra*, at 75–76.

11. *See, e.g.*, Lisa Shah, "Faith in Our Future," 23 *Whittier L. Rev.* 183, 203–4 (2001). On the dominance of psychological approaches to values, *see* Hunter, *The Death of Character*, note 7 *supra*, at 81–106.

12. *See* Hayes, "Secular Humanism," note 10 *supra*, at 371 n. 94.

13. One might, for example, so regard a comment that "self-actualization is the highest level of human need." *Id.*

14. However, I do not think "personal and subjective" is a precise or accurate way to communicate the liberty of citizens in respect to values. That phrase is analyzed and criticized in Winton E. Yerby III, "Toward Religious Neutrality in the Public School Curriculum," 59 *U. Chi. L. Rev.* 899, 920–23 (1989).

15. More likely, a religion will say that children of adults who believe *that* religion should follow what the parents say.

16. This dichotomy is rough, in part, because we might believe in an absolute value—say, love—and also believe how one should act depends heavily on context.

17. *See* Shah, "Faith in Our Future," note 11 *supra*, at 11.

18. I add the "more or less" because there will be nuances of difference.

19. Such an argument might be resisted on the basis that the particular ethical beliefs can be explained as peculiarly tied to religious views, and therefore are not sound if the religious perspectives are not sound. And any argument based on historical practice may be resisted on the basis that the practice has been misguided.

20. To be clear, I am not suggesting that either kind of argument is conclusive about what our morality should now be. Someone can make the counterargument that the world religions have all adopted a falla-

cious moral view—e.g., that women should not enjoy full equality with men—or that our particular religious tradition is seriously misguided in some respect.

21. See especially John Rawls, *Political Liberalism* (New York: Columbia Univ. Pr., 1993). My own doubts about more rigorous forms of this view are expressed in *Private Consciences and Public Reasons* (New York: Oxford Univ. Pr., 1995).

22. However, as I point out in chapter 2, students should have a chance to understand religious objections to a political life that depends on nonreligious premises.

23. In the interests of completeness, a teacher should probably also say that many practicing Catholics do not, according to polls, accept the church's stance on this topic.

24. I have read a fair amount of Roman Catholic literature about artificial conception and homosexual relationships, but, given historical developments in doctrine, divisions among Catholics themselves, and the abstraction of the arguments, I doubt my capacity to state fairly why the institutional church opposes these practices.

25. Nord, *Religion and American Education*, note 8 *supra*, at 342, concludes that schools should teach everyone's values. "When we agree, we initiate students into our moral tradition. . . . When we disagree, we teach students *about* everyone's values fairly (without taking sides in the case of public schools)."

26. This would exclude criminal penalties for consenting homosexual acts among adults. (Such penalties were declared unconstitutional by the Supreme Court in spring of 2003. Lawrence v. Texas, 539 U.S. 558 (2003)). Although it is minimally coherent to say that gays deserve equal respect as citizens, as do those with strong impulses to steal, but that homosexual actions, like thefts, may be punished, our modern notions of equal respect for gays include at least tolerance of sexual acts in private as well as of inclinations.

27. On the point that public schools need to teach values of democratic citizenship, *see* Amy Gutmann, *Democratic Education*, note 3 *supra*, at 39–40; Stephen Macedo, *Diversity and Distrust: Civic Education in a Multicultural Democracy* 3–10 (Cambridge: Harvard Univ. Pr., 2000); William Galston, "Civic Education in the Liberal State," *in* Nancy Rosenblum, ed. *Liberalism and the Moral Life* 89 (Cambridge: Harvard Univ. Pr., 1989).

28. On the other hand, if the vast majority of people in the country and in the community do not recognize something as a valid claim of social justice, public schools should not teach it as such, even if educators in the district disagree with the consensus. Claims of animal rights could now fit into this category.

29. I am oversimplifying to an extraordinary degree here, not raising the danger of AIDS, differences between gay women and gay men, the possibility of offspring who carry genes from both members of a couple, the prospect of homosexual marriage, the opportunities to be bisexual in practice, and so on.

30. Existing social prejudices (which have abated radically in the last few decades) and the complexities of child bearing and raising for gay couples might figure in whether one would encourage someone to pursue a gay life, if his or her inclinations were not strongly and exclusively homosexual. These considerations are distinguishable from the intrinsic desirability of homosexual acts.

31. When the issue is moral teaching, teachers do not have a responsibility to indicate religious opposition that has no significant representation in the culture.

32. On the virulence of some prejudice against homosexuals, *see* Theresa J. Bryant, "May We Teach Tolerance? Establishing the Parameters of Academic Freedom in Public Schools," 50 *Univ. Pitt. L. Rev.* 570, 580–90 (1999), summarizing the harsh facts of Nabozny v. Podlesny, 92 F.3d 446 (7th Cir. 1996).

33. Another, more obvious, illustration of the difficulties of distinguishing conclusions based on fundamental premises of liberal democracy from other moral conclusions is whether men and women should share equally the responsibilities of rearing children. This may be viewed as a matter of personal, noncivic morality, but many see it as an aspect of equal citizenship for women.

34. Our morality is laced with many judgments about various sexual practices. Oral sex (even between heterosexuals) is often regarded as wrong (or inferior); sexual relations between adults of widely variant ages (say a seventy-year-old and a twenty-one-year-old) are commonly regarded as inappropriate (and not just because of inequality); masturbation has come to be fairly broadly accepted, but many people still regard it as a poor substitute for sexual relations between two people; sexual relations with animals are generally regarded as disgusting, and are forbidden (and not mainly because the animals don't consent). I recognize that these examples do not bear very directly on the problem of gay relationships, but they do suggest that many people in our society are very far from the opinion that sexual relations, in general, are just matters of personal preference, like ice cream flavors.

35. *See* Warren A. Nord and Charles C. Haynes, *Taking Religion Seriously across the Curriculum* 194–95 (Alexandria, Va.: ASCD; Nashville: First Amendment Center, 1998). However, the fact that a position is dominantly based on religious premises and could not be otherwise

supported is a powerful reason for public schools not to teach it as *the* correct position. *See infra.*

36. Further complications arise if the local community has views that differ substantially from those prevailing nationally. Rosemary Salomone argues that public schools should be substantially responsive to local sentiments outside of "core" values, "Common Schools, Uncommon Values," note 6 *supra,* at 172, 224–28. That she treats the social roles of women as outside of core values is some indication of how controversial application of that principle could become.

37. *See* Gary J. Simson and Erika A. Sussman, "Keeping the Sex in Sex Education: The First Amendment's Religion Clauses and the Sex Education Debate," 9 *So. Cal. Rev. L. & Women's Stud.* 265 (2000). *See also* Kristen S. Rufo, "Public Policy vs. Parent Policy: States Battle over Whether Public Schools Can Provide Condoms to Minors without Parental Consent," 13 *N.Y. L. Sch. J. Human Rights* 589, 592–99 (1997).

38. Simson and Sussman, "Keeping the Sex," note 37 *supra,* at 284–96. *See also* Naomi Seiler, "Abstinence-Only Education and Privacy, 24 *Women's Rights L. Rep.* 27, 33 (2002) (doubting whether a challenge under the religion clauses would succeed unless programs contained religious teachings).

39. Simson and Sussman, "Keeping the Sex," note 37 *supra,* at 284–87.

40. According to a 1992 study of the Center for Disease Control, by the time they reach twelfth grade, over 70 percent of students report having had sexual intercourse. Roger J. R. Levesque, "Sexuality Education: What Adolescents' Educational Rights Require," 6 *Psych. Pub. Pd. & L.* 953 (2000).

41. Simson and Sussman, "Keeping the Sex," note 37 *supra,* at 289. On the other hand, apparently the instruction about condoms given so far may not increase their use significantly. *See* Levesque, "Sexuality Education," note 40 *supra.* Levesque contends that sexuality education should be revised to focus on "responsibility, individual decision making, and concern for the general treatment of human beings." *Id.*

42. On teenage infection with HIV, *see* Rufo, "Public Policy," note 37 *supra,* at 600–604.

43. Simson and Sussman, "Keeping the Sex," note 37 *supra,* at 291–95, conclude that a religious perspective is being endorsed, but they do so without any detailed analysis of what exactly it takes to endorse or promote religion.

44. *See id.* at 265–82.

45. On condom distribution, see Curtis v. School Committee of Falmouth, 652 N.E.2d 580 (Sup. Jud. Ct. Mass. 1995); Alfonso v. Fernandez, 606 N.Y.S.2d 259 (App. Div., 2d. Dept. 1993); Rufo, "Public Policy," note 37 *supra.*

46. In Brown v. Hot, Sexy and Safer Prods., Inc., 68 F.3d 525 (1995), the Court of Appeals for the First Circuit declined to find any violation of legal rights in a particularly provocative form of sex education. Whether students whose parents object should be excused raises a separate question I consider in chapter 14.

47. Nord and Haynes, *Taking Religion Seriously*, note 35 *supra*, at 97–104.

48. Jay Wexler, "Preparing for the Clothed Public Square: Teaching about Religion, Civic Education, and the Constitution," 43 *Wm. & Mary L. Rev.* 1159, 1200–1220 (2002), has developed a powerful argument that training students to be citizens of our liberal democracy is the most important reason for educating them about religious understandings. From this perspective, the "civic" reasons for teaching about religion extend far beyond civics courses. Wexler suggests that teaching about religion is valuable to improve intellectual reasoning skills, to impart a knowledge of the historical influence of religious communities and ideas, to allow informed evaluation of government actions that affect religion, to generate an understanding of the role of religion in public debate and decision-making, and to increase tolerance.

49. In many cultures, people themselves would perceive no distinction between religion and other cultural aspects, and outsiders could not differentiate the two in any simple way.

50. *See* Nord and Haynes, *Taking Religion Seriously*, note 35 *supra*, at 2–8, 172–78. *See generally* Robert J. Nash, *Faith, Hype, and Clarity: Teaching about Religion in American Schools and Colleges* (New York: Teachers College Pr., 1999). In "Darwin, Design and Disestablishment," 56 *Vand. L. Rev.* 75 (2003), Jay Wexler proposes a course about various religious perspectives on the origins of life as the best way to help students understand alternatives to scientific approaches.

51. Were it said that this is a course in religion, not skepticism, the answer is that no other course treats atheism and agnosticism in a serious way, and these are significant perspectives about religion. Such a course might, for example, examine Marx's view that religion is the "opiate of the masses."

52. Of course, much about Judaism would come out in coverage of Christianity, but Christians tend to perceive many events in the Old Testament as prefiguring the life of Jesus, obviously not a Jewish view; and a focus on Christianity would omit developments in Judaism after the beginning of the Christian era. My brother Kim, who teaches world history to high school students, spends more time on Judaism than any other religion because of its striking history, its influences on Christianity and Islam, its importance for the United States and the crisis between Israel and the Palestinians, and because of the interest of his (mainly non-Jewish) students.

53. The course should probably be an elective. At a minimum, students whose parents wished should be excused. *See* Wexler, "Clothed Public Square," note 48 *supra*, at 1261.

54. Obviously this is not possible with oral traditions, but even with these it might be helpful to have some account of how the religion is understood from the inside, as by a telling of a story in the oral tradition.

55. Nord and Haynes, *Taking Religion Seriously*, note 35 *supra*, at 49, 172–73.

56. *See* Charles H. Haynes and Oliver Thomas, *Finding Common Ground: A Guide to Religious Liberty in Public Schools* (Nashville: First Amendment Center, 2001).

57. Wexler, "Clothed Public Square," note 48 *supra*, at 1256, provides examples of sharply divergent views within the Buddhist and Confucionist traditions.

CHAPTER 13. CONSTITUTIONAL CONSTRAINTS AND OTHER LEGAL LIMITS

1. Lemon v. Kurtzman, 403 U.S. 602 (1971).

2. *E.g.*, County of Allegheny v. A.C.L.U., 492 U.S. 573 (1989).

3. Lee v. Weisman, 505 U.S. 577 (1992).

4. If the state cannot endorse, obviously it cannot condemn. In her concurring opinion in Capitol Square Review and Advisory Bd. v. Pinette, 515 U.S. 753, 778 (1995), Justice O'Connor wrote that government practices must be reviewed to see if they constitute "an endorsement or disapproval of religion."

5. *See* Grove v. Mead School Dist. No. 354, 753 F.2d 1528 (9th Cir.), cert. denied, 474 U.S. 826 (1985), in which the Court rejected a challenge to teaching of *The Learning Tree* in a literature class; the book has comments denigrating Christianity. *See also* Fleischfresser v. Directors of School Dist. 200, 15 F.3d 680 (7th Cir. 1999) (rejecting challenge to stories of the occult). In Jabr v. Rapides Parish Sch. Bd., 171 F. Supp. 2d 653 (W.D. La. 2001), the court held that it did violate the Establishment Clause for a school principal to present each student with a copy of the Bible.

6. This judgment is based both on what appear to be the implications of what the Supreme Court has said and on my own appraisal of sound constitutional doctrine, reflecting in part my analysis of the hazards of teachers offering arguments in favor of particular religious positions. Note, however, that I do draw a distinction between the permissibility of offering arguments and the permissibility of asserting them as true.

In Helland v. South Bend Community School Corp., 93 F.3d 327 (7th

Cir. 1996), the court held that a school district could remove from its list of substitutes a man who failed to follow lesson plans and improperly interjected religion into his classroom.

7. Just how to conceptualize this range is arguable. One might think each educational authority is more constrained by the religion clauses than even a fully informed court would rule, or one might conceive the range of the constitutionally permissible as congruent with what a fully informed court would allow.

8. Comment of Frank Manuel during a conference on religion and education, *Daedalus*, Spring 1988, 29.

9. Winton E. Yerby III, "Toward Religious Neutrality in the Public School Curriculum," 56 *U. Chi. L. Rev.* 899, 923 (1989), proposes that courts should treat as establishments "a *pattern* of choices about the curriculum that either (a) *directly promotes or disparages a religious viewpoint* or (b) *presents an exclusive view of an inherently religious issue.*" I think this approach is helpful, although I am troubled by a sharp distinction of treatment between issues that are "inherently religious" and those that are not, and I am inclined to think that individual instances of teaching religious propositions are constitutional violations, though not ones courts should correct.

I do not specially address the complex issue of how much power individual teachers should have under free speech concepts that include academic freedom. I am broadly sympathetic with criticisms that some courts have gone too far in assigning authority away from individual teachers. *See* Karen C. Daly, "Balancing Act: Teachers' Classroom Speech and the First Amendment," 30 *J. L. & Educ.* 1 (2001); Kara Lynn Grice, "Striking an Unequal Balance: The Fourth Circuit Holds That Public School Teachers Do Not Have First Amendment Rights to Set Curriculum in *Boring v. Buncombe Co. Board of Education*," 77 *N.C. L. Rev.* 1960 (1999); Kevin G. Welner, "Locking Up the Marketplace of Ideas and Locking Out School Reform: Courts' Imprudent Treatment of Controversial Teaching in America's Public Schools," 50 *U.C.L.A. L. Rev.* 959 (2003); Theresa J. Bryant, "May We Teach Tolerance? Establishing the Parameters of Academic Freedom in Public Schools," 60 *U. Pitt. L. Rev.* 579 (1999). But I do think higher authorities have a substantial responsibility to see that teaching *about* religion does not slip into teaching religion and to safeguard against unfair treatment of religious points of view. Thus, higher authorities should have wider-ranging powers to avoid teaching that trespasses on the values of the religion clauses than they should have in respect to individual teaching that does not in itself threaten any constitutional violation. *See* Yerby, *supra*, at 909–19.

10. *See* Christopher L. Eisgruber, "How Do Liberal Democracies

Teach Values?" in Stephen Macedo and Yael Tamir, eds., *Moral and Political Education* 58–86 (New York: New York Univ. Pr., 2002). Students with a grievance could, of course, bring a hidden recorder to class, but a few publicized instances of that would have a baleful effect on spontaneity in school classrooms.

11. *See* People for the American Way Foundation, *The Good Book Taught Wrong: "Bible History" Classes in Florida's Public Schools* (1999). The history of litigation and settlement is briefly summarized in Jay Wexler, "Preparing for the Clothed Public Square: Teaching about Religion, Civic Education, and the Constitution," 43 *Wm. & Mary L. Rev.* 1159, 1245–57 (2002).

12. So long as courts are inclined to trust the good faith and competence of public school teachers (Justice O'Connor's approach for the Court in *Agostini*), they will insist on such supervision only if a program has already exhibited serious problems, or the teaching concerning religion is assigned to persons other than public school teachers.

13. I assume that a teacher *may* teach about religious subject matters in history or literature without having special training, although such training would be desirable.

14. There are limits, however. Teachers cannot be told to lie, and one can imagine instructions that are so detailed they would trespass upon free speech rights.

15. *See* Holly M. Bastian, "Religious Garb Statutes and Title VII: An Uneasy Coexistence," 80 *Georgetown L.J.* 211, 213 n. 14 (1991). In the spring of 2003, after a teacher's aide in Pennsylvania was suspended for wearing a cross necklace, the federal district court suggested that a prohibition of religious jewelry might well be a discriminatory restriction on speech that is unconstitutional. Nichol v. ARIN Intermediate Unit 28, 2003 U.S. Dist. LEXIS 10810 (W.D. Pa. June 25, 2003).

16. I pass over the point here that there are a small number of Episcopalian nuns, wearing habits ordinary people cannot distinguish from those of Roman Catholic nuns. In few, if any, school districts are Episcopalian nuns teachers.

17. *See* 42 U.S.C. § 2000e(j). Cases can also arise if someone seeks unemployment compensation after having been discharged for wearing religious garb. Mississippi Emp. Sec. Commn. v. McGlothin, 556 So.2d 324 (Miss.), cert. denied, 498 U.S. 879 (1990).

18. Bastian, "Religions Garb Statutes," note 15 *supra*, at 211. However, state commissioners or local districts may act under more general powers to restrict religious garb, even in the absence of a specific statute.

19. United States v. Board of Education, 50 Fair Empl. Prac. Cos. (BNA) 71, 82–85 (1989), rev'd, 911 F.2d 882 (3d Cir. 1990).

20. Anti-Catholicism almost certainly had an influence on initial adoption of such laws.

21. Of course, this constant reminder can turn students away from the religion if they take a strong dislike to the teachers or their methods. Being educated within strict Roman Catholic schools is a reason some "lapsed" Catholics give for falling away from the church.

22. *See, e.g.*, Hysong v. Gallitzin Borough School Dist., 30 A. 482 (Pa. 1894); Rawlings v. Butler, 290 S.W.2d 801 (Ky. 1956). *But see* Zellers v. Huff, 55 N.M. 501, 236 P.2d 949 (1951).

23. *See* Commonwealth v. Herr, 78 A. 68 (Pa. 1910); O'Connor v. Hendrick, 184 N.Y. 421, 77 N.E. 612 (1906); Cooper v. Eugene School Dist., 301 Or. 358, 723 P.2d 298, app. dism., 480 U.S. 942 (1986).

24. 911 F.2d 882 (3d Cir. 1990).

25. Bastian, "Religious Garb Statutes," note 15 *supra*, at 228–31.

26. I put the point this way because the law as a whole would not be justified if many teachers would like to wear religious jewelry that would be likely to have little effect on students.

27. It is a close question what a court should do if there is no real problem in the local region but there is a problem in other parts of the state.

CHAPTER 14. STUDENT RIGHTS TO RELIGIOUS FREEDOM AND TO FREE SPEECH ON RELIGIOUS TOPICS

1. One can also imagine suits brought by parents who object that, by allowing religious speech, a school violates the Establishment Clause.

2. We have seen in chapter 3 that the Supreme Court has determined that public schools cannot sponsor prayers in classrooms, at graduation ceremonies, or at football games, and in chapter 6 that schools must treat religious groups that want to use school facilities equally with nonreligious groups.

3. Matters *might* be different if most students in the class chose to speak from the same religious point of view.

4. Rosenberger v. Rector, 515 U.S. 819 (1995).

5. I contend in "Viewpoints from Olympus," 97 *Colum. L. Rev.* 697 (1997), that excluding *all* messages, positive and negative, about religion is not really viewpoint discrimination (because opposing viewpoints are treated equally), although it is viewpoint discrimination to admit nonreligious approaches to issues of public and private morality but not to admit religious approaches.

6. If a teacher's only reason for excluding religious subjects is a misconception that admitting those subjects would be improper, his decision may be unacceptable even if he otherwise has very wide latitude.

7. Settle v. Dickson County School Board, 53 F.3d 152 (6th Cir. 1995), cert. denied, 516 U.S. 989 (1995).

8. *Id.* at 153.

9. *Id.* at 156. Judge Batchelder, concurring, considered whether a teacher can determine an appropriate topic; Ramsey's decision was permissible because her reason for rejecting the paper was not because of its religious content.

10. The court relied on the Supreme Court's decision in Hazelwood School District v. Kuhlmeier, 484 U.S. 260 (1998), involving supervision over the content of a school newspaper, and an indication in Tinker v. Des Moines Independent Community School District, 393 U.S. 503 (1969),that teachers have broad discretion to administer the curriculum. In his concurrence, Judge Batchelder regarded the problem as significantly different from the published newspaper in *Hazelwood*.

11. Presumably the four Gospels would have counted as one source, not four, for this purpose.

12. The risk that Settle would write a paper about her "personal religion" is a kind of compendium of risks that she would not use nonbiblical sources, would not learn something new, and would not take an "objective" approach to the paper.

13. Lisa C. Shaw, "Student-Initiated Religious Speech, the Classroom, and the First Amendment: Why the Supreme Court Should Have Granted Review in *Settle v. Dickson County School Board*," 18 *Pace L. Rev.* 255 (1998), is highly critical of Ramsey's educational judgments and believes courts should involve themselves much more in protecting the rights of students to rely on religious subjects. She cites, among other things, a speech by President Clinton. Remarks on Religious Liberty in America, July 12, 1995, *available at* http://www.ed.gov/PressReleases/07-1995/religion.html. Other relevant secondary literature is Jay Alan Sicilian, "Proposed Guidelines for Student Religious Speech and Observance in Public Schools," 46 Mercer L. Rev. 1017 (1995); Robert S. Peck, "The Threat to the American Idea of Religious Liberty," 46 *Mercer L. Rev.* 1123 (1995); Michael McConnell, Testimony before the House Judiciary Committee, June 8, 1995, available at www.house.gov/judiciary/2108.htm.

14. C. H. v. Oliva, 226 F.3d 198 (en banc 2000).

15. C. H. v. Oliva, 990 F. Supp. 341 (D.N.J. 1997).

16. C. H. v. Oliva, 195 F.3d 167 (3d Cir. 1999). This opinion was vacated when en banc review by the entire court was granted, 197 F.3d 63 (3d Cir. 1999).

17. In DeNooyer v. Livonia Public Schools, 779 F. Supp. 744 (E.D. Mich.), a teacher and principal agreed that a student should not, for show and tell, play a videotape of herself singing a proselytizing reli-

gious song before a church congregation. One reason was that playing the videotape would not involve the student in making an oral presentation to the class, the purpose of show and tell; another reason was that second graders might think the school endorsed the message of the song about a young child accepting Jesus as Savior, or might be embarrassed or offended by the song. Although the court found public forum analysis to be appropriate, it said the school classroom is a closed forum and that school authorities might regulate the content of speech "in any reasonable manner." *Id.* at 749. The school had legitimate pedagogical reasons for its decision.

In this instance, the independent reason that playing a tape does not involve an oral presentation was enough to sustain the decision. Suppose, instead, all students were told they could play videotapes of activities in which they were engaged. Barring special circumstances, the teacher could eliminate the worry about endorsement by reminding students that the child's choice of subject was purely her own, but the proselytizing content of the song might still be a sufficient basis not to risk discomfort and offense of the other students.

18. The teacher who had restored the poster to a "less prominent position" was not a party, and it was not alleged that she had acted because of the poster's religious theme or that defendants were aware of what she had done. Thus, the complaint failed to allege any responsibility of the defendants for any possible violation.

In a case that has so far reached only a procedural stage, parents complained that a child had been treated unconstitutionally when the teacher rejected an initial religious poster and concealed part of a second religious poster made in response to an assignment to make an "environmental poster" for display. Peck v. Baldwinsville School Board of Education, No. 00–9054, 2001 U.S. App. LEXIS 5281 (2d Cir. Mar. 28, 2001).

19. *Oliva*, 226 F.3d at 210. Ironically, any Thanksgiving poster may be implicitly religious, but being thankful for Jesus is religious in a sense in which being thankful for one's family is not.

20. *Id.* at 213, 193 F.3d at 170–72.

21. For Judge Alito's position to be a robust one, we have to assume that teachers cannot avoid the demand of equal treatment simply by creating an exception in their original assignments. That is, were the teacher to say, "Make a poster about anything you are thankful for except anything religious," that exclusion would have to pass strict scrutiny. Otherwise teachers and schools could sidestep strict review just by formulating assignments to contain the exclusions they wish.

22. *See* note 5 *supra*. On whether Hazelwood School District v. Kuhlmeier, 484 U.S. 260 (1988), authorizes schools to engage in viewpoint discrimination, see Downs v. Los Angeles Unified School Dist.,

228 F.3d 1003 (4th Cir. 2000); Fleming v. Jefferson County School Dist. R-1, 298 F.3d 918, 926–29 (10th Cir. 2002).

23. Gernetzke v. Kenosha Unified School District No. 1, 224 F.3d 464 (7th Cir. 2001).

24. John 3:16.

25. *Gernetzke*, 224 F.3d at 466.

26. The court determined that the First Amendment suit could not be maintained against the defendants in their official capacities.

27. *Gernetzke*, 224 F.3d at 467.

28. I am assuming restricting the content of the mural of a religious club would constitute unacceptable discrimination against the club under the Equal Access Act (and the First Amendment) if the school lacked a legitimate justification.

29. Put differently, school officials should not be able to rely on the specter of litigation that would definitely be unsuccessful. Were such litigation to justify action, unhappy parents could provide sufficient bases for school officials to act merely by threatening to sue.

30. For a summary of cases that deal with disorder or controversy, see *Fleming* 298 F.3d at 925–26.

31. *Id.*

32. *Fleming*, 170 F. Supp. 2d 1094 (D. Col. 2001). In answer to the argument that in subsequent years people entering the school would assume that the tiles might bear the school's imprimatur, the court said that what would count is the perception of a reasonable and informed observer, drawing from the language of Justice O'Connor's endorsement test. We have examined the problems with Justice O'Connor's approach—and particularly the divide between ordinary reasonable people and (hypothetical) ones as well informed as she envisions—for the temporary displays to which that approach has been applied. These problems are magnified when one considers items that may stay in a building for half a century. Perhaps the Columbine shooting was such a major event that people will have a sense many years later about the origins of the tiles, but one cannot expect that for most decisions to decorate school walls. It is bizarre to imagine forty years from installation that the "reasonable observer" who counts is familiar with all the history of how the tiles came to be as they are.

A better judicial response on this point would be to say that the very diversity of the tiles would suggest that the symbols and expressions on any single one would not reflect school policy *and* that the school might meet the concern about endorsement by posting a modest sign that either summarizes the history of the making of the tiles or states simply, "The tiles in these halls were painted by members of the community and are expressions by them; they do not represent the view-points of the school."

33. *Fleming*, 298 F.3d at 933. The court found it unnecessary to address the claim that religious references would serve as a reminder of the shooting. *See also* DeLoreto v. Downey Unified School Dist. Board of Education, 196 F.3d 958 (9th Cir. 1999) (holding that a school district could refuse to have an advertisement containing the Ten Commandments on the fence of its high school field).

34. Muller v. Jefferson Lighthouse School, 98 F.3d 1530 (7th Cir. 1996).

35. Orin v. Barclay, 272 F.3d 1207 (9th Cir. 2001), did not involve a student, but a man who was told he could demonstrate against abortion on the campus of a community college as long as, among other things, he did not couch the protest in religious terms. The court held that having given Orin the right to express himself, officials could not preclude religious language. The result was dictated by Widmar v. Vincent, 454 U.S. 263 (1981), and, as in that case, a desire to avoid a violation of the Establishment Clause could not justify the restriction.

36. *Muller*, 98 F.3d at 1534.

37. *Id.* at 1440. Judge Rovner, concurring, would have employed the standard from Tinker v. Des Moines Independent School District, 393 U.S. 503 (1969), which is more protective of free speech, requiring school officials to show that speech would "'materially and substantially interfere with the requirements of appropriate discipline in the operation of the school.'" *Muller*, 98 F.3d at 1546. Judge Rovner recognized that speech innocuous in high school might interfere with work in grammar school, but she did not think that was a reason to apply a different standard of judgment.

38. In Isaacs v. Board of Education, 40 F. Supp. 2d 335 (D. Md. 1999), for example, the court rejected an argument that plaintiff had a free speech right to wear an African head-wrap to celebrate her cultural heritage. *See* Canady v. Bossier Parrish School Board, 240 F.3d 437 (5th Cir. 2001).

39. Vines v. Board of Education, 2002 U.S. Dist. LEXIS 382 (N.D. Ill.).

40. Plaintiff's argument that there was nonetheless a violation because the requesting letter had to be on official church stationery (thus, plaintiff claimed, limiting the "opt out" to "officially recognized" churches) had not been raised in time.

41. Chalifoux v. New Caney Independent School District, 976 F. Supp. 659 (1997).

42. *Tinker*, 393 U.S. 503.

43. Employment Division v. Smith 494 U.S. 872 (1990).

44. *Chalifoux*, 976 F. Supp. at 671.

45. Were a court to use a more "relaxed" standard for ordinary symbolic speech, any heightened free exercise scrutiny could make a significant difference.

46. See Elaine Sciolino, "French Assembly Votes to Ban Religious Symbols in Schools," *N.Y. Times*, February 11, 2004, A3, col. 1.

47. Worry that Muslim scarves represent a subordinate role for women would presumably not be sufficient.

CHAPTER 15. EXCUSING STUDENTS WHEN THEY OR THEIR PARENTS OBJECT

1. The primary constraint on what schools teach flows from nonestablishment; the primary basis for being excused is free exercise. Also relevant for constitutional purposes are general principles of free speech and a possible parental right, under due process clauses, to control the education of their children.

2. Some states have their own Religious Freedom Restoration Acts. Philip C. Kissom, in "Let's Bring Religion into the Public Schools and Respect the Religion Clauses," 49 *Kan. L. Rev.* 593, 616 (2001), notes that Kansas has a law exempting students, upon parental request, from activities "contrary to the religious teachings of the child." I do not share Kissom's strong doubts that a law limited to religious objections is constitutional.

3. Mozert v. Hawkins County Board of Education, 827 F.2d 1058 (6th Cir. 1987), cert. denied, 484 U.S. 1066 (1988).

4. Stephen Bates, *Battleground* 19 (New York: Poseidon Pr., 1993).

5. *Id.* at 204.

6. *Id.* at 44.

7. *Id.* at 82.

8. *Id.* at 207.

9. *Id.* at 206–7. (The ellipsis in the text omits Peter's response to Anne's initial comment, as well as some of what Anne said.) The reader also contains the fable of the blind man and the elephant, suggesting that all religions contain some part of the truth but not the entire truth.

As Stephen Bates puts it, "To the plaintiffs, who believe that Jesus is the only way to salvation, such statements were sacrilege." *Id.* at 207.

10. *Id.* Diane Ravitch has written that after the *Mozert* litigation, educational publishers took to heart Fundamentalist objections to texts: "Consequently, the content of today's textbooks and tests reflects a remarkable convergence of the interests of feminists and multiculturalists on one side and the religious Right on the other." Ravitch, *Education after the Culture Wars*, *Daedalus*, Spring 2002, 5, 15.

11. Bates, *Battleground*, note 4 *supra*, at 54.

12. *See* George W. Dent Jr., "Religious Children, Secular Schools," 61 *S. Cal. L. Rev.* 863, 867 (1988). Frost also objected to the suggestion in the teachers' manual that students assume roles and act out stories. *Mozert*, 827 F.2d at 1066.

13. Bates, *Battleground*, note 4 *supra*, at 33–38.

14. *Id.* at 71.

15. *Id.* at 72–77.

16. *Id.* at 86–90.

17. *Mozert I*, 579 F. Supp. at 1052. I have omitted two items and renumbered the remaining ones.

18. *See* Nomi Maya Stolzenberg, "He Drew a Circle That Shut Me Out: Assimilation, Indoctrination, and the Paradox of a Liberal Education," 106 *Harv. L. Rev.* 581, 596–97 (1993). I have omitted ten items and renumbered the remaining ones.

19. The uncertainty about the scope of the parents' complaints may have affected whether they were afforded any remedy at all.

20. Bates, *Battleground*, note 4 *supra*, at 255.

21. *Mozert*, 827 F.2d, at 1063.

22. We have seen in the earlier chapters of this book that, insofar as secular humanism constitutes a coherent set of ideas about human beings and the universe, including atheism or agnosticism, public schools may not present that set of ideas as true, in comparison with (false) traditional religions. Given the fundamentalist religious convictions of most residents of Hawkins County, we can be confident that the teachers were not teaching the truth of atheism; and the educational authorities did not understand the Holt readers to do so. Insofar as the materials conveyed ideas such as tolerance and respect for opposing beliefs that might be held by proponents of secular humanism and by many religious believers, that would not count as teaching secular humanism. Insofar as the materials failed to propound the true religion and to assert that religion should be central in people's lives, that can be understood as the inevitable consequence of the state's not taking a position about religion. The parents' complaint about secular humanism might be seen as revealing the extent to which the parents perceived the readers to be inhospitable to their sense of the true religion and how it should be taught to young people. In this sense, the "secular humanist" objection became another way of complaining that it was the overall cumulative effect of the materials that the parents took as so damaging.

23. *See* Spence v. Bailey, 465 F.2d 797 (6th Cir. 1972).

24. *See* West Virginia State Bd. of Educ. v. Barnette, 319 U.S. 624 (1943); Sherman v. Community Consolidated School Dist. 21, 980 F.2d 437 (7th Cir. 1992). One *might* think pledges of loyalty, which the

Supreme Court said could not be coerced nearly sixty years ago, are special because they involve affirmations of belief, or because they are not part of the regular curriculum, but the principle of the *Barnette* case should not be taken so narrowly.

25. In Moody v. Cronin, 484 F. Supp. 270 (C.D. Ill. 1979), the court ruled that parents with religious objections could keep children out of coeducational gym classes. Charles C. Haynes, in *Religion in American History: What to Teach and How* 149–51 (Alexandria, Va.: Association for Supervision and Curriculum Development, 1990), has reproduced a letter sent by the Islamic Society of North America to many public school officials. Among the requests are separate gym classes for boys and girls and no required dancing. In itself, the request not to dance is innocuous enough, but it may fit into a religious view in which boys and girls are expected to play different roles. A school might be concerned that to make all the accommodations the Muslims request would compromise an aim to promote gender equality.

26. Whether educators should take the religious views of parents into account at all in designing a curriculum raises a more subtle question we have briefly examined in the book's previous parts. To construct an example from the facts of *Mozert*, suppose English teachers regard the Holt series as slightly better than the (imaginary) Dolt series of readings. If they estimate that most parents are indifferent between the two, but that a significant minority has strong educational objections to the Holt series, educators might reasonably decide to use the Dolt series, which enjoys the broadest acceptance among parents. Such a decision would be uncontroversial *if* the parents' reasons had nothing to do with religion. But suppose the minority parents object to the Holt series on religious grounds. I believe educators are justified in finding acceptable common ground, so long as their judgments are not self-consciously based on their own religious views and they are confident they are not significantly sacrificing educational value.

27. In Pierce v. Society of Sisters, 268 U.S. 510 (1925), the Court found such a right as a matter of substantive due process. More recently, many have assumed that the Free Exercise Clause is what mainly supports this right. On this view, the constitutional right would probably not extend to nonreligious private schools.

28. According to James G. Dwyer, "The Children We Abandon: Religious Exemptions to Child Welfare and Education Laws as Denials of Equal Protection to Children of Religious Objectors," 74 *N.C. L. Rev.* 1321, 1339–40 (1996), "States that do require state approval or accreditation for some or all private schools typically do not attempt to control the content or methods of instruction in licensed schools beyond mandating that they offer certain core subjects." *See* New Life Baptist Acad-

emy v. East Longmeadow, 885 F.2d 940 (1st Cir. 1989) (collecting cases upholding state regulations that assure minimum educational quality), cert. denied, 494 U.S. 1066 (1990). *See also* Suzanna Sherry, "Responsible Republicanism: Educating for Citizenship," 62 *U. Chi. L. Rev.* 131, 205–6 (1995).

The degree of regulation of home schooling, estimated in 1999 to involve 850,000 children, varies radically among the states. *See* Judith G. McMullen, "Behind Closed Doors: Should States Regulate Home-schooling?" 54 *S. Car. L. Rev.* 75 (2002).

29. As chapter 2 indicates, some scholars believe that states should require more education in liberal democratic values from private schools than they now do.

30. I do not discuss in the text the treatment of nonreligious objections. Briefly, religiously based objections will usually be stronger than those based on nonreligious grounds, but school authorities should respond to some nonreligious objections. If pacifist nonreligious parents object to military training, the children should not have to undergo it. However, for something like the Holt reading series, it is doubtful whether any secular objection would be strong enough to justify excusing children.

31. I pass over here whether biology is a basic subject and whether one can be competent in biology without being taught anything about evolution.

32. It is not that the state is setting out to prefer liberal to conservative religion; but students are likely to receive an implicit message that modes of inquiry relevant for other areas of life also apply to religion. And, of course, it may be argued that states should do more to constrain the education given by private schools. See note 29 *supra*.

33. However, the private school option does not necessarily undermine the state's claim to enhance autonomy altogether. The state can say that its interest in broadening the entire range of student choice is very great; even though it gives way to a right of parents to choose nonpublic schools if they feel intensely about that, the state maintains its interest in promoting autonomy for children in public schools.

34. Wisconsin v. Yoder, 406 U.S. 205 (1972).

35. *See* note 33 *supra*. What that note says about promoting autonomy also applies to democratic education.

36. For a case holding that parents of a student receiving home schooling did not have a right to choose certain public school courses for their child, *see* Swanson v. Guthrie Independent School Dist. No. I-L, 135 F.3d 694 (10th Cir. 1998). *See generally* William Grob, "Access Denied: Prohibiting Homeschooled Students from Participating in Public School Athletics and Activities," 16 *Ga. St. U. L. Rev.* 823 (2000).

37. Were a school to try to make all the accommodations requested by the Islamic Society of North America, *see* note 25 *supra*, the total effect on a school's program could be significant.

For circumstances in which school authorities did excuse children of objecting parents, *see* Grove v. Mead School District No. 354, 753 F.2d 1528 (9th Cir.), cert. denied, 474 U.S. 826 (1985); Wallace v. Knox County Bd. of Educ., 1993 U.S. App. LEXIS 20477 (7th Cir. 1993).

38. *Mozert*, 827 F.2d 1058 (1987), cert. denied, 484 U.S. 1066 (1988).

39. *Yoder*, 406 U.S. 205 (1972).

40. Employment Division v. Smith, 494 U.S. 872 (1990).

41. The *Smith* Court treated *Yoder* as a hybrid case involving free exercise and parental rights over their children's education. *Mozert*, also involving free exercise and parental rights, must also be classed as a hybrid case, for which the compelling interest approach of *Yoder* is apparently still apt. As far as it goes, this analysis is unexceptionable; but the Court in *Smith* may have created this hybrid category just to take care of *Yoder*; and it was highly unsympathetic to the actual inquiries necessary to resolve *Yoder*. Thus, one cannot predict that the Supreme Court will give that category its natural extension. In a case involving a parental claim that children could not be compelled to attend a sexually explicit program in AIDS and sex education, the First Circuit treated *Yoder* as inapposite. Brown v. Hot, Sexy and Safer Productions, Inc., 68 F.3d 525 (1st Cir. 1995), cert. denied, 516 U.S. 1159 (1996). The decision is criticized in a Recent Case, 110 *Harv. L. Rev.* 1179 (1997). *See also* Leebaert v. Harrington, 193 F. Supp. 2d 491 (D. Conn. 2002), using rational basis review to assess a claim to have a child completely excused from a mandatory health class (a state statute gave parents a right to have children exempted from lessons about family life, physical growth, and AIDS). For a more sympathetic response to a similar complaint, *see* Ware v. Valley Stream High School Dist., 75 N.Y.2d 114, 550 N.E.2d 420, 551 N.Y.S.2d 167 (1989).

42. For a discussion of the significance of exposure to obnoxious ideas, see *Ware*, 75 N.Y.2d at 126–27, 550 N.E.2d at 428, 551 N.Y.S.2d at 175.

43. *Mozert*, 827 F.2d at 1069. He relied on the famous decision in *West Virginia Board of Education v. Barnette*, 319 U.S. 624 (1943), discussed at 827 F.2d at 1066, that students could not be compelled to profess beliefs they did not hold, and he cited a court of appeals case involving conscientious objection to military training in school, among others, as suggesting that students could not be forced to commit acts they found objectionable. *Id.* at 1063, commenting on Spence v. Bailey, 465 F.2d 797 (6th Cir. 1972). Nomi Stolzenberg discusses whether reading silently

can reasonably be considered as less active than reading aloud, "He Drew a Circle,"note 18 *supra*, at 603–6.

44. As Nomi Stolzenberg points out, the parents also claimed that forcing them to allow their children to be exposed to the objectionable materials violated their own religious exercise. Stolzenberg, "He Drew a Circle," note 18 *supra*, at 600–601.

45. The court recognized that *Wisconsin v. Yoder* was a case involving undesired exposure, but the opinion said it rested on a singular set of facts, involving a wish to be free of the entire high school curriculum. *Mozert*, 827 F.2d at 1067.

46. Among other things, the parents argued that the New Testament orders Christians only to fill their minds with what is true, and to "avoid worldly and empty chatter."

47. He worried about the constant threat of lawsuits, and his treatment of *Yoder* shows that he supposes that withdrawal of children from the entire school system is much less troublesome than parents picking and choosing among courses.

48. *Mozert*, 827 F.2d at 1079–81.

49. *Id.* at 1081.

50. *Id.* at 1071. On this point, Judge Boggs responded that it was unfair to sustain the need to teach students in this way if the inadequacy of alternatives for children of objecting parents could not be revealed by testing. *Id.* at 1071. However, insofar as what the school is teaching is independence of choice and civic virtues, it is doubtful if these will be confidently revealed by standard testing.

51. *Id.* at 1071–72.

52. *See* notes 29, 32, and 35 *supra*.

53. A similar conclusion was reached in Fleischfresser v. Directors of School Dist. 200, 15 F.3d 680 (7th Cir. 1994). In Axson-Flynn v. Johnson, 151 F. Supp. 1326 (D. Utah 2001), a court held that a university drama student did not have a right to participate in an acting program without being willing to speak certain words and phrases in performances.

54. *See* George Dent, "Religious Children, Secular Schools," note 12 *supra*, at 863, 928–30 (1988), suggesting alternative instruction as a remedy and pointing out the schools often spend more money per pupil "on slow learners, handicapped students, gifted children, non-English speakers, and children in special programs" than on ordinary pupils. *See also* Bates, *Battleground*, note 4 *supra*, at 313–17. Stephen Macedo, who emphasizes civic education, is more sympathetic with the court's approach, *Diversity and Distrust: Civic Education in a Multicultural Democracy* 157–64 (Cambridge: Harvard Univ. Pr., 2000).

55. In *Ware*, 75 N.Y.2d 114, 550 N.E.2d 420, 551 N.Y.S.2d 167, the New

York Court of Appeals said that the state had a compelling interest in preventing AIDS, but had not shown the necessity of insisting that members of the Brethren attend the public school course.

56. Gary J. Simson and Erika A. Sussman, "Keeping the Sex in Sex Education: The First Amendment's Religion Clauses and the Sex Education Debates," 9 S. *Cal. Rev. L. & Women's Stud.* 265, 272–78 (2000). *See Brown*, 68 F.3d 525 (using a weaker test than compelling interest). For a case holding that schools need provide no "opt-out" for a program of condom distribution, because no one was compelled to take the free condoms, see Curtis v. School Committee of Falmouth, 652 N.E.2d 580 (Sup. Jud. Ct. Mass. 1995). The opposite result was reached on statutory grounds and on the basis of parental rights to control their children's sexual education. Alfonso v. Fernandez, 606 N.Y.S.2d 259 (App. Div. 2d Dept. 1993).

* Index *

Abington Township v. Schempp, 19–20, 38, 40–41, 58, 64, 80

agnosticism, 64–65, 150, 220n.35; of standard modern history, 126–27

Alito, Samuel, 167–68

Amish, the, 21, 182

Arkansas, 94, 110, 122

assignment topics, appropriateness of, 2, 164–68

atheism, 64, 81, 98, 126

authority to make educational decisions, 33–34

Balanced Treatment Acts, 94, 110

Bauchman v. West High School, 54

Behe, Michael, 103

Bible, 2–3, 67, 70–71, 112, 129, 131, 167, 169; as authoritative word of God, 119, 136; belief in literal truth of, 93, 95, 175; devotional reading of in schools, 8, 19, 37–44, 76, 79–80; as literature, 136–37; as source for school research paper, 165–66; use of in early public schools, 8, 15–16

"Bible-reading" case. See *Abington Township v. Schempp*

Big Bang theory, 94, 99

Boggs, Danny, 184

Brennan, William, 41, 122

Brown v. Board of Education, 38

Buddhism, 42, 130, 150, 164

C. H. v. Oliva, 167–68

Catholicism, 14, 28, 31, 128, 130–31, 134–35; and anti-Catholic attitudes, 14–15; attitudes toward homosexuality, 146–47; and Catholic schools, 18; and communion, 55; and rosaries, 172–73; and secular clothing, 156

Chalifoux v. New Caney Independent School District, 172–73

Christianity, 3, 8, 42, 52–54, 64–65, 92, 129–31, 134, 136, 150; fundamentalist

understandings of, 3, 93, 175, 179, 181–82

Christmas, celebration of, 1–2, 51–52, 54–56; and Hanukkah, 56

Church of England, 28

civic education, 24–25; and religion, 28

Civil Rights Act of 1964, Title VII of, 156, 158–59

Clark, Tom, 40, 64

clubs, 2, use of school facilities by, 22, 69–76

coercion, as a standard for Establishment Clause violations, 45

Columbine High School, 171

Commager, Henry Steele, 15

communion, 4, 49, 55

comparative religion, courses in, 149–51

constitutional doctrine, development of, 43–44

Creation Research Society, 114

creationism, 1, 88, 101, 115; constitutional principles and, 122–25; promoting negative challenges to evolution, 102–6; scientific plausibility of, 106–12; as teaching religion, 90, 116; theoretical framework of, 92–93. See also evolution; intelligent design

cultural diversity, in teaching literature, 136–37

"culture wars," 9

curriculum, parental objections to, 174–77

Darwin, Charles, 91–92, 97, 120

Darwinism. See evolution

Dembski, William, 225n.12

Dewey, John, 16, 214n.12

Diary of Anne Frank, The, 175

Doe v. Duncanville Independent School District, 53

Douglas, William, 19

dress, of teachers, 155–59; of students, 172–73

earth, age of, 91, 92, 95, 107
economics, 134–36
Edwards, Jonathan, 130
Edwards v. Aguillard, 94, 122
Eisgruber, Christopher, 195n.11
Elk Grove Unified School District v. Newdow, 206n.91
Employment Division v. Smith, 21, 173, 183
endorsement, as a standard for Establishment Clause violations, 61–62
Engel v. Vitale, 38, 40–41, 58
Engels, Frederick, 127
Epperson v. Arkansas, 94, 122
Equal Access Act, 70, 169–70
equal facilities, 69–76
Establishment Clause, 17, 38–39, 47, 57, 82, 116, 152, 156, 158, 176
Everson v. Board of Education, 18–19, 38–41, 81
evolution, 1, 83, 88, 80, 92–98, 114–17, 120–21, 146, 175; constitutional principles and, 121–25; and *Epperson v. Arkansas*, 94–95, 122; government treatment of, 93–94, 117–18; and Kansas Board of Education, 94; negative arguments against, 102–6; neo-Darwinism as scientific plausibility of, 101–2, 107–8, 117–20; neo-Darwinian synthesis, 91–92; omission of from textbooks, 94; state laws forbidding teaching of, 93; as subject of textbook disclaimer, 231n.5; theoretical framework of, 91–92. *See also* creationism; intelligent design
exemptions, of students from curricular requirements, 174–86; from otherwise valid laws, 21

First Amendment, 17, 20, 38, 43, 90, 168–70. *See also* Establishment Clause; Free Exercise Clause; Free Speech Clause
Fleming v. Jefferson County School District R-1, 171
Flood, 107
Florey v. Sioux Falls School District, 54
Fortas, Abe, 64, 94, 122
Fourteenth Amendment, 17, 20, 38–39

Free Exercise Clause, 17, 38–39, 156, 173, 176
Free Speech Clause, 156, 164, 173
Freudianism, 131
Frost, Vicki, 174–75
fundamentalism, 218n.20

garb. *See* dress
Genesis creationism. *See* creationism
Gernetzke v. Kenosha Unified School District No. 1, 169
Good News Club v. Milford Central School District, 71–72, 74
Gould, Stephen Jay, 219 nn. 28 and 30, 220n.39
graduation speakers, 2, 44–46
"Guidance on Constitutionally Protected Prayer in Public Elementary and Secondary Schools," U.S. Department of Education, 49–50
Gutmann, Amy, 24, 33

Hamburger, Philip, 203n.36
Hanukkah, 56
Hawkins County, Tennessee, 174–84
Haynes, Charles, 129
Hinduism, 42, 64, 127, 130, 150, 164
history, teaching of, 127–34
holiday observances, 1–2, 155–56
Holt, Reinhardt & Winston reader series, 175–79, 183–84
home schooling, 179–181, 253n.28
homosexual relationships, 2, 144–47

Institute for Creation Science, 114
intelligent design, 1, 88, 95, 101, 115; constitutional principles and, 124–25; promoting negative challenges to evolution, 102-6; scientific plausibility of, 106–13; as teaching religion, 90, 116–17; theoretical framework of, 93. *See also* evolution; creationism
Islam. *See* Muslims

Jackson, Robert, 40–41, 64–81
Jefferson, Thomas, 18
Jeffries, John, Jr., 192n.44

Jehovah's Witnesses, 21
Jesus, 2, 42, 67, 164–68, 175–76
Johnson, Phillip, 219n.33, 221n.41
Judaism, 18, 42, 56, 129–30, 150

Kansas Board of Education, evolution
  controversy and, 84
Kauffman, Stuart, 104
Kennedy, Anthony, 45, 73–75
Kennedy, Cornelia, 184–85
King, Martin Luther, Jr., 127
Kitcher, Philip, 91, 115

Lamb's Chapel v. Center Moriches Union Free
  School District, 72–73
Laudan, Larry, 110
Lee v. Weisman, 44–46, 49, 51, 56, 65
Lemon v. Kurtzman, 20, 57, 62, 70, 122,
  152–53
literature, teaching of, 136–37
Lively, Pierce, 183
Lord's Prayer, 51, 199n.2
Louisiana, 94
Luther, Martin, 130–31

Macedo, Stephen, 13, 30, 32
Madison, James, 18
Mann, Horace, 14–15
Manuel, Frank, 153
Marshall, Thurgood, 1
Marx, Karl, 127
Marxism, 126, 131, 135
Massachusetts, 13
McConnell, Michael, 25
McGuffey reader, 15
McLean v. Arkansas Board of Education, 110
Messiah, Handel's, 52
methodological naturalism, 95, 97–98, 105,
  113, 126
miracles, 99–100. See also supernatural
Moberly, Walter Hamilton, 83
moments of silence, 58–63
morality, teaching of, 25–26, 155
Mozert v. Hawkins County Board of Educa-
  tion, 174, 183–85
Muller v. Jefferson Lighthouse School, 172
Murphy, James, 194n.5

Murphy, Jeffrie, 101
music, 1–2, 51–54; carols, 1, 51–52, 53; devotional, 52–55; sacred, 51–53, 64; standards for use of religious music in
  schools, 52–53
Muslims, 31, 42, 134, 158, 173, 201n.33

Native American worship, 21
natural selection, 91, 98, 102–4, 121
Newdow v. U.S. Congress, 206n.93
Newton, Isaac, 102
Noah's flood, 107
Nord, Warren, 15–16, 81–82, 129, 131

O'Connor, Sandra Day, 60–63, 63, 70,
  74–75
O'Hair, Madalyn Murray, 37
omissions, of standard material as teaching religion, 117–18
On the Origin of Species (Darwin), 1, 91
"opting out." See exemptions
Orwell, George, 136

Paluxy River fossils, 93
parental rights, 33, 139
parental views, 120–21; objections to
  courses, 2, 174–87
Pennock, Robert, 218n.18
peppered moth, 102, 217n.14
permitted teaching, about religion, 85–87;
  that conflicts with religious views,
  67–68
personal beliefs, expression of, —by
  teachers, 131–33; —by students, 164–65
Plantinga, Alvin, 98
Pledge of Allegiance, "under God" in,
  56–57
Pledge case: See Elk Grove Unified School
  District v. Newdow; Newdow v. Congress
Posner, Richard, 169–70
Powell, Lewis, 60
prayer, in classroom, 37–44; at football
  games, 46; at graduation, 44–46; guidance of United States Department of
  Education on, 49–50; investigations into
  power of, 99; invocations by guest
  speakers, 48–49

private schools, public financing of, 6, 18, 33

Protestantism, nondenominational, 7–14, 64, 65, 128, 175, 179

Protestant Reformation, 127–28, 130

Puritans, 27–28, 126–29, 142

"Rainbow Curriculum," 2

Rawls, John, 143

Rehnquist, William, 201n.31, 203n.33

religion clauses, 38; application of against states, 17, 39. *See also* Establishment Clause; First Amendment; Free Exercise Clause; Fourteenth Amendment

religious diversity, and immigration law, 42; of United States, 137

Religious Freedom Restoration Acts, 250n.2

religious symbols, use of in displays, 169–72; wearing of, —by students, 172–73, —by teachers, 156

religious propositions, and moral views, 66–67

report topics, appropriateness of, 2, 164–66

Robertson, Pat, 48

Roe v. Wade, 38

Rosenberger v. Rector and Visitors of the University of Virginia, 73–75, 157, 164, 171

Ryan, James, 192n.44

Salomone, Rosemary, 194n.5, 240n.36

Scalia, Antonin, 21, 45–46, 122–23, 203n.53

school boards, authority of in making educational decisions, 33–34

science, and religion, 88–100; limitations of, 111–14

scientific creationism. *See* creationism

Scopes "Monkey trial," 218n.21

secular education, effects of, 81–84

secular humanism, 80–83, 175, 179

secularization, 81–84

Settle v. Dickson County School Board, 164–66

sex education, 1, 33 , 143–44, 147–48, 185–86; distribution of condoms, 148, 240n.37; 256n.56

Silver, Marjorie, 207n.5

Simson, Gary, 147

simulated religious practices in school, 55–56

Smart, Ninian, 151

Smith v. Board of School Commissioners, 82

Smith, Steven D., 199n.8

Society of Friends, 58

Souter, David, 46, 72–74

spillover effects, 4–5, 23, 28–33

Stevens, John Paul, 46–47, 72, 74

Stewart, Potter, 41

Stolzenberg, Nomi, 176

students, excusing from class, 174–87; rights of, —in fulfilling assignments, 163–168, —out of class, 169–71

student initiatives, 172–73

supernatural, 99; causal effect in evolution, 111; investigations of, 99; objections of parents to literature dealing with, 176

Supreme Court of the United States, 3, 8, 58, 88, 121, 183, 185; criticism of purported neutrality of, 57; implication of doctrines of, 49–50; interpretation of constitutition by (generally), 7, 17, 43–44, 66; interpretation of Establishment Clause by, 8, 17–20, 37–42, 44–47, 51, 60–63, 64–65, 69–72, 75, 94–95, 122–23, 152–53; interpretation of First Amendment by, 21, 80, 122; interpretation of Free Exercise Clause by, 8, 21, 45–46, 184; interpretation of Free Speech Clause by, 8, 69–76, 157, 164; public attitudes toward decisions of, 9, 79; speculation about future doctrinal development of, 56–57

Sussman, Erika, 147

teachers, authority of to make educational decisions, 33–34, 243n. 9; conduct outside of schoolroom, 133-34; latitude of, 133, 154; restrictions on dress of, 155–59; as role models, 133-34; training of, 27, 244n.13

Ten Commandments, 6, 51, 209n. 3

textbooks, judicial authority to review, 152–55; parental objections to, 174–77

theistic science, 98

Thomas, Clarence, 71, 203n.53

Tinker v. Des Moines Independent Community School District, 173

Title VII of Civil Rights Act of 1964, 156, 158–59

Tomasi, John, 30–32, 139

Unitarianism, 37, 64

United States v. Board of Education, 158

U.S. Department of Education, "Guidance on Constitutionally Protected Prayer in Public Elementary and Secondary Schools," 49–50

values, teaching of 139–48; clarification approach to moral issues, 83, 140, 175

viewpoint discrimination, for school assignments, 164; and student clubs,

69–76; relation to content discrimination, 22, 72–74, 164

Vines v. Board of Education, 172

Virginia, University of, 74

Vitz, Paul, 175

vouchers, 6

"wall of separation," 18, 39, 41

Wallace v. Jaffree, 60, 62

Webster, Noah, 13

West Virginia Board of Education v. Barnette, 21

Westside Community Board of Education v. Mergens, 70, 74

Westside High School, 70

Wexler, Jay, 213 nn. 26 and 28, 216n.28, 241 nn. 48 and 50

Wide Awake, 73–74

Widmar v. Vincent, 69–70, 173

Wisconsin v. Yoder, 21, 182–84

Wizard of Oz, The, 175

Wolterstorff , Nicholas, 228n.35